STUMPED

STUMPED

THE FOREST INDUSTRY IN TRANSITION

KEN DRUSHKA

Douglas & McIntyre
Vancouver/Toronto

Douglas & McIntyre Ltd.
1615 Venables Street,
Vancouver, British Columbia
V5L 2H1

Canadian Cataloguing in Publication Data

Drushka, Ken.
Stumped

Includes index.
ISBN 0-88894-419-5

1. Forests and forestry – North America.
2. Forest products – North America. I. Title.
SD140.D78 1985 634.9'097 C84-091224-2

Jacket photograph by Richard Krieger
Design by Barbara Hodgson
Typeset by Evergreen Press
Printed and bound in Canada by D. W. Friesen & Sons

Contents

Preface

I GOT MY FIRST timber sale in 1969.

I had no job at the time. The wood was there in the forest, and I needed the money it could bring. Obviously, the thing to do was to apply for permission to cut it and sell it. The British Columbia Forest Service agreed. The day formal approval of my licence arrived in the mail, I became a timber baron.

Now I was my own boss. I would decide when I would go to work, how I would do it and to whom I would sell the product. I was lord of a few acres of ground at Thurston Bay on Sonora Island. According to the forest ranger who handled my application, it was the smallest disposal of Crown timber in the entire history of the B. C. Forest Service.

My knowledge of the wider issues and controversies that raged, and still rage, in and around the forest industry was no greater than this tiny operation. My education began that afternoon in the bar, where most of us — gyppos, handloggers, beachcombers — would gather after the twice-weekly mail was delivered. My companions congratulated me, bought me a few beers, and of course I had to buy a few more, and good-natured advice flowed as freely as the beer.

But after a while, the conversation took a new direction and a new tone. As they began to discuss wider issues in the industry, talking of quotas, Tree Farm Licences, scale sheets and other terms I had never heard, there was an element of bitterness and confusion.

These people were men of action, courage and energy. Difficulty or danger did not intimidate them. Most of them could crop a 2 m (6 foot) diameter, 61 m (200 foot) tall Douglas-fir exactly where they chose, then move it over some of the roughest terrain on the face of the earth with as little fuss as most people would make going to the corner store for a newspaper. They had been down to their last penny a dozen times, and they had all hit it big at least once. Accidents, death, breakdowns, bankruptcy — these were all part of the game. If you could not face them and laugh later, then maybe you should go to town and work for wages in the sawmill.

Sudden problems and immediate danger, dealt with by swift and decisive action by which you would either win or lose — that was their style, a style that was, in part, the very definition of a logger in the first half of this century. But that afternoon, as the glasses left their marks on the table and the ashtrays overflowed, I began to see that these independent loggers — these gyppos — were beset by problems they could not meet head-on, problems that would not yield to a logger's style.

They were being killed by concepts. They were being destroyed by words and phrases draped with ambiguity and vagueness. They were being put out of business by terms like "multiple use" and "forest management."

Yet the concepts themselves seemed inoffensive enough. "Multiple use" — the idea that a given land mass can support a number of activities — seemed reasonable to a logger who fished or hunted on the same land he had logged the previous week. And "forest management" — well, whatever it was, the words themselves had a certain ring. But when combined with warnings of a future timber shortage, the phrase became suspect. As far as my beer partners could see, the trees were growing faster than they could be cut down.

There seemed to be yet another implication. "Forest management," it turned out, involved the allocation of huge tracts of timberland in the form of perpetually renewable leases to a handful of big companies. The reasoning seemed to be that these large corporations had the financial stability for the proper management of forests.

Somewhere in the process, the small loggers became villains. They were no longer hard-working, independent businessmen; they were now the despised, irresponsible "cut-and-get-out loggers."

Of course they were the first to notice, timber famine or no, that the big companies were beginning to mount logging operations that dwarfed anything that had ever existed in the province. But who would believe a cut-and-run gyppo?

Out of all this grew a bitterness that is very close to the heart of forest resource politics in British Columbia as well as other provinces of Canada and in the western United States. It was a bitterness I could hear that afternoon of my first timber sale. Although I could not fully understand it then, it was the bitterness of people whose way of life was being brought to the verge of extinction.

Still less could I understand then that the entire matter rested on a single question: what is the proper use of publicly owned forest land? This book concerns that question.

Acknowledgements

THE INFORMATION AND IDEAS in this book come from many sources. It was conceived during after-dinner conversations in logging camps, during lunch breaks on spacing and thinning contracts, in the back seats of crummies on the way to and from work. From there it led to public and corporate information offices, through the intricate mazes of state and private bureaucracies, into libraries, archives and museums. In the six years that I have lived with it in my mind and on paper, I had many jobs in the forest industry which provided me with an unparalleled opportunity to test the theories on the practical men and women of experience. Everywhere I received a lot of advice, criticism and information. I wish I could acknowledge all this assistance, but a cardinal rule of the forest industry is that one does not rock the boat. Few people knowledgeable about the industry feel secure enough in their jobs to speak publicly about what they know and think. I have dealt with my debt to all these people by not naming anyone who works in or around the industry.

However, I am able to express my gratitude to Garry Nixon, whose timely application of carrots and sticks — not to mention his generous contribution of Georgist economics — made possible the writing of this book. Jim Douglas convinced me it was worth doing and taking seriously. Wayne Richards's sense of humour helped in a crucial period. Judith Alldritt did a superb editing job. And Les and Helen Weiss provided encouragement when the undertaking was not a lot of fun. I am enormously indebted to the librarians at the Council of Forest Industries, MacMillan Bloedel, the Ministry of Forests, the Special Collections Branch at the University of British Columbia, the B. C. Provincial Archives and the Campbell River and District Museum and Archives.

ONE

What Kind of Forests Do We Want?

THE FORESTS OF BRITISH COLUMBIA, and of the world, are undergoing profound changes.

There are no limits to the potential breadth and depth of these changes. The natural forests with their jumble of sizes and species are giving way to forests of uniform size, uniform species, uniform age, all neatly spaced, marching to market in serried ranks like Napoleon's soldiers marching to meet Wellington's cannon.

The trees themselves are being transformed. The once casually created love-children of wind pollination are becoming wise children; both parents are known, having been carefully selected for strengths and qualities that suit not nature's purposes but man's.

These changes and yet more — to the fungi, the bacteria, to the very soil of the forest — are being brought about by one other change, the most fundamental of all: a change in our relationship to the forest. We have begun to "manage" the forests, and in so doing, we ourselves are being transformed. Where once we were simply wood-cutters — harvesters — we are attempting to become as well growers — forest farmers.

Done well, forest management can yield almost incredible benefits. Done badly, the hazards are appalling. The differences will lie in the choices we make and the decisions we take.

Some decisions are based on what we know — data that have been tested and verified by scholars and professionals. Our fund of known data is at present tiny, though it is growing. Some decisions come from experience; but we are as yet very inexperienced at growing trees. Some decisions are based on what we think we know, but in fact do not know. These are far more dangerous than decisions made in a state of confessed ignorance. When we are wise enough to admit ignorance, we are usually wise enough to be careful.

A growing number of decisions are small *p* political, in the sense that they carry out the expressed will of the citizens. A forest might be managed for jobs or a large cash return in one area, for greater recreational opportunities in another, as an aid to agriculture in a third. The people of Smithers, B. C., quite reasonably want the forest on the mountain facing their town to be managed primarily for scenic value. The inhabitants of Nelson, B. C., have the same attitude towards their area.

As small *p* political activity grows, it can soften and sometimes reverse capital *P* decisions, those based on party advantage or dogma. This is all to the good; capital *P* decisions have often been injurious to forests.

Whatever the basis of the decisions, there are risks involved in forest management. As an example, admittedly extreme but nevertheless possible, we might plant many large areas throughout the province with some carefully bred, genetically altered strain of fir. These trees may, unknown to us, have a weakness, a failure factor, that does not become apparent for perhaps thirty years. This weakness may be an unusual susceptibility to an insect or mold. Whatever the agent of destruction, suddenly trees throughout the province begin to weaken and die.

Combining widely dispersed stands of dead timber with a hot, dry summer and a few lightning strikes gives us a dramatic scenario — the province in flames. As the fires spread from dead forests to dry, gone would be the game, the camping grounds, the protection against soil erosion and mud slides. Rain, when it came, would no longer be held and then slowly released by the forests. The province would be all flash flood and desert. The salmon fishery, already in serious trouble, would instantly be snuffed out. Agriculture would disappear almost totally.

Extreme though the example may be, it serves to illustrate how much we depend on our forests. Further, such a scenario is entirely possible on a smaller scale. Entire watersheds could well be wiped out by bad forest management practices. Where we know little, we would do well to be cautious. What can realize a dream can also cause a nightmare.

The idea of forest management is neither new nor original to North America; it was introduced from Europe almost a century ago. What is new is the conviction that we must bring every hectare of forest land on the continent under some form of management. Until recently, forest management had been a fairly limited concept, applied primarily to forests suitable for timber production, and even then usually limited to certain phases of their growth. Vast areas of forest had been regarded as wilderness and beyond the scope of forestry practices; now it is argued that all forest land needs the benefits of management.

Because of the increased demands on forests as their uses multiply, the ability to grow trees to ensure continuing supplies is assuming enormous importance. Intensive forest management will, its proponents claim, enable us to maintain or even increase our timber harvest without having to forfeit the other benefits obtainable from our forests.

When foresters use the phrase "intensive forest management," they are referring to a range or set of silvicultural practices aimed at dramatically increasing the growth of the forest. Intensive forest management compares to conventional North American forestry in much the same way as the growing of vegetables by modern agri-business compares to the activities of a casual weekend home gardener.

Intensive forest management is accepted by the three components of the forest industry — labour, management and government. For labour, it promises a massive potential for creating jobs; for management, it offers the means of avoiding projected timber shortages; for government, it is the key component in an integrated management policy to obtain the wisest use of other forest resources, including water, fish, wildlife and recreation.

Increasingly, all three components of the forest industry use sophisticated propaganda campaigns to convince the public that intensive forest management will deliver unending benefits. These campaigns are necessary because intensive forest management requires huge expenditures which will not yield a return on the investment for perhaps a century. Because most of the forests upon which this management will be practised are on public lands, and because the landowner is usually the one who has to make such investments, much of the money required will have to come from the public purse. Therefore, the majority of people must be convinced that such expenditures are worthwhile. Hence the propaganda — and the politics.

The politics of forest resources in North America are determined to a large extent by who owns the land in the various regions. A general rule is that the more publicly owned the forest land, the more conflict over its resource use. On this continent, it has always been widely accepted that whoever owns the land has the right to do as they wish with it, provided this does not adversely affect others beyond its boundaries. Thus, conflicts over the forest land base are generally limited to provincial, state and national forests.

Most of these public lands, and their attendant conflicts, are in the western part of the continent. Historical processes have determined that pattern. Private ownership of a particular, carefully defined piece of land is a European notion. European settlement of North America began in the East at a time when the prevalent government policy was to encourage private ownership. It was also policy to encourage deforestation of a heavily forested continent.

By the latter half of the nineteenth century, settlement had proceded into the West and North, at which time governments on both sides of the border adopted policies of retaining actual ownership of the land, thereby keeping it in the public domain. By doing so, they were able to control the private utilization, or extraction, of the land's resources.

Most of the United States's productive forests are in the East.[1] They cover 1 450 000 km^2 (560,000 square miles), nearly three times the 520 000 km^2 (200,000 square miles) of the West. About 62 per cent of the eastern area consists of the spectacular hardwood forests — maple, oak and other deciduous species. Half of the eastern forest lies in the northern states, and 82 per cent of this is privately owned, most of it in small holdings.

Until the turn of the century, the main land-use strategy in this area was to cut the forests to create farms. Since then, however, a new, fast-growing hardwood forest has developed on these relatively small parcels of privately owned land.

Although these parcels account for close to a third of the nation's forest growth, only one-sixth of the total U. S. harvest is taken from them. One reason for this disparity is that a large proportion of these forest lands is owned by city dwellers, for their recreation.

The forests of the Southeast are even more predominantly in private hands — 91 per cent, with 70 per cent of this in small holdings. Until a few decades ago, these lands were treated in much the same way as those in the North, where trees were being cleared for crops such as cotton. More recently, changing economic circumstances have led to the reversion of large areas to forest, much of it softwood — pine — destined for the pulp market. Today, about half the U. S. annual forest growth is to be found on these lands, and from them comes almost half the annual harvest.

The resurgence of the Southeast's small, privately owned tracts as a source of softwood timber is one of the outstanding features of the North American forest industry. These tracts are the fastest growing, most accessible and intensively managed forests on the continent. A major political consideration in this area is not so much resource-use conflict as the tensions created by corporate wood processors having to rely on a large number of small owners for their wood supply.

A far different situation exists in the western U. S. forests, which consist of a Pacific Coast region and a Rocky Mountain region. Large-scale timber harvesting did not begin in the West until the 1890s. It expanded until the end of World War II and then began to level off. Because the area was settled relatively recently, its pattern of ownership contrasts markedly with that of the East and Southeast, reflecting the general policy shift that took place at the turn of the century. Hence, a much higher proportion of the western forests remained in public ownership, with the major portions being held by the federal government in National Forests. Ninety-three per cent of these forests are softwood species.

In the Pacific Coast region, there are about 280 000 km^2 (110,000 square miles) of commercial forest land, 46 per cent of it classed as National Forest land and managed by the U. S. Forest Service. The large forest companies own about 18 per cent, and another 22 per cent is held by smaller, private owners. Although this region contributes something less than one-sixth of the annual national forest growth, it provides about 30 per cent of the U. S. annual harvest; 42 per cent of that harvest comes from the 18 per cent of land owned by the forest industry.

The Rocky Mountain region's 250 000 km^2 (96,000 square miles) of commercial forest show an even greater proportion of public ownership: 65 per cent is classified as national forest, 4 per cent is held by the forest industry and another 20 per cent by other private owners. The harvest from this region, less than 7 per cent of the national total, utilizes only two-thirds of the annual growth in the region. Yet over 20 per cent of the Rocky Mountain harvest comes from the 4 per cent of the land owned by the forest industry.

The key to the western timber supply, and the source of most of the land-use conflict in the western United States, is the National Forest land held by the federal government. This contains an estimated two-thirds of the western U. S. softwood inventory, yet it provides only a little over one-third of the region's annual cut. Perhaps even more important, it contains almost all the virgin forest in the nation. For this reason it is of great concern to the growing numbers of people in the United States demanding the preservation of wilderness areas. At the same time, the industrially held forest lands are being heavily overcut relative to their growth, and industry increasingly looks to the national forests for future wood supplies.

In Canada, the situation of forest ownership is much different, at least superficially.[2] Provincial governments own 87 per cent of the almost 2 000 000 km^2 (800,000 square miles) of forest land in the country. The federal government's 5 per cent ownership consists mainly of the untapped forests of the Yukon and Northwest territories. Only 8 per cent of the national total is privately owned.

The only provinces with significant portions of their forests in private hands are Nova Scotia (76 per cent) and New Brunswick (56 per cent). In both Quebec and Ontario, less than 10 per cent of the productive forest is privately held. A negligible amount of private forest land exists in the three Prairie provinces, and British Columbia's government holds about 94 per cent of that province's immensely productive forests.

Although it is difficult to calculate the inventories of these Canadian forests with any degree of accuracy, comparing the allowable annual cut figures with the actual timber harvest in each area reveals a disproportionate reliance on the forests of certain specific regions, similar to the situation in the United States.[3] The Atlantic provinces, with 8.4 per cent of the Canadian allowable annual cut, provide 9.7 per cent of the annual harvest. Quebec, with 14.8 per cent of the allowable cut, accounts for almost 22 per cent of the Canadian harvest. The Prairie provinces have 15.9 per cent of the allowable cut, but contribute only 7.1 per cent of the harvest. Ontario has 23.9 per cent of the allowable cut, but accounts for only 13.4 per cent of the actual volume. British Columbia, with an estimated 36 per cent of the allowable cut, contributes 48 per cent of the Canadian timber harvest each year.

Thus, throughout Canada we can see a pattern of forest land ownership (Nova Scotia and New Brunswick excepted) which closely parallels the pattern that in the United States is found only in the western states: the forest land is government, which is to say publicly, owned. It is hardly surprising that the kind of resource politics found in the western United States are prevalent as well throughout Canada. And given the disproportionate concentration of the Canadian industry in British Columbia, we need not be amazed that some of the most intense conflicts are found in that province.

The above figures also reveal one of the main features of North American resource politics: the Pacific Coast states — primarily California, Oregon and Washington — along with the province of British Columbia, provide the rest of the continent with roughly 40 per cent of its timber supply. This portion is taken from just under 19 per cent of North America's commercial forest lands, which contain about 36 per cent of the continental growing stock.

This area, generally known as the Pacific Northwest, already has substantial amounts of its productive forest land classified for uses that do not permit timber harvesting. About 5 per cent of the Pacific Coast states' productive land is either reserved for parks and wilderness areas, or is under study for possible inclusion in these classifications. In British Columbia, the percentage is only slightly lower. During the last decade or so, legislation passed by the various state, provincial and federal governments has created a number of mechanisms whereby still more productive land can be taken out of the reach of timber harvesters. Although the legislation has not yet resulted in any marked increase in actual removals, it has increased the potential and the probability of such removals, and pressure for further reclassification of forest land usage has resulted.[4]

Most predictions for the future of the Pacific Northwest timber industry indicate reductions in both the land base available for harvesting and the volumes of timber to be harvested. But like most forest resource statistics, these figures vary enormously, depending on who is doing the predicting. In 1980, the B. C. Ministry of Forests released figures projecting "reductions to the provincial productive land base" of about 25 per cent over the next twenty years. But 40 per cent of these so-called reductions consist of land so inaccessible that it is uneconomical for harvest in any case. An almost equal "reduction" was included to allow for environmental protection of other forest resources that could coexist with timber. It seems fair to argue that these are most improperly called reductions, either because they are not genuine exclusions from the forest base or because they should never have been included in the first place. At the same time, the ministry's projections included a notation that the "estimates do not meet the level of reductions necessary to satisfy all other resource agencies' objectives." A strange situation: reductions of dubious authenticity, and a confession that they are inadequate anyhow. In either case, the much-publicized 25 per cent reduction in the provincial productive land base figure is nonsense.

Whether or not these reductions and reclassifications actually take place, the Pacific Northwest has and will continue to have a problem common to all publicly owned lands on the continent: the conflict between the economic value of the timber harvest, based on quantifiable data (harvest dollars, payroll dollars, tax dollars) and other values which are less obvious, either because the data to support their value are not readily available, or because their value is inherently unquantifiable.

In its 1980 technical report, the B. C. Ministry of Forests outlined the economic value of some of the other resources dependent upon the same forest land base as the forest industry.[5] The salmon-producing streams of the province provide spawning grounds for an estimated 10 million fish each year. Spawning salmon produce an annual crop from which almost 23 million fish are harvested. In 1977 the wholesale value of the salmon catch was estimated at $232 million. The salmon spend most of their lives in the ocean, but are dependent for their reproduction on the preservation of the streams. The problem in this instance is that for any given area it is impossible to predict the quantitative effect of a specific timber harvesting program on the production of that area's salmon. So even if the participants in the timber-versus-salmon debate were willing to settle the matter on a purely economic basis — which they are not — there is no way of appraising in fish terms the cost of logging in a certain manner or, conversely, the cost to the timber industry of protecting the salmon stocks.

The question becomes even more difficult with resources that do not have dollar value. In 1977 there were 390,000 licensed freshwater sports fishermen in British Columbia. They and their spokesmen have produced many studies detailing the numbers of fish caught, the average number of fishing days per licencee, expenditures on fishing equipment and so on. But until someone can put a precise dollar value on the enjoyment a fly fisherman feels from a day spent slowly wading up a secluded river, compared with the value of a cubic metre of spruce growing along the banks of that same river, much of the figure-flaunting that goes on in resource politics is meaningless.

A different sort of conflict arises in the province between the B. C. Hydro and Power Authority and other users of the forest. In a 1979 memo to the Ministry of Forests, B. C. Hydro stated that its plans for the next decade would require the permanent removal of about 171 000 ha (422,000 acres) of forest land for proposed reservoirs, dam sites, roads and transmission lines.[6] An enormous public opposition to this program can be expected, largely centred on the effects these projects will have on fish, wildlife and recreational resources. The forest industry will also oppose the reduction of forest lands, but it will never fight B. C. Hydro as energetically as it fights conservationists. This probably has a lot to do with the fact that although these power projects are detrimental to the forest industry in the long run, the industry will take sizable short-term profits from the timber harvested during the site clearances.

Only one thing is certain from all this: the conflicting demands on the Pacific Northwest forest resource base, which have developed over the past two or three decades, are not going to diminish. The now-traditional reliance of North Americans on this region for their softwood lumber and pulp supplies promises a continuing source of revenue that both industry and government want to maintain or even increase. At the same time, a growing number of other forest users, some whose interests are compatible with timber harvesting and some whose are not, are lobbying at the political level to have their requirements met from the same land.

The present era has been called "the period of the great land-grab." At this point, the noisiest battle for control of public forest lands is being fought in the Pacific Northwest. Here, a large established timber industry depends on access to public lands — lands that also support a variety of less tangible but equally desirable resources. But given the nature of the conflict and the political climate of the times, there can be little doubt that the public land-use struggle that is in full cry in this corner of the continent will intensify in other regions containing significant areas of public land.

The conventional solution to these conflicts is the concept of multiple use, or integrated resource management. The theory is attractive: the various groups interested in a particular area of forest land will sit down together and use inventories of the various resources to work out a resource-use plan that satisfies everyone to the greatest possible degree. It is an extension of the utilitarian philosophy of the greatest good for the greatest number.

In practice, the policy is a disaster. Like so many other theories being applied to our forests, the multiple use concept came to North America from nineteenth-century Germany, where the owners of large private estates, unlike their North American counterparts, controlled not only the trees on their lands but also the wildlife in the forests and the fish in the streams. It was economically logical for them to treat their forests as ecological entities, investing time and money in fish and wildlife as well as in trees. They found profit from these investments by selling hunting, fishing and recreational privileges to the public.

That situation has never existed in North America. Ownership of land here does not normally confer such comprehensive rights. And in the case of public lands, the various resources have over the years become the responsibility of a wide variety of government departments, ministries, branches and agencies, each of which usually has jurisdiction over just one resource. The confusion is compounded by the existence of three levels of government — federal, provincial or state, and regional or municipal — each of which is likely to be pursuing different policies.

Therefore, the utilization of public lands is almost always restricted to a single use per user. Within a single watershed, separate licences or permits will probably be required for sport fishing, commercial fishing, hunting, water rights, recreational activities, timber harvesting and so on. The holder of a timber permit need feel no particular concern over the state of the water or fish. Conflicts arise, and as they do there is a tendency for the various user groups to form shifting alliances with each other and with certain government agencies. The result is often a glorious free-for-all as the various factions flog each other with dubious statistics, irrelevant data and a great deal of public posturing. All too often the dust settles to reveal a sort of compromise in which the ecological realities of the land are lost.

Until the last decade or so, the chief beneficiaries of this procedure were the timber companies. Their ability to generate from the forests quick and enormous revenues, a share of which was paid to government, gave them a definite advantage. But in recent years they have begun to lose a lot of ground — literally as well as figuratively. Now, even where the facts speak otherwise, they behave as though they are fighting a rearguard action against a mounting coalition of bureaucrats, "eco-freaks" and a largely unsympathetic public which, in theory at least, owns the bulk of the productive forest lands in North America.

The "land grab" of the past few years is a reflection of this chaotic conflict. It is a response by various resource users —

notably the forest industry — designed to tie up as much productive forest land as possible, preferably in perpetuity. These attempts to secure long-term land tenure emphasize the importance, or at least the possibilities, of resource management, whether it be the management of fish, wildlife, timber, water or whatever.

The basic principle of resource management in North America is that whoever owns the resource pays for its management. The owner can expect to recover the management costs when the resource is utilized. Because most forest land in western Canada is publicly owned, the vested interest groups and the relevant government agencies are generating tremendous pressure for the expenditure of enormous sums of money on the management of the various resources. Ultimately, the public must approve these expenditures. For a government like that of British Columbia, which has been in the habit of regarding its forests as a source of income rather than an expense, the prospective costs of intensive forest management — costs that will not pay off for decades — themselves become a highly charged political issue.

The potential costs of long-term management of North America's 2 400 000 km² (930,000 square miles) of publicly owned commercial forest land over a single crop rotation — anywhere between thirty and one hundred years — are indicated by the costs of the various silvicultural treatments now being applied to the forests. During 1979 and 1980, the B. C. Ministry of Forests spent $6.1 million on the reforestation of 7800 ha (19,274 acres) — $782 per hectare ($316 per acre), $78,200 per square kilometre ($30,200 per square mile).[7] And that is just reforestation. Juvenile spacing — thinning the young stands — took $13.3 million for 21 000 ha (52,000 acres) — $633 per hectare ($256 per acre), $63,300 per square kilometre ($24,450 per square mile). Fertilizing 19 700 ha (48,700 acres) cost $2.8 million — $142 per hectare ($57 per acre), $14,200 per square kilometre ($5,480 per square mile). Together, these various efforts amounted to about $1,550 per hectare ($628 per acre), or $155,000 per square kilometre ($403,000 per square mile). A similar program applied to the continent's 2 400 000 km² (930,000 square miles) of public commercial forest would cost $372 billion. Of course, these are

B. C. figures and cannot be applied to the rest of the continent quite so simply. On the other hand, the B. C. figures are probably low since the treatments were carried out on some of the most accessible areas in the province.

The figures must be further qualified. The planting and thinning costs can be apportioned over the time span involved in the rotation of the forest in question. However, fertilizers must be applied more frequently. Further, many important silvicultural treatments have been omitted from these estimates — disease and pest control, research, firefighting and so forth.

Let us put dollar figures on the most conservative picture. Assuming a full one-hundred-year rotation and applying only the most basic silviculture — planting, thinning and fertilizing — to a mere 25 per cent of the productive lands gives us a public expenditure in North America of nearly $1 billion a year.

Of course, we are not spending that kind of money now. In 1979, the total public expenditure on all silvicultural treatments in Canada was $156.2 million. Critics delight in pointing out that governments spend on forest managment only a small fraction of the revenues they collect from the forests. That $156.2 million was only 5 per cent of the more than $3 billion the governments reaped from forest activity.

The forest industry, most professional foresters, a growing number of conservationists and other users of forest resources all argue that silvicultural treatment and expenditure must be increased far beyond present levels or else massive timber shortages will occur, with a concomitant depletion of all other resources associated with forests. The expectation, of course, is that the various public treasuries will bear these expenses, plus the billions more for environmental protection, road building, research, administration and so on.

If a crisis is indeed upon us, surely the only sensible thing to do is spend whatever is needed to avoid it. But what if there is no crisis? The figures dazzle us. Who can grasp the reality of a billion dollars, a hundred million cubic metres of wood, a million square kilometres of forest?

If we fear a crisis in our forests, we can either accept the arguments for increased silvicultural expenditures, or alternatively we can remember that all the figures to support these arguments have been pulled from data bases and inventories that more often than not are outdated, speculative or just plain wrong. Indeed, most of the dire predictions come from an industry that sustains itself on publicly owned forest lands. The same predictions are gravely supported by government bureaucracies that have never been known to turn down a chance to spend extra money.

Even more important than the questionableness of the crisis is the fact that the proposed solution — intensive forest management — is based on a European theory which has never been made to work on this continent. The theory of sustained yield assumes that we can get through the crisis with intensive management; but without more silvicultural knowledge than we now possess, we cannot accurately predict the consequences of such a policy. Until we know more about how to manage our forests, we cannot be sure that intensive management will guarantee a perpetual supply of timber without ruinous long-term effects on the character and quality of our forests.

Nor can intensive management by itself resolve the social, economic and political conflicts that dominate resource-use policy in North America. Until these problems are solved and until we know more about growing trees and forests, sustained yield will remain a chimera. Yet the theory of sustained yield is the major weapon in the industry's battle for control of the forest land resource in western Canada.

The real solution lies not in intensive management or sustained yield, but in a profound change in our attitudes and relationship to the forest. Somehow we must learn to manage the forest in the same way that farmers manage their land. We must cease to be merely exploiters of the forest resource and become instead cultivators and nurturers. But in order to do this, we must also establish a relationship to the forests that will allow us to accumulate the knowledge and experience essential for sound silvicultural practices. Only if we acquire this knowledge through intimate, long-term study and experimentation in a variety of particular forest environments will we be able to preserve our forest heritage while at the same time enhancing its social and economic benefits.

In many respects, the situation is comparable to the effort of convincing a tribe of hunters and gatherers to invest their energies and resources in tilling the soil. Such transitions bring about what anthropologists call a "cultural shift," a period of conflict for the individuals directly involved and for their society. Given the primitive state of silviculture in most of North America, it is not surprising that cultural conflicts are developing as we shift from a forest-cutting to a forest-farming economy, displacing as we do so many habits and hallowed concepts.

TWO

How Did It All Begin?

HISTORICALLY, THE DEVELOPMENT of the forest industry and the practices of forest management on public lands in North America has consisted of a series of conflicts and uncertain resolutions. There is little reason to expect that the present stage of the process will be any different. We are still in the process of sorting out appropriate methods and concepts.

The lumbering industry on this continent began in the East with the arrival of the first European immigrants. Their primary concern was to clear land for agriculture, and they used the timber for their homes and barns and fences.

This early logging was accomplished almost totally with muscle power of both man and beast. Only the best logs were removed from the woods, and only the best logs were put through the early sawmills. There was little sense of what we today would call waste — the forest seemed endless.

Until late in the nineteenth century, forests were viewed as a resource to be exploited and, in the end, eliminated in the name of a higher economic use for the land. As the Euro-American civilization spread westward across the continent, virtually no consideration was given to the preservation or perpetuation of forests. In much of the United States, most of the land passed into private hands, but in Canada, with a smaller population and an inherited British tradition of Crown lands, a much larger proportion remained in public ownership. There was little concern in either case for the supply of timber. The western forests lay virtually untouched and there was a widespread belief that the forests were inexhaustible. By the middle of the last century, the vast hardwood and white pine forests of the East had been devastated.

A reaction against this devastation set in and during the 1860s and 1870s, state and provincial governments initiated tree planting programs. Railway companies, with their insatiable need for ties and timbers, began tree nurseries, and by 1880 plantation forestry was well established in eastern Canada and the eastern and midwestern United States. The sandy wastelands of Cape Cod, created by the lumbering of the pilgrims, were reforested with pine. Tree planting programs were initiated in the American Midwest and the Canadian Prairies, areas that had been stripped of trees to create farmland. During the 1880s, the Canadian Pacific Railway was establishing plantations along its right-of-way in the Prairies. By 1883, 100 000 ha (250,000 acres) had been planted in Nebraska alone.

Very little of this activity, however, was concerned with forestry or forest management — at least as those terms are understood in North America today. Such plantations were, in part, a branch of agriculture. In part they were the outgrowth of a conservationist movement which began then. The idea of managing an existing, natural forest was unknown, and such an approach would have been strenuously resisted, particularly by conservationists.

Until 1876, there did not exist in North America one professionally trained forester. The forestry movement, if it can be called that, was in the hands of botanists, agriculturalists, naturalists, lumbermen and conservationists. Public concern and enthusiasm manifested itself in arbor days, when trees were planted in large numbers but with little or no thought for providing a future timber supply. Some northeastern states began acquiring land, most of it already cut over, to create forest reserves. In later years, these efforts were ridiculed by professional foresters because they were not undertaken according to the principles — nor in a spirit of — "scientific forest management."

A young Prussian visited the United States in 1876. Bernhard Fernow was twenty-five at the time. He had been trained as a forester in Germany with the thought that he would eventually take over the management of his uncle's large forest estate. However, in Germany he met an American woman, followed her to the United States, married her and remained.

Because there were no jobs available for a professional forester, he worked as a mining engineer for a number of years before being appointed chief of the division of forestry of the U. S. Department of Agriculture in 1886.

At this time, a pitched battle was being waged between lumbermen and conservationists, the latter being known at the time as "denudiatics" — roughly equivalent to today's "ecofreaks." The lumbermen wanted to log and move on; the conservationists were adamantly opposed to logging, especially to the cutting of second-growth forests in state reserves which had often been assembled as a result of their efforts.

Fernow's position placed him initially in the camp of the denudiatics. He argued for the protection of water resources and for "legislation looking towards the preservation of the remaining natural forests." But as a forester he also maintained that "forests grow and are grown to be cut and to furnish valuable material to man. Their influence, climatic and hydraulic, is by no means destroyed or checked, by a well-conducted, systematic forestry, which utilizes the ripe timber, taking care for its immediate regeneration for the continuity of the forest as well as the timber supply. . . ."[1]

This approach, which he had learned in Germany, and which was known as sustained yield forestry, appeared to offer the best of both worlds and to be an acceptable middle ground in the controversy. In 1900, 12 100 ha (30,000 acres) of the Adirondack reserve were set aside as a demonstration forest to be managed by Cornell University, which then established a school of forestry with Fernow as director. The existing forest was predominantly hardwood, with some spruce. Fernow's plan was to create a dominant spruce forest, since it was the most valuable wood with the best market. The area would be a multiple-use forest which, in addition to producing a steady flow of commercial timber, would protect the watersheds and provide for recreational activities. The techniques Fernow proposed to demonstrate the advantages of scientific management included clearcutting and replanting half of the forest. The remaining stands would benefit from such silvicultural practices as thinning, selective cuttings and coppice cuttings — taking out small trees and undergrowth. The clearcutting was barely begun when protests started. The conservationist movements which had been largely instrumental in creating the forest reserve were outraged. The Association for the Protection of the Adirondacks was formed and Fernow was accused of wanting to clearcut the entire Adirondacks. Some of the most active objections came from a group of wealthy cottage owners with property near the forests to be clearcut; they launched legal actions to prevent the logging. In the uproar, the state cut off funding for the forestry school, and it was forced to close down. Thus, the first attempt at sustained yield forestry in North America died in its infancy.

The concept of sustained yield forestry that Fernow had proposed for North America was workable within the stable, fixed social structures of nineteenth-century Germany where there were no virgin forests, but it was less appropriate in the highly mobile society of North America with its vast areas of untouched forest lands. It is also clear, from Fernow's writings, that his concepts of forestry were inextricably bound up with the social, economic and political views of mid-nineteenth-century central Europe. Among these was a well-developed sense of historical determinism.

> The history of the woodlands has been the same in all parts of the world, progressing according to the cultural development of the people. First the forest was valued as a harbour of game, then it appeared as an impediment to agricultural development, and relentless war was waged against it, while at the same time the value of its material stores made it an object of greedy exploitation, and only in a highly civilized nation and in a well-settled country does the conception of the relation of forests to the future welfare of the community lead to a rational treatment of forests as such for continuity and to the application of the principles embodied in the science of forestry.[2]

Such concepts were alien to North American thinking in the mid-nineteenth century. Fernow perceived two major obstacles to the adoption of scientific forest management in North America. The first was North America's love of small, independent businesses, and its acceptance of the theories of Adam Smith, which advocated removal of the restrictive practices of government and opposed the state as property owner. Fernow looked ahead to the day "finally when the ideal, the socialistic, co-operative, most highly organized state will have developed, the policy will be that the community shall own or control and devote to forest crops all the poorest soils and sites, leaving only the agricultural soils and pastures to private enterprise."[3]

Fernow was not so much a socialist as an advocate of large organizations: "Trusts . . . properly organized for continuous business, may prove next to governments the most hopeful agencies for practicing forestry, since they control large areas under uniform and continuous policy."[4] And in a speech he gave at Kingston, Ontario, on sustained yield forestry: "Only governments and perpetual corporations or large capitalists can afford to make the sacrifices which are necessary to prepare now for such a management."[5]

The second major obstacle to the implementation of sustained yield forestry on this continent, in Fernow's mind, was the enormous area of its virgin forests.

> The virgin forest and the forester's forest will necessarily differ, inasmuch as the former is merely the result of a natural evolutionary struggle among the different forms of vegetation, in which the "most fit" survivors may not be the economically desirable, while the forester substitutes artificial selection for natural selection, and makes sure of the protected survival of the most useful.[6]

Fernow called this cultivated forest the "normal forest." It was an ideal, designed for many uses, yet providing a constant volume of timber forever. The object of sustained yield forestry was to create the ideal, or "normal," forest. Given the available technology and the timber markets of Fernow's day, this task appeared overwhelming.

Although Fernow's ideas had suffered a major setback in the Adirondacks and had encountered opposition elsewhere, there was cause for optimism in the fact that the major forested areas of North America still resided in public hands. In the western United States, the federal government had, in creating National Forests, retained control over enormous areas. In Canada, particularly in British Columbia, provincial governments leaned towards policies that maintained public ownership of forest lands.

Forestry was also gaining acceptance as a science, particularly in government circles, and when the Society of American Foresters was formed in 1900, Fernow became a member. The believers in a rational approach to forestry were almost religious in their devotion to scientific methodology. Fernow and like-minded professional foresters saw themselves almost as a kind of priesthood. They corresponded with each other about the best means of achieving sustained yield forestry as discussed in Fernow's standard text on the subject, *The Economics of Forestry,* published in 1902. Over the next few years, this relatively small group was to have enormous influence on the development of forest policy, both in the western United States and in Canada, and particularly in British Columbia. Fernow was even strongly opposed to making forestry techniques available to everyone, partly because he feared the errors which would come from superficial knowledge, but also because he was afraid of flooding the employment market with professionally trained foresters.[7]

Following the closure of the Cornell forestry school, Fernow became dean of forestry at Pennsylvania State College. Then a year later, in 1907, he occupied the same seat at the University of Toronto when Canada's first forestry school opened. The next year, he organized the Canadian Society of Forest Engineers, which demanded professional status for membership, in contrast to the existing Canadian Forestry Association to which anyone interested in forestry could belong.

One of Fernow's students at Cornell had been a young man named Judson Clark. After graduation, Clark spent six months studying in Germany and returned to teach forestry at Cornell. When the Cornell forestry school closed, Clark was hired by the Ontario government and thus became the first government-employed professional forester in Canada.

At the turn of the century, a series of events occurred which was to transform the face of the continental forest industry. The U. S. lumber industry had for some time been concentrated in the northern forests of Wisconsin, Michigan and Minnesota. By the end of the nineteenth century, the U. S. industry had spilled over into Ontario, and in 1898 that province prohibited the export of logs cut on Crown land. Three years later, Theodore Roosevelt came into power in the United States on a platform of conservation of natural resources. Within a few years, Roosevelt had placed almost 61 000 000 ha (150,000,000 acres) of forest land in National Forest reserves and out of reach of lumbermen.

The lumbering industry gravitated towards the nearest source of available timber — British Columbia. The McBride government of that province, anxious for increased revenues, welcomed the U. S. lumbermen and encouraged them to take out twenty-one-year renewable timber leases and licences. The licencee was given ownership of the timber, but title to the land remained with the Crown. The Americans liked this arrangement and an enormous timber rush started. During 1900, 143 leases and licences were issued, producing revenues to the B. C. government of about $135,000. In 1907, when the rush was in full flow, 10,456 licences were issued and provincial revenues had increased to $1.25 million. The government of the wealthiest forest lands of North America had discovered a rich new source of funds.

Perhaps the first professional forester to realize the opportunities available in British Columbia was Judson Clark. He quit his job with the Ontario government in 1906 and became managing director of the Continental Timber Company in Vancouver. His professional training and experience placed him in an excellent position to locate and appraise valuable timber stands for his company. At the same time, he advised the B. C. government on forest policy and served as a liaison between the government and Fernow, who was in Toronto.

Fernow's advice was valued by both the McBride government and Fred Fulton, the land commissioner who chaired the first B. C. Royal Commission on forest resources. Fernow made a number of suggestions, including the establishment of a provincial forestry service and the taking of an inventory of the province's forests. When the government acted on Fernow's recommendation and established a provincial forestry service in 1912, it also accepted his suggestion for British Columbia's first chief forester — H. R. MacMillan.

MacMillan wrote to Fernow: "We are the only Forest Branch in Canada having actual control of all timber business of one province, or jurisdiction. For this reason we shall require a large number of foresters of administrative ability. . . ."[8]

Fernow recommended that MacMillan employ Judson Clark in the proposed survey of timber resources; so, in that same year, Clark set up the province's first forest engineering firm working under contract to the new Forest Branch. When MacMillan organized the Society of B. C. Foresters, Clark became its first president. Two years later, Fernow was elected president of both the Society of American Foresters and the Canadian Society of Forest Engineers. In March 1914, Fernow received one of his regular communications from MacMillan:

> . . . at the present we are trying to bring about cleaner logging and slash disposal that will facilitate the best natural reproduction. Forest management of British Columbia is, I think, merely a question of the success or failure of those men whom we now have in the Forest Branch. I myself am extremely optimistic and think that there will be Province-wide forest management here before any place else in Canada.[9]

As it turned out, MacMillan's optimism was premature. That year, World War I threw the B. C. forest industry into chaos. The ranks of the Forest Branch were decimated as young foresters volunteered to fight in Europe. It would be another thirty years before British Columbia's forests would be brought under any form of scientific management. By that time, Bernhard Fernow was gone; he died in 1923.

How could a handful of men, all students of a German-trained forester with limited practical experience, exercise such a profound influence on the direction of North American forestry? Part of the answer probably has to do with Fernow's belief that the state or, secondly, large trusts were best suited to managing forests. In the Canadian case, and particularly in British Columbia, this argument undoubtedly appealed to politicians striving to secure the power of their governments while dealing with a lumber industry controlled largely from the United States.

Fernow's ideas appeared at a critical point. The lumber industry at the turn of the century operated on an ethic of "cut the best, leave the rest and move on." At the same time, a large and powerful conservationist movement was successfully removing large areas of forest land from the reach of loggers. An enormous conflict was developing, and Fernow's theories appeared to offer something to both sides. He proposed a "scientific" form of management which would preserve timber resources while allowing commercial exploitation of the forest.

Scientific methods were first applied to North American forests in an attempt to quantify them, to conceptualize them in terms both of area and of the amount of resources they contained. A scientific method of measurement known as "mensuration" was the first step in forest management. Fernow brought the science of forest mensuration to North America and taught it at Cornell and Toronto. His first recommendations to the B. C. government included a suggestion that the government conduct an inventory of the province's forests; Fernow and his successors wanted to achieve an objective, scientifically accurate description of the forests. Yet measurement also had another function: the practical value of the inventories lay in identifying the areas of forest that could most profitably be exploited for timber.

The mensuration arsenal includes many techniques for calculating the timber resources of a forest, but basically the method involves determining the volume of standing trees in certain sample areas. Statistical methods are then employed to provide estimates of timber volume, species, disease and so forth for large areas of forest land. When growth rate data are added in, the result is an estimate of the future state of the forests. Since Fernow's day, mensurationists have acquired new and improved tools. Statistical sampling and processing have both been refined; aerial photography, then three-dimensional photography and most recently satellite photography have eased the mensurationists' task. Computers now process large quantities of information in less time than it takes to cut down a tree.

Nevertheless, the procedure allows considerable room for error. How can we with certainty rely on statistical samples for areas as obstinately unique as fingerprints? And to extrapolate from samples to the entire forest region requires the correct choice between several highly debatable statistical formulae. If we cannot plan a sunny picnic even a week hence, how can we predict the state of a forest ten years from now, during which time the unpredictable weather will have directly affected not only the growth rate of the forest but also the nature and severity of disease and insect infestation?

Since Fernow's time, there have been many attempts to measure the forest, and each attempt has been spawned by some inadequacy of a previous effort. Indeed, so frequently have these inadequacies been revealed that one can only marvel at the assurance with which politicians and bureaucrats quote the latest inventory data. Since these assessments never agree, one can only assume that measuring the forest is far from being a simple matter. Forest measurement is in fact fraught with subtleties and difficulties.[10]

One difficulty is the matter of definition. What is "forest land"? Where does the forest end and the Prairie or tundra begin? Is it a question of the number of trees per hectare? If so, how many? And what is the basis for that figure? Similarly, what is a "productive forest"? Or a "commercial forest"? These definitions, difficult enough to establish initially, change over time with changes in legislation, in technology and in the uses made of the various forest components.

Yet again, how can one measure something that is in a state of perpetual change, and which changes at no fixed or constant rate? One could perhaps factor in some average growth rate were it not that forests, at a certain point of maturity, actually experience negative growth — they lose volume. The forest cycle of birth, growth and death is profoundly influenced by an infinite number of variables, almost all of them unpredictable.

The sheer enormity and variety of the wooded land is yet another factor. About one-third of North America is covered with forest. Of this third, no one spot is quite like another. Over the entire forest area, the variety and complexity passeth all understanding.

The statistical process is not immune to criticism, either. Mark Twain observed that "there's liars, there's damned liars, and there's statistics." Although he was referring to the deliberate or accidental abuse of statistics, he could as easily have been discussing the very science itself.

Statistics always deals with uncertainty, and so fundamental is this relationship that the results are expressed in terms that are themselves uncertain. Statistical terms define the limits within which an event may be expected to happen, and how many times in one hundred that it will happen within those limits. This last expression implies a certain lack of confidence in the defined limits, since it indicates the number of times in one hundred that the event will fall outside them.

Despite its uncertainty, statistical method is a valuable tool for dealing with one variable. As the number of variables increases, however, so do the uncertainties. Worse, the various levels of uncertainty may not simply be added together; they must be multiplied. Conclusion: the more magnificently variable the forest, the less confidence we may have in our attempts to quantify and qualify it.

The point here is not to question the competence or integrity of the mensurationists; nor is it the point to question the motives of those who use the figures with such confident assurance of their accuracy. The point is simply that we have never had, nor do we have now, an accurate quantitative or qualitative measurement of our forests. Yet scientific forest management, as defined by its own proponents, requires an accurate appraisal of the forest under consideration.

Loggers generally take a more shirt-sleeve approach to forest management. An experienced logger or timber cruiser would spend the morning walking through a stand and work out the calculations over lunch. "It should run about fifty thousand feet to the acre, maybe a little thinner at the top end. If we work up that ridge, along the bluff to the creek and down again, there's maybe a hundred acres. Say five million feet to be safe. That'd get us out of here by Christmas next year."

If the Forest Service were to send in someone to apply scientific techniques of measurement to the same stand, they might arrive at a figure of three million feet. When the timber was harvested, the logs measured and the waste calculated, the final figures would be as likely to show the logger right as the Forest Service expert.

As late as 1980, I worked a show that was cruised, with the most up-to-date techniques, at 26 cunits (100 cubic feet) an acre (7 m^3 per ha). We took out 40. This is a 65 per cent margin of error. I would submit that this scale of error does not necessarily disappear when measurement techniques are applied to the entire forest resources of a province, a country or a continent.[11]

Right or wrong, figures are to forest economists and planners what logs are to sawmill operators. They are added and subtracted, multiplied and divided, proportionalized and decimalized, cross-referenced and compared, converted to and from metric, and used and abused to bolster just about any argument from just about any interest group. In large part they are used by the timber harvesting industry to convince the politician and the public of the crucial economic importance of the timber harvesting industry.

Actually, there is little reason to doubt that economic importance. In 1978, wages totalling some $5.5 billion were paid to 300,000 workers in the Canadian forest industry. This compares with $1.1 billion paid to 693,500 agricultural workers, or $3.1 billion earned by 234,200 miners.

Governments find various ways to share in the economic benefits of timber harvesting. By means of stumpage charges, royalties, land rents and personal and corporate income taxes, the Canadian government received $1.3 billion in 1979. The provincial governments did even better: they realized $1.7 billion, of which the government of British Columbia received 55 per cent.[12]

Industry people are quick to point out that only a small portion of those government revenues ever returns to the woods in the form of forest management. Of the $3 billion collected by all governments in Canada during 1979, only 5 per cent was spent on forestry. In that same year, the B. C. government took in $759.1 million more than it spent on management of the forests. That "profit" amounted to 10.9 per cent of provincial revenue.

There is a hidden problem with statistics which purport to show the economic value of forest lands: they create a distorted assessment of the forests' true worth. There is more to the woods than trees and taxes. Forests generate a variety of benefits which have little to do with their industrial importance. They provide habitat for fish and wildlife, they are critical in regulating water resources, they produce an important share of the world's oxygen, they offer recreation — the list is almost endless. Most of these benefits cannot be measured in dollars.

A major factor in attempting to assess the relative importance of the various forest resources or values is that the keystone forest policy, sustained yield, concerns itself almost exclusively with commercial timber values. The shortcomings of this policy are the subject of the next chapter.

THREE

What's Wrong With Sustained Yield?

IN 1908 MARTIN GRAINGER CREATED this classic portrait of the brutal logger in his novel about turn-of-the-century British Columbia logging, *Woodsmen of the West.* Here is Grainger's description of Carter, the logging boss:

> Much he cared that he was spoiling leases for future working, like a mine manager who should hurriedly exhaust the rich patches of his mine. Leases, he said, were going up in value. Someone would find it worthwhile, some day, to buy from him the stretches of forest whose sea-fronts he had shattered and left in tangled wreckage. As for him, he was going to butcher his woods as he pleased. It paid.[1]

Two years later, in 1910, Grainger served as secretary to British Columbia's first Royal Commission on forest resources. In his report, a document that was to shape the province's forest policy for forty years, he wrote: "Everywhere, in the early developments of lumbering, cheap stumpage is seen to have been accompanied by butchery of wood; for human nature is careless of anything of low commercial value, especially when the supply seems inexhaustible and waste costs nothing to the waster."[2] Six years after this, Grainger became the province's chief forester.

Grainger's report did not recommend the adoption of sustained yield forest policy for British Columbia; that was not to come until after the second Royal Commission in 1945. But the philosophy of sustained yield, as imported from Germany by Bernhard Fernow and eventually promulgated throughout North America, shared the classic view of the independent logging operation as a selfish exploiter of the forest resource.

The classic sustained yield theory developed in Germany during the eighteenth and nineteenth centuries was quite simple: in order to sustain productivity, employment and a constant flow of forest products, the annual cut should equal the annual growth. The growth would occur on the younger trees; the harvest would come from the older, mature trees on which growth had slowed. One did not cut more than the annual growth in a given year since this would bring about future shortages. Nor did one cut less, for this would tie up land that could be stocked with young, fast-growing trees.

In practice, the theory was applied to a management unit, which might be a private estate or a state-owned forest. For example, if this unit were 10 000 ha (24,710 acres) in area and consisted of uniformly productive land that grew trees which matured at an age of one hundred years, then 100 ha (247 acres) would be harvested annually. If each hectare produced 10 m^3 (353 cubic feet) of wood each year, the annual harvest would be 100 000 m^3 (3.5 million cubic feet). Deductions from this volume would be made for losses due to fire, disease and insect damage. Increases in the cut could be made only if productivity were increased through the application of various silvicultural practices that would boost the growth rate. After a century of this type of management, the forest would contain an even distribution of age classes, and each year 1 per cent of it would be harvested and planted. German foresters called this a "normal" forest. Creation of a normal forest was one of the primary objectives of their forest policies. Once achieved, the normal forest would sustain itself perpetually.

A sustained yield policy requires that landowners be both willing and financially able to resist the temptation to increase their immediate revenues, which they could do by either increasing the annual cut or by decreasing the expenditures required to secure the annual growth. An increased demand for timber tends to drive prices up, creating an immediate incentive for the forest owners to realize a quick profit. Since a heavier cut would not decrease the future supplies for perhaps another century, why not cut? Fortunately for the European enthusiasts of sustained yield forestry, increased demand during the nineteenth century could be met by importing timber from the unregulated forest lands of North

America. To a certain extent sustained yield forestry was possible in nineteenth century Europe because it was not being practised elsewhere.

Transplanting sustained yield theory to North America required dealing with social and economic difficulties. When Fernow and his disciples began broadcasting their ideas on this continent, the twin bases of the forest industry were speculation and exploitation. One invested in forest land or leases with the expectation of selling them when the price of timber increased, not to obtain a perpetual timber supply. One did not invest money in the growing of trees when the continent was covered with a natural forest that grew itself gratis.

Fernow was not blind to this. He realized that "all that can be expected from private forest owners is that they may practise more conservative and careful logging of the natural woods, avoiding unnecessary waste, and as far as possible paying attention to silviculture, the reproduction of the crop, leaving to the future the attempt to organize a sustained yield management."[3] Overall, he concluded that governments and large corporations were in the best position to undertake such a program of management.

The major physical difficulty with transplanting the sustained yield theory to this continent was that the North American forest, which consisted of millions of square kilometres of unmanaged timberland, was about as different as it could possibly be from the European concept of the normal forest. As Fernow explained:

> In the actual forest, some one condition or all conditions will usually be found abnormal. The normal accretion may be deficient, because the area is not fully stocked or the timber is past its prime, old timber growing at an inferior rate, or rot offsetting increment. The age classes are usually not present in proper gradation and amount; some of them are probably entirely lacking, others are in excess, either too many stands of older or of younger timber, so that even if the normal stock of wood in amount be on hand, it may be in abnormal distribution."[4]

The challenge for sustained yield foresters, then, was to liquidate the "abnormal," actual North American forest in order to replace it with the scientifically managed "normal" forest. The central problem was deciding how rapidly to harvest the natural forest so that an even flow of timber could be obtained during the transition from a natural to a managed forest system.

Sustained yield policies received no legal recognition in North America for more than half a century. Yet the theory provided a coherent set of principles around which foresters, and particularly government-employed foresters, could rally, principles which could be used as the basis of an argument against unrestricted harvesting. Until after World War II, two essential viewpoints dominated the shaping of forest management legislation: one view held that the wood supply was without limits, that forests were growing faster than they could be cut; the other held that the forests would eventually be cleared for agricultural use. It was against these viewpoints that Fernow's successors put forth the idea of continuous timber production. But they were confronted not only by an industry that would accept only the market restrictions of rising and falling demand but also by governments that had become accustomed to steadily increasing revenues from timber harvesting on public lands.

The debate could continue to rage because no one knew how much timber was available. In part this was because inventory methods were crude and inaccurate. Every survey of forest resources came up with widely divergent figures. In British Columbia, for example, the 1910 Forest Service estimates indicated reserves of 240 billion board feet; seven years later a new calculation indicated 336 billion board feet. Twenty years later, in 1937, the figure had dropped to 254 billion, then over the next twenty years the estimates rose again to 760 billion board feet. These dramatic changes could be justified: technological changes not only made previously inaccessible timber available but also increased the amount of lumber that could be recovered from each log at the mill. Few people in industry or government were willing to accept the professional argument that the future of the industry depended on regulating the cut and a long-term yield policy. Every logger knew from experience that Forest Service timber estimates on a particular piece of land might be off by as much as 50 per cent — and they were invariably low.

But the main issue in British Columbia during the immediate postwar years was not the threat of timber shortages. Each participant in the debate had a different interest. The great concern of industry, as revealed in testimony before the Sloan Commission in 1947, was to assure itself of a long-term timber supply in order to finance the building of new pulp- and sawmills. The chief concern of the Forest Service was that it be given a set of revamped laws and regulations to steer its way out of the bureaucratic mess it had created for itself in three decades of operation. The professional foresters' main interest was that some form of scientific management be instituted, as opposed to what they called "cut-and-get-out" policies. Sloan tried to make everyone happy.

Conventional wisdom has always held that Sloan was the architect of sustained yield forestry in British Columbia. In fact, the policies and legislation were created by the Forest Service and its chief forester, C. D. Orchard. The Sloan Commission served as a convenient and acceptable means of introducing the concept to the public. Orchard left documented evidence of this process in the forest history project he undertook for the University of British Columbia after his retirement from the Forest Service in 1958. The essence of the Sloan report, and the legislation that followed it, appeared in a confidential document prepared by Orchard in 1942. In 1959 he said of this document:

> This memorandum was prepared and submitted to the Minister of Lands, the Hon. A. Wells Gray, in August 1942. There were about half a dozen copies of which this was my personal copy. Mr. Gray read it, discussed it with me, and took it to the Premier, Hon. John Hart, who kept it for more than a year, discussing it with me and with his friends in the industry, some of whom he sent to me to argue the matter and then to report back to him. Some prominent industrialists, amongst them, I recall particularly Syd. Smith, had it for review. As I remember it didn't cause any great stir amongst any such — just another crazy Civil Service brain wave that wouldn't be heard of again.
>
> In December 1943 the Premier, Mr. Hart, called me to his office, when he told me that the Government was "sold" on my proposals, but that he couldn't hope to get such a radical change

> of policy through the legislature if it were introduced "cold." He, therefore, proposed to appoint a Royal Commission, he thought one man and hoped that it would be the Chief Justice, Hon. Gordon Sloan, to canvas [*sic*] the proposition, both for the value of his findings and as a measure of public education.
>
> The Commission was appointed accordingly as of 31 December, 1943, and the rest of the story is public property. The Commission, approved, and the sustained yield policy was introduced in the Legislation of 1947.[5]

Couched in the language and framed around the concepts of classical sustained yield forestry, Sloan's recommendations were designed to bring the provincially owned timber lands under a regulated form of management which would maximize the productive capacity of the forests. He defined sustained yield as "a perpetual yield of wood of commercially usable quality from regional areas in yearly or periodic quantities of equal or increasing volume."[6] The great hope was that a sustained yield policy would stabilize the regional economies which were based on forest industries, as well as maintain a continuing forest cover "adequate to perform the invaluable functions of watershed protection, stream flow and run-off control, the prevention of soil erosion, and of providing recreational and scenic areas, and a home for our wild bird and animal life."

Sloan's first objective was to set in motion a cut-control policy that would "normalize" the province's natural forests. There has long been a misconception that sustained yield forestry began with the implementation of Sloan's recommendations in 1947. What actually occurred then was a decision to begin regulating the harvest of natural, mature forests to create — but only at some unspecified time in the future — forests containing that even distribution of age classes which would then yield a constant volume of timber in perpetuity. This may seem like a subtle distinction, hinging on mere semantics, but it has been at the core of some of the most controversial issues of B. C. forestry for more than thirty years.

The impact of this decision was enormous, though not immediately apparent. Sloan and the government of the day that implemented his recommendations were committing the province to a decades-long course of action that had only one objective: the realization of that somewhat hazy abstraction brought to this continent by Fernow — the creation of the "normal" forest.

When a decision is made to convert a large forest jurisdiction to sustained yield regulation, as in British Columbia in 1947 or in the U. S. National Forests in 1960, the first step is to break up this area into a number of management units, each of which will ultimately constitute a "normal" forest complete with an even distribution of age classes yielding a more or less steady annual harvest. Creating the management units is more than just an administrative convenience. North American sustained yield forestry has always been seen as an instrument of government economic and social policy, especially as a tool to influence regional economic development. To this end, Sloan clearly stated that the management unit must be manageable under one plan. No nineteenth-century European estates were available in twentieth-century British Columbia to serve as convenient management units, so Sloan offered this model:

> The "regional area" of my definition is therefore a sustained-yield unit capable of being managed under the provisions of one and the same working plan. It should not be so large that objectives having social implications cannot be achieved, nor so small that it does not include the necessary range of growing stock to provide an annual yield large enough for profitable operation. It may or may not coincide with an administrative forest unit. It may include more than one type of forest and be managed to supply more than one type of conversion plant, but to satisfy the essential criteria of a sustained-yield unit, it must be organized regionally to produce a sustained annual yield under a single working plan.[7]

In some areas it was deemed wise to shape the management units to reflect the existing patterns of timber usage; to define a management unit as the area providing timber for a processing mill or a number of mills. In areas dependent on land transportation, there are natural economic limits to the size of the area; the cost of transporting timber by truck or rail is proportional to the distance. In coastal areas, the main cost of transporting logs is getting them to the salt water and prepared for towing to a mill; once they are in this state, it costs little more to tow them 500 km rather than 50. In remote areas containing no processing plants, the defining of a sustained yield management unit could be used as an instrument to encourage development of a timber processing industry.

In British Columbia, the coalition government of the late 1940s created two major types of sustained yield management units. One, Forest Management Licences (later Tree Farm Licences, or TFLs), were to be managed by private industry. They were given to individual companies and were intended to supply the timber needs of a particular processing mill or complex. Public Sustained Yield Units (PSYUs) were those managed by the provincial Forest Service, the timber in them being sold to private companies. In 1980, when there were thirty-four Tree Farm Licences and eighty-four PSYUs, the latter were reorganized into thirty-three Timber Supply Areas, which among other things recognized the concentration of the timber processing industry that had occurred since 1947.

The next stage was to calculate how much timber should be harvested per year from each unit so that the maximum possible volume could be cut annually and forever. The volume figure, known as the allowable annual cut (AAC), was calculated on the Tree Farm Licences (TFLs) by the companies and approved by the Forest Service, which also performed the calculations as part of its management responsibilities in the PSYUs. Because most of the timber in these units was mature, the adoption of the German regulatory policy required a means of calculating the harvest so that it would not drop when the conversion from natural to "normal" forest was completed, while at the same time maximizing the perpetual annual harvest. The mechanism selected for making this calculation was a formula devised in 1922 by an American forester, E. J. Hanzlik. He modified the European concept of equating harvest, or yield, with growth. In Hanzlik's system, a volume figure was obtained by dividing the volume of mature timber in the unit by the number of years in the rotation of the future sustained yield forest and then adding the average or mean annual growth of the immature trees in the unit:

$$\frac{\text{Mature (timber)}}{\text{Rotation (term)}} + \underset{\text{(MAI)}}{\text{Mean Annual Increment}} = \underset{\text{Annual Allowable Cut}}{\text{(AAC)}}$$

In order for this calculation to produce a realistic AAC, a number of factors needed to be known accurately. One was the volume of mature timber that could be utilized by the existing processing mills obtaining timber supplies from the unit. Rates of growth of the immature stands also had to be calculable. And the rotation period of the "normal" forest being created needed to be calculated. Unfortunately, very little of this information was available in British Columbia in 1947. Gathering inventory data had not been a high priority in an era that believed timber would last forever. Figures did exist, of course, but few were accurate, and who could know which they were? The Forest Service's approach was to take the most conservative of these guesses and, acting as if truth had been revealed, approve an allowable cut for each unit. And they began gathering data. On the other hand, industry began a campaign to have these figures revised upward in order to take advantage of the growing demand for timber products. Thus, the calculation of the AAC and the concept of sustained yield itself became a matter of widespread political and economic controversy. Much of this controversy centres on details of the actual AAC calculation. The relatively simple sounding Hanzlik formula, in fact, ends up as a vague summary of a complex procedure for arriving at a figure that is crucial to both present industrial activity and the long-term future of the forests.

Knowing the volume of mature timber in a sustained yield management unit is not a matter of going out on foot and measuring it. That approach is impossible; before the task could be completed, the forest would have changed so much that any results would be meaningless. The procedure is to use aerial photographs and existing inventory information on file to prepare forest-cover maps. This method, too, has its limitations. In spite of the millions of dollars spent since 1947 (the 1979–80 inventory budget was \$5.4 million), the forest-cover maps in use in many areas today are fifteen to twenty years out of date.

The areas of mature timber are classified by species and checked against growth curves or equations. There is a curve for each forest type and each site class — some four hundred in all. Among other things, these curves reveal the theoretical point at which a given species on a given site will begin to experience a declining annual growth rate — the culmination of its mean annual increment. The volume figure obtained by matching the area of mature timber with the growth curves for particular stands is then divided by the culmination age of that stand, which also represents the rotation figure. To the result of this equation is added the annual growth (MAI) of the immature stands in the unit; the MAI is obtained from growth tables and area estimates of young growth. The final figure represents the tentative annual cut for the unit.

In order to give this procedure some realistic basis, sample measurements are made in a statistically defined number of locations. By 1980, information was available from about 53,000 sample plots within the province. The volume and growth data they contain provide a check and a means of adjusting the growth and yield curves. A further check on the procedure is obtained when a stand is harvested and the logged timber measured during the scaling process that is used to assess stumpage payments to the government.

Experience has shown that the results obtained from this process are not particularly accurate, though they are improving. Perhaps the strongest criticism is not so much with the procedure itself as with the Forest Service's insistence, or at least the Inventory Division's insistence, that each successive calculation be the accurate one. Of course, there has always been a good reason for this insistence: it would be administratively and politically unacceptable to restrict the activities of timber harvesters to the limits of the allowable annual cut if at the same time it were admitted that the accuracy of the figures used to calculate it were questionable.

Once the tentative AAC figure was obtained, the procedure until recently was to subject it to an allotment check to ensure that the forest would be able to sustain that yield throughout the rotation. The next step was to make reductions in the AAC figure for a number of factors: allowances for parks, rights-of-way, urban expansion; main logging roads which would be kept free of new growth; a delay in the regeneration period of the new crop; losses due to fire, insects, disease, wind and other factors; breakage during harvesting operations, and utilization at a lower level than originally calculated.

This was the end of the calculation procedure; but the figure obtained, the indicated AAC, could be modified yet further for a host of other reasons — administrative, economic, political — by others in the Forest Service hierarchy. Eventually the chief forester, the top person in the Forest Service bureaucracy, would settle on an amount that became known as the Approved AAC. By the 1970s, the entire question of yield regulation was under criticism from a number of directions, on levels ranging from the purely technical to the basic validity of the sustained yield policy itself.

The technical disagreements focus on the fundamental question of whether the allowable cut levels would produce a "normal" forest, ideally during its first managed rotation. At any given time there are really only two positions on this issue: the allowable annual cut is either too low or too high. This debate may pertain to individual sustained yield units and, in a rather loose, theoretical sense, to all the forests within a jurisdiction — the B. C. provincial forests, the U. S. National Forests and so on. In a way this is a very academic debate. It is about a type of forest and a type of timber processing industry that may not come into existence for another century. While the discussion is spangled with such phrases as "timber shortages" and "maintaining employment and economic activity," these phrases are not immediately relevant. The reason for this is simple: there is no shortage of timber. In British Columbia, for example, somewhere between 40 and 50 per cent of the productive commercial forests have never been touched by loggers.[8] If Ministry of Forests inventory figures are taken at face value, logging every mature tree in the province and loading it on highway logging trucks would create a line-up 6 to 8 million kilometres long, depending on your choice of truck. The cost of harvesting and processing much of this timber may be more than its end products will sell for, but it does exist.

What is really at issue is whether the current cutting levels will create a future forest that will produce a perpetual annual harvest of sufficient volume or value or both to sustain the forest industry and satisfy other forest users. This question presupposes the acceptance of sustained yield policies. It is in this context that inventory accuracy becomes important. But as we have seen, inventory accuracy, though basic to the proper implementation of sustained yield, is a frustratingly elusive Grail.

There are also certain assumptions involved in the definitions and judgements made in formulating the inventory data. For instance, the volume figures used to quantify mature and immature trees presuppose a certain level of utilization, a defined concept of merchantability not only for the present but also into the future. The concept of sustained yield is by its very nature a future-oriented idea, yet fifty years hence the forest harvest will be determined by demand; demand will depend on perceived usefulness, and who knows what kind or age of tree will be considered useful in half a century?

Utilization levels refer to the kinds and sizes of timber that go into the volume figures, as well as to the kinds of timber a logging or forest company is required to take out of the woods. The "close utilization" standard, which applies in most cases, includes any tree cut off at a stump no higher than 12″ (30.5 cm) that produces a log larger than 9.1″ (23.1 cm) in diameter at breast height on the coast, and in the Interior, 7.1″ (18 cm) with the top cut off at 4″ (10.2 cm).

Whether all this wood is economical to log and process, either now or in the foreseeable future, is a question that has been tossed back and forth for a long time. Some people argue that there are stands of timber included in the inventory that are so difficult to get at, and the costs of processing them so high, they should not be harvested, at least at the present time. Therefore, the argument goes, these stands should be excluded from the inventory until they are economical to log. A counterargument maintains that this timber — much of it decadent and losing volume each year — should be cleared to make way for new crops that would mature at much higher volumes per hectare.

The rotation decision is also influenced by the utilization level. As explained earlier, with the maximum volume type of rotation used by the Forest Service, the rotation is the same as the culmination of MAI — the point at which the annual growth rate begins to fall off. This culmination point occurs at an earlier age on the curves as utilization standards are increased, that is, as a larger proportion of a log is used.[9]

A criticism of the type of rotation used is that the policy does not take economic factors into account, even though one objective of sustained yield policy is to ensure economic stability. The determination of the rotation and its function in the calculating process ignores the differing values between species, stand ages, quality of wood and so on. It assumes every cubic metre of wood is of equal value. A further criticism of the maximum volume rotation is that it does not take into account effects, whether negative or positive, on the productivity of the forest soils of taking out a perpetual succession of harvests at the maximum volume level.

The uneven distribution of age classes of forests throughout the province creates a dilemma. It is unlikely that any management unit would have roughly equal areas of each ten- or twenty-year age class. All types of rotation assume timber stands will be harvested when they reach the culmination point — the end of the period of maximum MAI. In practice, however, many more trees will culminate some years than in others. To harvest at culmination in all cases would produce erratic annual harvests, conflicting with the objective of steady yields. On the other hand, harvesting before or after culmination, according to the preferred method of calculation, results in a lowering of the potential yield.

A key ingredient of most discussions on yield regulation is the threat of timber shortages at some point in the future. One factor of this concern is known as the "fall down." This phenomenon will occur, it is argued, because second-growth stands harvested at rotation will not contain as much volume per hectare as the natural stands now being harvested, many of which have been growing for centuries. Consequently, allowable annual cuts following the first managed rotation will have to be lowered from the volumes taken from natural stands.

A further shortcoming of the allowable cut calculating process is that it tends to distort the worth of certain forest management activities. In forestry jargon this is known as the "allowable cut effect," or ACE. For example, since any increase in the growth rate could permit an increase in the tentative annual cut, normal accounting procedures can find the cost of obtaining that increased growth — by fertilizing, thinning young stands, brush control and so on. This would be the cost of obtaining an immediate increase in the annual harvest. Depending on how the figures are juggled, one can obtain a theoretical return on silvicultural investments many times more than would result from calculating only the value of increased wood growth. In a similar sense, the ACE indicates that it is more profitable to invest in silviculture treatments which will increase timber volume than in treatments which will increase timber quality and, hence, the value of each unit of timber grown. A current manifestation of this in British Columbia was the obsession with juvenile spacing during the 1970s, which in theory will produce higher yields in the future. By contrast, pruning the trees is ignored because, while it would probably increase the quality of the timber, it would not produce greater quantity.

A reverse effect of the ACE is to discount the value of expenditures on protecting the forests against fire, insects and disease. In the calculating procedure, the timber volumes lost in this manner are spread over the rotation and so in the short term do not reflect the actual value of the timber lost.

Many critics have questioned the loss factors which reduce the initial AAC figures to figures that represent the indicated annual cuts. They have pointed to the speculative nature and subjective judgements involved in estimating how much land would be taken out of production in the management unit for such items as small parks, rights-of-way, roads and urban expansion, and the fact that these potential reductions are factored in over the entire length of the rotation. The question of reserves has always been a contentious one, though it is not a part of the calculating procedure and has never had any legal basis other than Forest Service regulations. The so-called reserves are actually that portion of the allowable annual cut in the PSYUS or TSAS that the Forest Service simply declines to harvest. While there are a number of rationalizations for this practice, it is mostly a reflection of the Forest Service's conservative bias which has developed after decades of dealing with business and political interests intent on milking the forest resources for whatever can be siphoned off. The amount of timber held back in these "reserves" is substantial — at times more than a third of the combined AAC of the various Timber Supply Areas.[10]

Another area of sometimes heated debate is the enforcement of cut controls, as it affects licencees. Holders of TFLs and licencees who work under annual volume allocations in PSYUs must cut within a certain percentage of their allocation or they may be penalized, with fines of some sort if they cut too much and reduced allocations if they cut too little. The operating principle in the latter case, as expressed by B. C. minister of forests Tom Waterland, is "use it or lose it." In the TFLs, these provisions have been rigidly upheld, forcing the operators to continue harvesting during market slumps when they might otherwise prefer to shut down and wait for an improvement in timber demand. In the PSYUs there is more leeway, albeit somewhat arbitrary and subject to the interpretations of the minister of forests and the senior officials of the bureaucracy. There are many arguments, most of them economic, against the *allowable* annual cut being construed as *required* annual cut. But to do otherwise would mean abandoning the concept of the maximum volume rotation.

Beginning around 1960, a new form of criticism of sustained yield policy began to appear, mainly in British Columbia. These complaints have grown in volume and sophistication until the future of the policy is now seriously under question in some areas. One of these criticisms reflects what could be called the ecological perspective.[11] This point of view takes issue not so much with the basic policy itself as with the reliance on the idea of the maximum volume rotation and the stolid way in which sustained yield practices treat a wide diversity of forest sites as if they were identical.

The maximum volume rotation, as described earlier, is the period over which the mean annual increment is maximized. Culmination is the termination of this period. When it is used in calculating the allowable annual cut and as a criterion for establishing the "normal" forest, obtaining the largest possible volume from the forest on an ongoing basis becomes the primary concern. While it is possible to make allowances at later stages of the calculating process for treating sensitive sites in less demanding ways, this approach does not have built into it from the outset a means of recognizing and protecting the variety of ecological conditions found in a forest.

To appreciate this, it is only necessary to walk through an intensively managed forest in Washington or Oregon states, or visit the Sayward forest on Vancouver Island. From the point of view of conventional practice, these plantation forests are impressive. They are well stocked, containing little or no denuded land. The trees, usually Douglas-fir, are uniform and well developed. Many of the areas have been spaced. There is a certain sense of order and vigour not found in natural, unmanaged stands. Rare are the areas containing rotting snags, tangled brush patches or the haphazard mixture of species common in forests allowed to determine their own growth. Such a forest is beautiful in the way a wheat field or a well-tended garden is beautiful, but not in the way a natural forest is beautiful.

These managed forests can be depressing, particularly if one has spent any time in unmanaged forests. There is a lot missing in most of these tree farm forests. If the snags have been removed, there will be a few woodpeckers heard. Once the stands have reached a certain age and choked out the undergrowth, there will be few deer or elk. Many types of trees one expects to find are not there: in the spring, one rarely comes across a dogwood in full, flowering splendour. Then comes the realization that these forests are temporary, that they will be harvested at a relatively early age and replaced with an identical forest. This raises a disquieting question: how long can this process go on? This is the question to which ecologists address themselves.

An ecological rotation can be defined as that period required for a forest site to return to its preharvest condition with a given level of management technology. Although ecologists have been accused of wanting to preserve or restore every last gnat and lichen to a forest site, in fact they are talking about a rotation in which the overall productive capacity of the site will be maintained or enhanced. This "productive capacity" refers to something more than the trees alone. It means the entire complex web of life which occupies the site. From an ecological standpoint, the timber-producing capability of a site can be sustained at maximum levels only if these interdependent life forms can be preserved.

Under current concepts of management, with the attendant means of controlling harvesting, the ecological rotation can be violated in a number of ways. One example involves the degree of site disturbance during logging. If the site is not able to recover fully from this disturbance during the rotation period, there will be a gradual, or perhaps even a rapid, decline in its productivity.

To illustrate: A cubic metre of healthy forest soil may contain anywhere from 1000 to 1400 species (50 to 250 species per cubic foot) of various organisms, numbering in the tens of thousands of individuals, most of them involved in interdependent life cycles. Undisturbed forest soil might be composed of 25 per cent air, which is critical for the lives of its inhabitants. If the logging operation uses heavy equipment that compacts this soil, squeezing out the air, many of these life forms will die. Some of these organisms, such as mushrooms, live in symbiotic relationships with trees. The mushroom roots penetrate the tree roots, drawing sugars from the tree. In return, they provide the tree with certain mineral nutrients which the trees cannot obtain for themselves. The ecological rotation has to include the time it takes the mushroom population to restore itself.

This sort of scenario can be pursued indefinitely. One way mushrooms are spread is by mice and other rodents carrying the spores, dropping them along burrows and tunnels. If regeneration of the logged site is obtained by broadcasting seeds treated with poison to protect them from mice, as was commonly done in the past, the ultimate effect is to lengthen the ecological rotation. Yet the conventional, scientific approach might well look upon the application of poisoned seed as a silvicultural practice which would increase the immature growth, thereby providing an increase in the allowable annual cut.

Ecologists are also concerned about the effects of harvesting on the nutritional elements of a site. It was once believed, and Fernow taught, that wood was composed of carbon, hydrogen, oxygen and nitrogen, elements taken by trees from the air and water.[12] According to this reasoning, forests take little from the soil and harvesting them does not remove nutrients. It is now understood that this is not the case; certain nutrients are indeed depleted by harvesting operations. Nevertheless, the idea of a perpetual succession of rotations on the same site, without any allowance for the effects of nutrient deficiencies, remains deeply ingrained in sustained yield policy and practice.

The point ecologists and others make is that if the rotation is a shorter period than that required to replenish the nutrients on a site, the nutrient capital will fall below a critical point. Then the productivity of the site itself will fall.[13] Adoption of current management proposals, most of which are geared towards producing larger volumes of timber in shorter rotations, would further exaggerate the decline. The ecologists' contention is that much contemporary sustained yield forestry is really a form of timber mining which, if continued, will actually convert many forests into nonrenewable resources. They will be nonrenewable in the sense that they will not recover their productive capabilities in an acceptable socio-economic time span.

Few ecologically oriented critics appear to advocate an abandonment of sustained yield policies in favour of some other approach. Yet the logical thrust of their viewpoint seems to be in that general direction. The alternative they propose centres around site-specific decision-making in regard to harvesting cycles, silvicultural practices and so on. Sustained yield forestry, as it has always been carried out, deals with large forest units that can be classified into site categories, each of which is treated in a uniform way. Site-specific forestry ultimately deals with each tree on an individual basis. It is hard to imagine a reconciliation of these two perspectives within the context of classical sustained yield theory.

In contrast to the ecologists, some forest economists actively suggest that sustained yield forestry be totally abolished in North America. Since about 1960, a growing chorus of economists has been arguing that sustained yield policy and practice are products of a forestry profession that ignores basic economic criteria.[14] The economists offer a number of arguments, almost all of which call for increased harvesting levels in one way or another.

One of the first requirements of sustained yield policy which economists find hard to accept is that of an even annual flow of timber from a sustained yield unit. The argument that sustained yield promotes stability is disputed by these economists for both the short and long terms. The contention that regional employment and income levels are stabilized by a constant harvest rate are countered with the observation that in such an export-oriented industry short-term changes in demand are caused by fluctuating international markets. These markets are hardly affected by controlling supplies. In fact, it is argued, controls on supply aggravate price fluctuations. When demand is high, supply restrictions force prices even higher; when demand drops, surplus inventories quickly accumulate, rapidly driving prices down. Economists argue that if harvest rates were responsive to changes in demand, rising and falling with it, they would cushion the impact of such changes. Although this method of regulation would preclude the creation of the "normal" forest and seriously affect the available timber supply a rotation or more into the future, the economists argue that it is unreasonable to expect the present generation to bear some unknown future cost now, especially since those costs could as easily turn out to be benefits.

The economic critics also maintain that there is an unaccounted cost in holding mature timber inventories, rather like a retail business cramming its shelves. Related to this factor, according to the economists, are the foregone costs of the second-growth crops that cannot be grown until the mature timber is harvested. These costs are the highest on the so-called decadent mature sites which experience an annual loss of volume when instead they could hold stands of rapidly growing young trees.

Economists also have been unhappy with the way sustained yield policy and practice concentrates on maximum volume of wood, rather than maximum value. This tendency leads to such practices as establishing utilization levels that require the harvesting of timber that costs more to log and process than it will bring on the market. Economists view the costs of harvesting this timber as a waste of money which could be invested in reforestation or silvicultural treatments, in the end producing a larger volume of better-quality timber.

The alternatives proposed by the economic critics include the concept of an economic rotation, which can be defined as that period which would yield the highest average annual return on investment — the maximum quantity of dollars rather than the maximum quantity of timber. In terms of the rotation during which the mature forest is liquidated, as well as the rotation of the managed forest which replaces it, this period would invariably be shorter than the maximum volume rotation commonly used. The direct effect of adopting this type of rotation for purposes of yield regulation would be to increase the allowable cut — at least during the harvesting of natural stands. In the long run, over a number of rotations, the effect of applying this kind of economic criterion would be the creation of intensively managed, short-rotation forests.

It is precisely this type of forest that is being developed on some of the private, industrial forest lands in the United States, and to a limited extent in British Columbia. The objective in these forests is to obtain a high volume of uniform timber in the shortest possible time. Typically, plantations are intensively managed — spaced, thinned and fertilized — and harvested on a thirty- or forty-year rotation, compared to eighty- or one-hundred-year rotations on comparable sites managed on a maximum volume basis. And, it almost goes without saying, they are the antithesis of the forests proposed by ecologists and site-specific foresters. What is required to resolve this conflict is a perspective that synthesizes the concerns of both the ecologist and the economist. Ecological limits for a stand or a forest need to be established within which economic procedures can be applied. Then the integrity of the site can be maintained without an escalation of costs.

Probably the most articulate and outspoken advocate of the economic viewpoint during the 1960s and early 1970s was Peter Pearse, a forest economist at the University of British Columbia. He was a key participant in a decade-long debate on basic policy. This debate, primarily concerned with forests in British Columbia, was conducted in academic circles, the pages of professional journals and at forestry conferences.

Pearse saw forest policy as the result of changing influence among three interest groups: conservationists, industrial promoters and technologists. He believed that forest policy in British Columbia since 1947 had largely been determined by technologists, professional foresters and ecologists whose main interest was in the resource itself, rather than in the people who own it (the public) and use it (the industry). He also thought the Sloan Commission had been unduly influenced by technologists and that the sustained yield policy laid down by Sloan and adopted by the government ignored most of the fundamental economic considerations described above.

Pearse also maintained that economic tools could be used to help resolve the conflicts between timber producers and other forest users. Taking issue with the position of many foresters that multiple use is a viable concept so long as it does not interfere with timber production, he argued that nontimber forest values — such as recreation — were increasing at least as rapidly as timber values: "The fact that some of these benefits yield no market return does not mean that they are worthless. It does mean, however, that more effort is required in order to systematically assess these values."[15]

Appealing though this position may be, it has a familiar ring. The suggestion that one particular discipline, in this case forest economics, may be able to provide at least a partial solution to forest-resource conflicts is essentially the same suggestion that was offered by North America's first professional foresters around the turn of the century. They maintained that sustained yield forestry would resolve these conflicts; today, the forest economists, among others, are making much the same claim for themselves.

In 1975, Pearse was appointed as a one-man Royal Commission to examine and make recommendations "into the management, regulation and use of the forest resources in British Columbia." His exhaustive report, which appeared the following year, was built around an elaboration of his earlier economic critique of sustained yield policies. And though it was never explicitly stated, the hundreds of recommended changes in policy and practice scattered throughout the report created an overwhelming argument in favour of abandoning the sustained yield policies adopted almost thirty years earlier. In the section on yield regulation policy, Pearse said:

> It is no longer adequate to fix the goal of yield regulation as a more or less constant flow of timber volume over very long

> periods. Present circumstances call for a more flexible approach to yield regulation, with greater emphasis on protecting and enhancing the productivity of forest land and on the economic, social, and environmental implications of harvesting. Forest management policy for the future should be directed toward two related objectives: protection and enhancement of the capacity of forests to produce their potential range of industrial and environmental values; and within that framework the regulation of harvesting to produce the maximum long-term economic and social benefits from the timber resource.[16]

Two years after Pearse released his report, the provincial legislature approved a drastically revised Forest Act incorporating perhaps half of his recommended changes. Among them were a number of provisions for altering the policies and procedures for regulating yield. The PSYUs were reorganized into thirty-three Timber Supply Areas (TSAs), and a new method was adopted for determining the allowable annual cut of these larger management units. The significant feature of this new methodology was that it no longer depended on the use of formulae and mathematical calculations, but ultimately became a matter of choice. This choice, which is made by one of six regional managers in the Ministry of Forests, is intended to reflect the nature of the forest in the TSA, regional and provincial economic policies and conditions, and the amount of money available for silvicultural expenditures. It requires a number of value judgements by the manager. A computer-assisted procedure was adopted to assist in this choice. Essentially, the computer is programmed to predict the long-term (one or two rotations) consequences of harvesting at various cut levels over the next twenty years. The computer can also match the existing timber supply with the needs of an individual mill. Although it is called the "production forecast method," the process in fact provides a forecast of timber supply rather than production, which is largely determined by market demand. The production forecast method really indicates the amount of timber the Ministry of Forests will allow to be cut.

There are limitations on the harvest level in each TSA. Stated Ministry of Forests policy is to not allow the long-term annual harvest to fall below the sustainable yield as a result of short-term overcutting. The sustainable yield is defined as the volume that can annually be taken from productive sites in the TSA with the application of only the most basic silvicultural treatments designed simply to maintain the productivity of the sites — planting denuded areas and providing protection from fire, insects and disease. The sustainable yield figure is essentially the same one provided previously by the Hanzlik formula, in that it equals the culmination of mean annual increment. As such, it is subject to many of the criticisms outlined earlier — inaccurate inventory data, the definition of rotation and the problems of establishing realistic utilization levels. Yet under the new forecast method, sustainable yield becomes the major controlling factor in establishing current and future rates of harvest. What the new method does provide is a more accurate prediction of future supply problems — the "fall down" — as well as indicating when and where to spend money on intensive silvicultural practices designed to increase the timber supply. If the forecasts indicate that intensive silvicultural practices would fail to alleviate predicted shortages, a reduction in the current harvesting level might be made.

Built in to this computer projection are a number of reduction factors, which formerly were deductions from the calculated annual cut. These factors take into account other land uses, incompatible with timber harvesting, as well as restraints on harvesting for environmental reasons and the existence of uneconomic logging areas. As Bill Young, B. C.'s chief forester, said in explaining the new system to professional foresters:

> This is one of the more contentious aspects of the rate of harvest policy. Some argue that insufficient consideration has been given to the other resources and that the resultant allowable rate of harvest is too high. Others are equally adamant in expressing their opinion that too much allowance has been made and the economic well-being of the province is being jeopardized.
>
> I say that both may be right relative to the particular philosophy of the individual. But both cannot happen. However, this is one of the most important subjective decisions that must be made in establishing a rate of harvest which attempts to arrive at a proper "balance" of forest use.[17]

While the new yield regulation method has several advantages over the old method, it is not without its critics. One serious objection, given the fact that the rate of harvest in a TSA is closely tied to the productive capacity of the forest land within its boundaries, is that site productivity is still derived from the growth curves or equations. In somewhat simplified terms, this means that the site classification is calculated by relating the height of the trees in a stand to their age. This tends to confuse productivity with the condition of the standing crop. Simply because one species presently growing on the site grew at a certain rate does not mean that it will grow at the same rate in the future, or that other species will grow at that same rate.

One of the more valid criticisms of the old AAC figures had nothing to do with the calculation procedure, or even with the figures themselves. It was directed at the Forest Service's dogmatic insistence that its data were accurate, that its calculation methods were a reasonable reflection of what was going on in the woods, and that the allowable cut figures did not constitute over- or undercutting of the sustainable yield. If this bureaucratic attitude persists under the new method, there is at least one area where the results could be serious. As previously mentioned, the production forecast method can indicate where intensive silviculture is required to sustain existing harvest levels, or where it could be used to boost the current cut. This provision presumes that the growth response resulting from these treatments is known with at least some degree of accuracy — for example, that spacing a juvenile stand of fir and then applying fertilizer every five years will produce such and such an increase in volume on that stand. But at present these factors are not known. In the first place, very little research into this has been done in British Columbia; most of the existing information comes from the better-funded forestry research establishments in Washington and Oregon. And second, it is a dubious proposition to apply the results obtained from a very few research projects to the wide diversity of sites and situations throughout the province.

The danger of this situation is not so much that of undercutting or overcutting based upon faulty estimates of the response to silvicultural treatments — though these are distinct possibilities — as it is the trade-offs resulting from a belief or an insistence that the estimates are sound. Even now it is possible to predict a trade-off scenario: public pressure is generated to create a park in a TSA already being harvested at its sustainable yield. The political/bureaucratic response is to approve the park and at the same time allocate funds for intensive silviculture within the TSA in order to compensate for the timber locked up in the park. Forty of fifty years later, it is found that the expected growth increases have not occurred. Alternatively: the forecasts indicate future shortages requiring reductions in the current harvest equivalent to the needs of two mills in the TSA. The silvicultural response figures indicate that only half this predicted shortage can be avoided by undertaking a broad program of treatments. One mill shuts down and a decade or two later it is learned that the growth response has been double that predicted. The point is not that these sorts of decisions should not be made, nor that intensive silviculture should not be practised, but that the entire question of silvicultural response should be treated with a great deal of skepticism until the results of treatments on specific sites are known. The danger of the new method, like that of the old one, is that convenient numbers will be dropped into the appropriate slots and everyone involved will pretend they know what they are doing.

By January 1982, the B. C. Ministry of Forests had calculated the allowable annual cuts of the new TSAs, using the production forecast method. Although it is not easy to make a direct comparison between these figures and those used the previous year in the PSYUs, in general the new harvest levels appear to be slightly lower. Without a detailed knowledge of the inventory data used, and without making a detailed evaluation of the reduction factors used, it is difficult to say whether these figures are any more realistic than earlier ones. The one clear point is that the Ministry of Forests feels a lot more confident about its predictions.

If one is to go by the statements of politicians and bureaucrats and Ministry of Forests publications, a new policy is emerging in British Columbia which is more concerned with preserving and enhancing the forest land base than with maintaining an even flow of timber products by creating the ideal, or "normal," forest of classical forestry theory. Does this mean that British Columbia has abandoned the goal of sustained yield? One answer is no, because British Columbia has never actually practised sustained yield, even though from 1947 to 1978 it was the stated policy under which the forest industry operated on publicly owned land. Today, however, that is no longer the case. While the abandonment or retention of sustained yield policies may be an academic question, the real issue is what effect recent changes in government policy will have on the production side of forestry. Under the new order, questions involving employment and regional or provincial economic development will be influenced more by politicians and planners external to the forest industry than by the professional foresters who for over thirty years have attempted to manage the forest resource according to nineteenth-century German principles.The most optimistic view of present circumstances is that the makers of forest policy are at last beginning to recognize that North American forests are not European estates. One hopes we are entering a new and pragmatic phase in which the future development of the forest will reflect a reality and experience that is distinctively our own.

One legacy of the B. C. experience with sustained yield is the tenure system which was created through policies adopted in the 1940s. In theory, the various forms of licences granted to private companies on public lands were an integral part of the sustained yield system. In practice, as we shall see in the next chapter, there were other, less laudable motives involved. With or without a concerted policy of sustained yield, tenure remains the most volatile issue in forest resource politics.

FOUR

Who Owns the Trees?

TENURE IS FUNDAMENTAL to forestry. It is represented by the piece of paper a logger watches for in his mail, the scrap of printed pulp that permits him to cut trees on Crown land. Forest policy and politics come together at no point more critical than this — the government's legal and administrative apparatus giving private interest access to timber on publicly owned lands. Tenure not only defines the mechanics of the process but can — as it has in British Columbia for the past thirty-five years — determine who may or may not obtain this access. In some cases, it can entail rights over the forest land itself, beyond the mere acquisition of timber.

Tenure provisions are administrative procedures, established in law passed by the government and defined by bureaucratically applied regulations. Thus they are — at least in theory — subject to constant change and are often hotly debated. This is as it should be: in a province, state or country, the more land that is publicly owned, the more critical are tenure policies and procedures to the economic and political life of the area. In a province such as British Columbia, where almost all the land is publicly owned, the tenure provisions are important to every resident.

In theory, for example, a government newly in power in Victoria could pass laws abolishing all the existing forms of tenure and establishing a whole new set. Regardless of the merits of the new tenure policy, the change alone would severely shake the forest industry, and then the entire province. Although various political parties have suggested during their election campaigns that they would undertake such a complete change, once in power they have usually chosen to alter the tenure provisions by splicing new forms to the existing structure. As a result, just about every form of forest land tenure that has ever existed still survives in British Columbia, though many of them have been modified at various points along the way.

In British Columbia, the earliest form of forest land tenure was ownership. Beginning with the colonial administrations and carrying on for some time after the formation of a representative government, the primary means of obtaining access to timber was to buy the land from the Crown or otherwise obtain outright land ownership. Then, for three or four decades after Confederation, the main way of obtaining land was as exchange for some great task of public benefit: in other words, building a railway. The first of these enormous land grants — 5 665 800 ha (14 million acres) — was given by British Columbia to the federal government for building the Canadian Pacific Railway. At this time, the CPR's interests lay more in controlling the strategic urban lands in the centres created along the rail route, rather than owning vast areas of mountainous forest land. The timber on these lands was sold by Ottawa through a licence called a Timber Berth. Following completion of the CPR to the East, successive provincial governments attempted to duplicate this approach. Numerous schemes were negotiated with a long parade of promoters ranging from respectable businessmen to outright con artists. Although few of these notions went beyond the planning and talking stage, they indicated a basic policy approach towards the private use of public land.

One of the oddest schemes proposed involved a considerable slice of Vancouver Island containing large areas of agricultural land and vast coalfields, as well as some of the finest timber stands in the Pacific Northwest, perhaps in the world. When Confederation was being negotiated during the 1860s, the Crown Colony of Vancouver Island was part of an economic region stretching from California to Alaska. Victoria businessmen were oriented towards Seattle, San Francisco, Hawaii and the Orient, rather than to Toronto, Montreal or New York. For the most part, they were only interested in Confederation if the railway that was being promised by the Canadian government were to end at Victoria. In anticipation of this, local land speculators were busily engaged in obtaining property rights and encouraging one of their number, Alfred Waddington, in his promotion of a railway route to Victoria via Bute Inlet. The fact that this route was difficult, costly and not included in the railway construction contract seems to have escaped the Victoria interests, but it was quickly spotted by the railway builders. They ended the line at Vancouver.

While this was sufficient to bring the mainland into Confederation, residents of Vancouver Island were somewhat miffed. There were loud mutterings about joining up with kindred spirits in the U. S. territories to the south. In order to forestall this possibility, the Canadian government dispatched the Governor General, the Marquis of Lorne, to make a deal with the powers-that-were in Victoria. The end result was one of the more incredible deals in the history of the province. When the negotiating dust had settled, most of the strings were held by one man — Robert Dunsmuir, an ex-foreman in a Hudson's Bay Company coal mine. The Canadian government contributed a dry dock at Esquimalt and gave $750,000 to Dunsmuir. George Walkem's provincial government transferred 768 930 ha (1.9 million acres) on the eastern shore of Vancouver Island, from Campbell River to Victoria, to the federal government, which in turn passed the land title on to Dunsmuir. In exchange, Dunsmuir built 127.1 km (79 miles) of railway from Esquimalt to Nanaimo — the E & N, or Esquimalt & Nanaimo, Railway. One of the chief cargoes hauled on this line was coal from the mines Dunsmuir now owned.

Dunsmuir sold much of his land grant to lumber companies. Eventually, in 1905, the Dunsmuir interests were bought by the CPR for $1.25 million. Ostensibly, the CPR bought the E & N Railway, but, in fact, they were primarily interested in Dunsmuir's coal mines and forest land. The Railway has always been considered a liability which the company has consistently sought to shut down. Successive provincial governments have just as consistently threatened to revoke the company's purchased tenure on the forest land it still owns, about 121 500 ha (300,000 acres). This land makes Pacific Forest Products, a Canadian Pacific subsidiary, one of the largest private forest land owners in British Columbia.

Today, 2 630 600 ha (6.5 million acres) of B. C. forest land are privately owned, yet even before the turn of the century, outright land ownership had few advantages for a mill or logging operator. Once the land was logged, the operator still had to pay taxes on it, and few people wanted to buy logged-over land. In addition, after 1884 the government began placing charges and restrictions on the use of timber from granted lands. A royalty of fifty cents a thousand board feet was imposed, and after 1906 timber from Crown-granted lands had to be processed into lumber within the province. By 1947, when outright prohibitions were placed on the sale of Crown forest land, access to timber on Crown lands was gained almost exclusively by various forms of lease or licence which allowed the lease holder to harvest the forest crop while the province retained ownership of the land itself. The first Timber Leases were granted by the colonial administrations and were continued after British Columbia became a province. These leases could be of any size, were renewable and required the payment of an annual rent. But they could not be sold or otherwise transferred to someone else.

Around the turn of the century, a new form of lease, the Timber Licence, came into effect. These were normally 404.7 ha (1000 acres) in size, involved a rental fee on the land and a royalty payment on the harvested timber, and were renewable.

Shortly after Timber Licences came into existence, a series of events led to an unprecedented timber boom in British Columbia. The market was expanding rapidly, the eastern North American forests were running out of timber, and in 1905 the U. S. government established its National Forest system, locking up 68 800 000 ha (170 million acres) of forest land. The McBride government in British Columbia looked upon this situation as a heaven-sent opportunity to fill the provincial coffers. At this point, there was no Forest Service and few, if any, professional foresters to warn of the consequences. The rules on acquiring Timber Licences were relaxed — the so-called Special Licences were transferable — and a timber-staking boom ensued.

For two years, the forests of British Columbia crawled with people calling themselves timber cruisers. Some of these cruisers knew their business and understood the logistics of harvesting timber; many more did not. Some licences were taken out by mills which would legitimately require the timber in the foreseeable future; but most of them were staked by speculators. To obtain a licence, one had only to drive a single stake into the ground, write the appropriate information on it and file a claim with the government. The claim could be retained by paying the annual rent, or it could be sold.[1] Within two years, about fifteen thousand of these licences had been staked and government revenues from the forests had increased fivefold. This was the beginning of a policy which still prevails: that of financing provincial budgets through the sale of timber rights.

This scale of timber speculation was too much, even for the McBride government, and in 1907 the government stopped issuing licences and established the Fulton Commission to consider the warnings of professional foresters such as Judson Clark and H. R. MacMillan. The foresters were claiming that the province would soon run out of timber unless the government changed its policies.[2]

Prior to this, in 1901, various business interests in the province had persuaded the government to establish special leases to supply wood for pulp and paper mills. These pulp leases were small compared with the capacity of the mills, but they provided pulp-quality logs at half the royalty rate for saw logs. Supposedly, the leases required the construction of a pulp and paper mill within six months, but it was not until 1909 that the first mill went into production at Swanson Bay. Several leases were taken out at various points along the coast, and most changed hands, sometimes frequently, before mills were eventually constructed. No more of these Special Licences were approved after 1903, by which time 143 260 ha (354,000 acres) had been put under licence. Initially, Special Licences had a twenty-one-year life, but later became renewable. They were complemented by Pulp Licences, granted between 1919 and 1921, which were actually conversions from Timber Licences and contained wood more suitable for pulp than for lumber. Together, these two forms of tenure supplied the timber upon which the coastal pulp and paper industry was founded.

The only other significant form of tenure on coastal forest lands at this time was the handlogging licence. These were small patches of timber close to the shoreline which were available to small operators who worked without power equipment.

These handloggers would fall their trees towards the water; if they did not reach the water they were moved in with jacks. Hundreds of these licences were issued and, though the areas and timber volumes were relatively small, they were important for two reasons: they provided entry into the industry for independent loggers who had limited capital, and they created a log market which the coastal mills could draw upon.

Until the Forest Act of 1912 was passed, the only other means of getting Crown timber in British Columbia was through the federal government in the interior railway belt, on lands acquired from the province to finance construction of the CPR. These leases involved rental and royalty payments, and they also required their holders to operate sawmills. They were known as Timber Berths and were issued to meet a growing demand for lumber in the Interior and on the Prairies generated by the settlement that followed construction of the CPR. When the railway lands were returned to the province in 1930, those Timber Berth agreements still in effect were honoured by the Victoria government.

As the Fulton Commission had recommended, the 1912 Forest Act rejected all these existing forms of tenure except handlogging licences.[3] They became known as the Old Temporary Tenures, and were replaced by the Timber Sale Licence, which contained a number of features giving the newly created Forest Service increased control over the timber harvest. An area proposed for sale had to be cruised and classified; sales were advertised and sold by way of competitive bids. In addition to rental and royalty payments, loggers had to pay a minimum stumpage rate called the upset price, as determined by the Forest Service, as well as the amount by which their bid exceeded this price. They also paid the advertising, cruising and surveying costs. Timber Sale Licences were for fixed terms of three or five years and could not be used to tie up timber indefinitely. Until 1948, they were the only means of acquiring timber, apart from handlogging licences. They were given on demand with virtually no restrictions on their number. By 1945, they provided about 25 per cent of the provincial timber harvest.

Until its revision in 1948, the Forests Act's tenure provisions were not a critical factor in acquiring timberland. Anyone who wanted timber could get it, either by buying one of the Old Temporary Tenures or by taking out a handlogging or Timber Sale licence. But with the adoption of sustained yield policies in 1948 the whole concept of tenure changed drastically, and tenure became one of the basic instruments used by the Forest Service to control what was going on in the woods. Within a very few years, it became one of the hottest political issues in the province, a status it still maintains.

In the late 1940s, the economic and political climate of British Columbia was being influenced by a number of factors. North Americans were looking forward to a postwar economic boom. There were large accumulations of capital floating around the continent, looking for a place to land. An expected boom in the demand for forest products — lumber for housing, and pulp and paper for a wide array of uses developed during the war — made British Columbia's large forest reserves and relatively undeveloped forest industry an attractive investment possibility.

Another important political reality was the anticommunist sentiment sweeping the U. S. and spilling over into Canada. The agenda of the 1948 B. C. Truck Loggers' convention in Vancouver was dominated by two topics: the new tenure provisions and the communist threat. Guest speakers argued that free enterprise was the best antidote to communism and that free enterprise in the forest industry was dependent on a continuous and secure timber supply. Walter Owen, who was later to become British Columbia's lieutenant-governor, warned the delegates that communists had already taken control of the trade unions.

Provincial party politics at this point were chaotic. The province had been governed since 1941 by a coalition of Liberals and Conservatives; the 1948 Forest Act revisions were brought in by Byron "Boss" Johnson, a Liberal. The key ingredient of this coalition was its opposition to the growing strength of the socialist Co-operative Commonwealth Federation (CCF) led by Harold Winch.

Under the new Act of 1948, the major change to tenure was the new Tree Farm Licence, initially called a Forest Management Licence. The TFLs were composed of two categories of forest land: Schedule A land consisted of land held under Old

Temporary Tenures and private land owned by the licencee; Schedule B lands were any additional Crown lands obtained in a TFL. At the outset, these licences were issued in perpetuity. The TFL, taken as a whole, was to be a sustained yield management unit, with an allowable annual cut set at a level which, in theory, could be sustained forever. The licencee had an obligation to manage the land according to sustained yield policies and practices, as approved by the Forest Service. The applications for TFLs began to pour in, ultimately winding up on the desk of the minister of lands and forests. The legislation gave the minister unqualified discretion to decide how many licences would be issued, how large they would be and who would get them if there were competing applications. It was a procedure wide open to abuse.

The architect of the sustained yield policy, Chief Forester C. D. Orchard, and those working under him in the Forest Service, had imagined that the province would end up with two hundred, perhaps three hundred TFLs.[4] These would have been relatively modest operations, combining the grants, licences and leases of existing loggers and mill owners, with enough Crown land added to make up viable sustained yield units. What actually happened was something altogether different. A number of people in the B. C. forest industry saw TFLs as an opportunity to raise capital outside the province in order to build integrated pulp and lumber complexes, which in turn could be used to obtain licences covering large areas of forest land.

One of the first of these entrepreneurs to arrive in Victoria early in 1947 was R. J. Filberg of the Canadian Western Lumber Company, which had a mill on the Fraser River and large timber holdings around Comox and Campbell River. Filberg brought with him officials of the Celanese Corporation of New York, and their proposal was to create a TFL on the islands along Johnson Strait and in the Sayward forest. Since the Forest Service already had plans for this area of highly productive forest, they were turned down. Disassociating themselves from Filberg, the Celanese people then applied for and obtained TFL no. 1 near Prince Rupert. It contained 809 400 ha (2 million acres) of Crown land, that is, Schedule B land. Meanwhile, Filberg had turned his attentions to another U. S. company, Crown Zellerbach, and submitted a modified proposal for a TFL in the Johnson Strait area. This application was accepted, and British Columbia's second tree farm licence was awarded. Almost half consisted of private, Schedule A, lands formerly owned or controlled by Canadian Western Lumber. Filberg thus combined his own Canadian Western interests with those of the U. S. giant, Crown Zellerbach.

The new legislation gave the minister of forests the ultimate authority in awarding TFLS, and this was a key factor in the negotiation of these licences. The Forest Service no longer had the final word, as it had since the formation of the service in 1912. It is not surprising that, under the new policy, TFLS were likely to go to those making large political contributions to the party in power. The independent mill owners and loggers of the day who could not operate in this league certainly did not like this type of arrangement. But in those days that was how business was done. And because such payments could be seen as a means of combatting the spread of communism, not to mention the local socialists in the CCF, they had a certain legitimacy in the business world.

With the defeat of the coalition government in 1952 by the newly created Social Credit party under W. A. C. Bennett, the practice of awarding TFLS to those making political contributions expanded and eventually went beyond its earlier quasi-respectable status. The new government was very soon at odds with the Forest Service and Chief Forester Orchard. As Orchard later recalled:

> We didn't expect, and I wouldn't have credited the character of our new Cabinet. We had been accustomed to dealing with men of character and ideals. We now found ourselves in an entirely different atmosphere. . . . We drew, as our Minister, . . . R. E. Sommers fresh from his school teaching at Castlegar. His forestry training had consisted in seasonal work for a few summers with the Forest Service.
>
> In my opinion the Socred Government was a one man administration. Ministers were nonentities who referred the simplest routine matters to Mr. Bennett, the Premier, and parroted his decisions.

> Certainly the new government took office firmly of the opinion that every predecessor in office had been venal and that no civil servant could be trusted. . . . I was told that civil servants had no conception of economics. We were to do the purely routine work. The government would instruct us in all else. . . . I was told that the government was reliably informed that I was disloyal to and undermining the government, and should be carefully watched. . . .[5]

This was the atmosphere in which sustained yield forestry and Tree Farm Licences were introduced to British Columbia. By the time Sloan conducted his second Royal Commission into forestry in 1955, eighteen TFLs had been awarded, another twenty-eight were in the works and an additional one hundred applications had been received.

The forest industry was in an uproar. A large and growing number of loggers and mill owners were actively campaigning, not only against the awarding of TFLs but against the forest management concept itself. Foremost among these was Gordon Gibson, who with his three brothers had started from scratch and built a large logging and sawmilling business on the west coast of Vancouver Island. Gibson's opinion was shared by many independent loggers. He maintained that forest management should remain the responsibility of the Forest Service and that timber harvesting should be undertaken with licences acquired through competitive bidding at public auctions.

Gibson ran as a Liberal on this issue and was elected to the provincial legislature. At the Sloan Commission hearings he relentlessly grilled and harassed Orchard, the Forest Service and the battery of lawyers representing the big companies which had acquired TFLs. Having grown up in the logging and sawmilling industry, he had the advantage of first-hand knowledge. He was also fully aware of the role political contributions had played in obtaining timber rights. And he felt sure, but could not prove, that the Socred government was carrying this practice to highly questionable extremes.

Shortly before the Sloan Commission began hearings, the Forest Service had received an application for a TFL near Tofino on the west coast of Vancouver Island. It had been submitted by British Columbia Forest Products (BCFP), which had come into existence just before the creation of the TFL tenure. H. R. MacMillan is credited with persuading E. P. Taylor, a Toronto promoter, to get in on the TFL land-grab by buying up some existing mills and applying for additional Crown lands. The land the company wanted for TFL no. 22 included some that the Forest Service had already designated as a Public Working Circle. These PWCs had been created in 1948 by the same legislation that had established TFLs. They comprised forest lands not included in the TFLs and were administered by the Forest Service on a sustained yield schedule.

C. D. Orchard as chief forester refused to approve BCFP's application; Sommers approved it, in spite of the fact that the legislation required the chief forester's approval. Orchard described the event in the following terms:

> They [BCFP] wanted the Working Circle, which I opposed, and they proposed what I considered to be a dangerous overcut. In other words, a timber grab and legalized liquidation; or rather liquidation with government blessing and documentary approval. We, the Forest Service, would have nothing to do with it. . . . After I had condemned the application, and in my absence from the office, the Minister called on F. S. McKinnon, Assistant Chief Forester, February 1954, for a memo defining how this licence could be awarded; with a warning that he didn't want to hear anything about why it shouldn't be done, and that if we couldn't give him what he wanted they would have to get someone on the job who could.[6]

A number of people began pointing out irregularities in this approval, and in September 1955 Gibson publicly made accusations of bribery. Charging that "money talks," Gibson was expelled from the legislature. Then a Vancouver lawyer, David Sturdy, appeared before the Sloan Commission with details of a bribery conspiracy to obtain TFLs involving a number of individuals and companies — including Sommers and BCFP.[7] He had obtained his information from an accountant working for a forest consulting company which he said was the conduit and recipient of bribe money paid by a number of forest companies. This accountant, Charles Eversfield, had fled to California, taking records of these transactions with him. Sloan refused to accept Sturdy's submission. His commission report, which came out in 1956, glossed over the application for TFL no. 22 and generally whitewashed the government's handling of TFL approvals.

Meanwhile, the Socred attorney general, Robert Bonner, had been sitting on Sturdy's evidence and did so until after a provincial election in September 1956, when the Socreds — including Sommers — were re-elected. When the government presented the Forest Service budget in the legislature, the opposition grilled the minister of forests relentlessly. Sommers would not answer; Bennett finally demanded his resignation, and replaced him with Ray Williston.

In October 1957 the accountant Eversfield returned to British Columbia and produced receipts and details of payments which had been made. Two days later, Bennett appointed Sloan to look into the evidence. After half an hour's examination, Sloan concluded that charges should be laid, and on 21 November Sommers was arrested, along the C. D. Schultz and H. Wilson Gray. Schultz and Gray had started Pacific Coast Services Ltd., the company for which Eversfield had worked. Schultz was also the owner of the province's major forest consulting firm, C. D. Schultz and Company. It was well understood in the industry that an application for a TFL would be more favourably considered if the required timber cruise on the proposed area were prepared by Schultz's company. By the time the TFL no. 22 scandal erupted, Schultz had divested himself of any formal connection with Pacific Coast Services Ltd.

Less than a month later, Sloan resigned from his $15,000-a-year job as the province's chief justice and accepted a $50,000-a-year post as advisor to the minister of forests.

The day after Sloan accepted his new appointment, B. C. Forest Products was also charged. When the company's chief financial officer, Trevor Daniels, appeared in court the following February, he admitted that BCFP had allocated $30,000 to Sommers in order to obtain TFL no. 22.

C. D. Schultz was subsequently acquitted in court, as was B. C. Forest Products. Gray and Sommers were convicted. Some charges against others brought forth "not guilty" verdicts, but there was a hung jury on many of the charges against the big forest companies involved. Attorney-General Robert

Bonner (currently chairman of B. C. Hydro) intervened and ordered there be no new trials.

Although Sloan had recommended a five-year moratorium on the granting of Tree Farm Licences, twenty more were approved in the decade following his 1956 report, most of them before 1962, bringing the total to forty-three. Some were later amalgamated, and by the 1970s the number had stabilized at thirty-four. They occupied almost 4 050 000 ha (10 million acres) of Crown-owned land — more than 8 per cent of the total forest land — and provided about 26 per cent of the annual provincial harvest.[8]

The jailing of Sommers did nothing to stem the rising tide of dissatisfaction with the tenure system among loggers and mill owners who did not possess TFLS; their dissatisfaction increased, as under the new Socred minister of forests, Ray Williston, the pace of concentration increased.

The distrust and suspicion created by the Sommers incident were to persist for another twenty years. The basic political reality of the B. C. forest industry after 1958 was that, despite the Sommers case, the TFLS which had been issued while he was in office remained intact, and the TFLS issued after 1956 were awarded to the same kind of large, externally financed companies that had obtained the first ones.

The rationale for this practice, based on orthodox sustained yield theory dating back to Fernow, was that large companies were more efficient than the small operations, and that large companies had both the willingness and financial ability to manage the land on a continuing basis. Orchard later commented that:

> Forest management finally was possible in B. C. because of the increased values of the wood on an acre of forest land, arising out of prior liquidation, world markets, diversification of products, closer utilization, improved manufacturing, consolidation of forest properties into big holdings in the hands of wealthy and well-financed big companies and corporations, and a baffling complex of a thousand and one other less obvious factors. . . .
>
> And so, big forest business and forest management came to B. C., and the small logger found himself on the way out. He

> squealed like a stuck pig and blamed everything and everybody other than the real cause of his trouble. He gave the Forest Service and Government some anxious times and did his best to kill forest management. In 1960 he still grumbles and mumbles but the battle by this time is lost and won.[9]

There were, however, some other factors. Modernizing a mill or a logging operation requires a lot of expensive equipment, which in turn requires the ability to borrow large sums of money. Then, as now, borrowing power in the forest industry was directly related to the size of a company's timber reserves, which were counted as assets. Any company that obtained a TFL instantly increased its assets in proportion to the value of the timber in the licence area. It has been estimated that when B. C. Forest Products obtained the contentious TFL no. 22 from Sommers, its share value increased about $20 million in one day. A small logger or mill owner depending on short-term Timber Sale Licences for his wood supply had no chance of competing at the bank.

Throughout the 1950s and 1960s, the companies which obtained TFLs used them as leverage for taking over control of the wood supply in areas outside their TFLs. This was done with the active encouragement of the government and, to a lesser extent, the Forest Service, which still adhered to Fernow's belief in government and large corporations. The continued opposition of small operators served only to strengthen the Forest Service's belief that these independents intended only to "cut and run."

The timber in the Public Working Circles, later called Public Sustained Yield Units (PSYUs), was to be harvested on a sustained yield schedule administered by the Forest Service. The allowable annual cut would be taken by logging and milling companies bidding against each other at public auctions. In PSYUs, where the allowable cut was higher than the current level of harvest, there was no immediate problem of allocation. But in some areas, such as the southern coast, the harvest was higher than the allowable annual cut calculated by the Forest Service. A "quota system" quickly evolved which had no legal basis whatsoever. First begun as an administrative convenience, quotas soon became the controlling factor for tenure within the PSYUs.

It was a simple system which had a devastating effect. In a fully or overly committed management unit, the allowable annual cut was divided between the existing licence holders in proportion to what they had received before the harvest was regulated. This volume became the operator's "quota position," the amount of timber he was guaranteed each year. Initially, there was competitive bidding on this timber, but in time the regulations were altered to give quota holders certain advantages in the bidding process. They got the right to match the highest bidder, and all bidders were required to post a nonrefundable deposit before the sale. The prospect of losing as much as $150,000 or $200,000 in an unsuccessful bid to obtain timber effectively scared off most competition.

Naturally, "quota" quickly acquired a value of its own, as it conferred a continuing right to timber. And though initially it was not supposed to be sold or traded, this rule soon went by the wayside and an active quota market developed. In this market, the TFL-based companies were at a distinct advantage because of their ability to raise capital. By 1975, the fifteen largest forest companies directly controlled over half of the timber in the PSYUs and virtually all of the TFL timber.[10] In addition, these same companies held controlling interests in a number of smaller companies and effectively owned most of the private forest land in the province. As far as it is possible to calculate, in 1975 about 85 per cent of the timber in British Columbia was held by fifteen companies, almost none of which had been in business in the province prior to 1948, the year the revised Forest Act had created the TFLs.

During this same period, the province's allowable annual cut had increased dramatically, partly because of improved inventory data, but chiefly because of the ability of the new mills to work smaller and lower-quality logs. The greatest increases occurred in the TFLs, sometimes 500 and 600 per cent higher than when they were established. Between 1950 and 1975, the actual timber harvest in British Columbia more than doubled.[11]

During the 1960s, the higher utilization standards brought about a series of new tenure arrangements. Some PSYUs were designated as Pulpwood Harvesting Areas in order to superimpose a pulp industry on the existing sawmill industry which already accounted for the allowable annual cut in that unit.

Essentially, the government guaranteed companies building pulp mills a supply of wood chips from sawmills, which in turn received a higher annual cut in exchange for harvesting smaller and lower-quality trees. At the same time, quota holders who agreed to harvest to close rather than intermediate utilization standards automatically had their quotas increased — by one-third in the Interior and one-half on the coast. Since none of this increased allowable cut was sold competitively, the big companies grew even larger. In some PSYUs, quota holders did not receive the entire increase of the larger cut available from close utilization. The remaining volume — called "third band" — therefore became available; but the only companies eligible to bid on it were existing quota holders who had agreed to purchase specified processing equipment, or who could prove a need for it to maintain production at their mills.

The other major tenure innovation during the 1960s was the Timber Sale Harvesting Licence (TSHL), which was provided in exchange for a company's Timber Sale Licence. In fact, the TSHL simply formalized what had occurred in the PSYUs with the advent of quota. Whereas Timber Sale Licences were granted for the timber on a specific piece of land, and the amount of quota a company held determined the number and size of these sales, a TSHL gave the company the right to an annual harvest within a PSYU. The term of these licences ranged from ten to twenty-one years and, unlike Timber Sale Licences, required the holder to replant the logged areas — with the cost deducted from fees they would otherwise pay the government. By 1975, about 60 per cent of the timber harvested in PSYUs was through TSHLs.

Except for two minor considerations, by 1975 the province's forest industry was firmly in the hands of a few large corporations. One of these exceptions was TFL no. 26, the smallest in the province at 7690 ha (19,000 acres), held by the city of Mission. The other exception was a form of tenure available on Crown forest land, called Farm Wood Lots. These could be obtained by bona fide farmers and operated on a sustained yield basis along with farmland they owned. In 1975 less than 3640 ha (9000 acres) of Crown land was held under these licences by thirty-six farmers.

In reponse to the growing concern of small logging companies, all new TFLs from 1959 onward contained a clause specifying that 30 to 50 per cent of the harvesting had to be performed by independent loggers working under contract to the TFL holder. In some cases, this so-called contractor clause served as an inducement for quota loggers to sell their quota to a TFL holder, with part of the deal including a logging contract. Occasionally this worked out to the benefit of both parties — loggers were able to realize a large profit from their quota, which they could invest in new, modern equipment, and TFL holders obtained additional timber rights and were freed from the necessity of financing the equipment needed to log it. But this arrangement did not always have such a happy result. The clause was vague about just what stages of the actual logging operation were included in calculating the percentage. It was common for contracts to be verbal, for unspecified periods of time or unspecified volumes of timber. The system was wide open to abuse, and many a logging contractor found himself holding the short end of the stick when the market dropped or a major company found that for one reason or another it wanted to be rid of him.

For example, suppose a company holds a coastal Tree Farm Licence containing a mixture of its own private land and Crown land. It has its own logging crew which it uses on its own property. This Schedule A land is relatively cheap to log but is at high elevations. In order to maintain its crew, the company has to keep it working year-round, and this can only be done by logging during the winter on the low-elevation Crown (or Schedule B) land where a contractor is operating. Furthermore, the company mills are unable to utilize all of the allowable annual cut and the company is under pressure from government, the Forest Service and independent loggers to sustain its yield — "use it or lose it." When its own crew gets snowed out of the high elevation site, the company might evict the contractor from the lower areas, with perhaps only a few hours' notice, and move in its own crew. It might also decide to ask the Forest Service to ignore or suspend the contractor clause.

Another example: suppose there is a contractor in the area looking for work. The division manager and the contractor conclude a verbal agreement concerning the logging of 4000 cunits of timber. The contract price remains open, subject to approval from head office in Vancouver, but the manager says he thinks the company will be able to pay the contractor $20 a cunit. The contractor hires a crew, loads his equipment on a barge and arranges for a tug to tow it to the camp. There is still no agreement on the price, but the manager sounds hopeful. The contractor commits himself fully by taking out a bank loan to finance his start-up costs. The tug leaves with his equipment and an hour later the manager tells him, "Sorry, they'll only pay $18 a cunit." The difference represents the contractor's profit but, with no real choice, he goes to work. By the time he finishes the felling, bucking and yarding, he is losing money. And he still has to truck the logs to the beach. At this point, the company agrees to cancel the contract, paying him so much a thousand for what he has done. The company sends in its own loading and trucking crew to haul the logs. They leave all the small logs on the ground, knowing that the penalty chargesfor waste imposed by the Forest Service are lower than what they would have to pay the contractor if the logs were taken out and scaled. When the contractor gets his final payment, he is $60,000 in the hole, enough to bankrupt him.

By the early 1970s, the ranks of independent loggers and sawmill operators in the province had been thinned almost to extinction. Many of those who had gone into the contracting business were starting to feel like sharecroppers. Not many were amused by the irony of the situation: that this corporate takeover had been engineered by a government made up of small-town businessmen, schoolteachers and fundamentalist preachers who for two decades had proclaimed the virtues of free enterprise.

In 1972 the Socred government of W. A. C. Bennett was defeated by the New Democratic Party. A Vancouver urban planner, Bob Williams, was appointed minister of forests. Among the many other features of forest policy and practice thrown into question was the subject of tenure. Williams's first concern was to find ways of extracting increased revenues from the industry and of making the private companies pay what he considered to be a fair rent for the publicly owned resources they were using.

The issue of tenure was thrust at the new government after only a few months in office, and even then in an indirect manner. When the NDP came to power, there was by no means a uniform response towards the government from people in the forest industry. By and large, those working at the executive and management levels of the big forest corporations looked upon the new government as some sort of blight, to be eradicated as quickly as possible. But there were a lot of smaller, independent loggers and sawmill owners with a more open mind on the subject. From their point of view, it was hard to imagine a government more detrimental to their interests than the previous Socred administration. And many of them not-too-secretly looked forward to the day when the NDP would act on its election campaign rhetoric and turn out the multinational corporations that had taken over control of the public forest lands. For the most part they adopted a wait-and-see attitude.

A few months after the election, Crown Zellerbach announced that it was closing its sawmill complex in Ocean Falls. The government bought out the company and kept the mill running. This brought a great hue and cry from corporate levels about government interference in free enterprise. But what was not made public was that the Crown Zellerbach head office in San Francisco was making discreet enquiries to see if the government was willing to buy out their entire B. C. operation.

A month later, Williams further jolted the industry when he announced that the government would buy the Celanese Corporation's mills in Prince Rupert and Castlegar, including TFLs nos. 1 and 23, and would continue to operate them as a Crown corporation. Later, Williams would defend this decision on purely pragmatic grounds: it was a chance to regain public control over hundreds of thousands of hectares of Crown land, and it provided the government with an inside view of the workings of a major forest company. Within five years, the Crown company, Cancel, made $200 million in profits, on a government investment of $20 million.

However, many small operators in the industry were appalled. If the new government's response to concentration in the industry was to set up Crown corporations as huge as the private ones, and even more powerful, they wanted no part of it. Throughout the hinterlands of British Columbia, about the only first-hand experience people had with a Crown corporation involved B. C. Hydro, which many viewed as a dark shadow upon the landscape, a monolithic entity whose program of expansion often ran roughshod over local interests. For these people, Crown corporations were bad news.

In retrospect, it is clear that Williams was not launching a broad new policy with the government purchase of Cancel. He was not about to rescind tenure agreements and abolish quota by having the government take over the entire forest land base. But he was determined to bring about some major changes in the tenure system. Rather than bury himself in the complex of leases and licences which had evolved over more than a century, he assigned the job to a Royal Commission. Among other tasks, this Commission was specifically instructed to examine "all matters relating to the disposition of rights by the Crown to harvest timber and to occupy forested land in British Columbia."

Williams selected University of British Columbia forestry economist Peter Pearse to undertake this enquiry. Pearse had already made known his concerns about the degree of concentration of timber rights in the province. In 1973 he had been appointed to head a three-man task force on British Columbia's Old Tenures, which brought in very few revenues to the provincial coffers. His recommendations, while increasing some of the burden on the Old Tenure holders, advised that a clever use of the loopholes in the federal Corporation Tax Act be used, in effect, to raise B. C. tax rates on the holders while lowering the federal rates.

During the latter half of 1975, Pearse received more than two hundred submissions representing a wide range of views. All the major forest companies submitted briefs, the main theme being their desire to obtain even more secure tenure agreements. A number of independent loggers, contractors and their various associations argued that, one way or another, a larger proportion of the province's timber resources should be kept out of the hands of the major, integrated companies. Several briefs proposed a form of tenure which would allow small, family-sized operations to run silviculturally oriented forest farms on Crown land. In many ways, the Pearse Commission was dominated by the tenure issue. Many of the public hearings turned into full-fledged debates over who should have access to publicly owned forest resources.

While Pearse was digesting all this information and preparing his report, the picture changed dramatically. The forest industry slid into a market slump, the NDP government was defeated and a reconstituted Social Credit government came back into office. Although few small independent forest operators publicly supported Bob Williams, his appointment of the Pearse Commission laid the foundations for a shift in tenure policy which would eventually check almost thirty years of concentration of timber rights.

In his report, Pearse had some harsh things to say about the tenure situation:

> The forest policies we have pursued have not . . . been neutral; while they have not been deliberately biased to the disadvantage of smaller, non-integrated firms and potential new firms, there can be little doubt that they have nevertheless accelerated the consolidation of the industry into fewer, larger, and more integrated enterprises. . . . Some important forms of rights are designed to meet the needs only of large companies, and these have been awarded over the best Crown timber in some regions; whereas all of the significant licensing arrangements depended on by small firms are held by large corporations as well . . . privileges even beyond contractual rights have been conferred more generously on larger enterprises. . . . Nor, I want to emphasize, is my anxiety about the size, per se, of our large forest companies; it is the erosion of opportunities for others to play a constructive role in the industry, and the growth of regional monopolies as large corporations assimilate small firms with their resource rights. . . . In my opinion the continuing consolidation of the industry, and especially the rights to Crown timber, into a handful of large corporations is a matter of urgent public concern.[12]

As Bob Williams was later to observe, Pearse was a good Liberal — he was subsequently an unsuccessful Liberal party candidate in a federal election. Pearse pointed out that any changes in tenure had to honour existing timber rights, take into account the industrial structure which already existed and provide sufficient security of timber supplies to maintain and expand the level of capital investments. While these constraints make a lot of sense, Pearse ignored two important factors.

One of these surfaced with the decision of the Celanese Corporation to pull out of the B. C. forest industry, and the tentative approaches to the NDP made by Crown Zellerbach's parent office. Newspapers have called this factor the "exodus theory." Is is rarely discussed publicly, though it is occasionally debated in the pages of the high-priced forestry newsletters, such as *Beale's Letter* and *Forest Insight,* which are largely comprised of tidbits of news and views, most of them obtained from unnamed sources in the management and executive levels of industry and government. What the exodus theory proposes is that once the major forest companies have creamed off the mature timber on their TFLS, they will take their profits and leave the province, selling off their processing plants for whatever they can get; they will not bother to stick around and manage these lands for future crops. The predictions are that this exodus will occur in ten to fifteen years. If this theory is valid — and there are many well-placed people who believe it is — the concerns over secure timber rights are not nearly so important as Pearse indicated.

The second factor, which Pearse discussed very briefly, is closely related to the exodus theory. It has to do with the management functions the big companies assume when they receive TFLS, which they may then use as a base for taking over other tenures. No one, Pearse included, has ever seriously questioned how well these companies have managed the public lands they hold by tenure. Indeed, Pearse maintained that the TFL form of tenure has been successful in bringing about desirable forest management. As he said in his report,

> From the point of view of resource management, Tree-Farm Licences have met, if not exceeded expectations. . . . The proprietary interest that licencees have developed in these lands, the incentives the system has provided, and the priority given them by the Forest Service have produced the highest standard of forest management in the province — a standard that in

> many cases is high by international comparisons as well. With few exceptions both the Forest Service and the licencees are proud of the rapid improvement of resource management under these tenures.[13]

A considerable number of people would argue this point. Company foresters whose silviculture budgets and programs have been refused, or silvicultural workers or Forest Service field people who monitor the actual work done — all these and others could have provided Pearse, had he asked, with evidence to dispute his short, laudatory dismissal of the issue. If nothing else, such an examination would have indicated which companies were taking their management functions seriously. That in itself would have been a clue to the validity of the exodus theory.

Two years after the Pearse report, the new Social Credit minister of forests, Tom Waterland, tabled a revised forest act in the legislature. The tenure provisions in the new legislation were fairly consistent with Pearse's recommendations: the Tree Farm Licences remained intact, and though Pearse suggested their term be changed to fifteen years, Waterland set the figure at twenty-five. The contractor clause was applied to all TFLs at a rate of 50 per cent of the TFL harvest.

A number of provisions were included which were intended to bring tenure up to date with current practice. The most significant feature was to "legalize" quota by converting the old Timber Sale Licences and Timber Sale Harvesting Licences into Forest Licences, which provide a specified volume of timber annually over a fifteen-year term. Like the Tree Farm Licences, they contain what Pearse called an "evergreen renewal" clause. Every five years, licencees can obtain an additional five-year extension on the licence, which means they will never be in the position of having to renegotiate a licence that is about to terminate. They will be renewing for a period ten or twenty years down the line.

Streamlined administration of the pulpwood, third band and Old Temporary Tenures had the overall effect of increasing the security of the licencees. This was increased further when a 1981 amendment actually approved transfer of cutting rights from owners of overcut areas to undercut ones the companies did not even own. The amendment also allowed TFL boundaries to be expanded so as to increase allowable cut while still permitting companies to cut only the profitable areas. Pearse had recommended that the extra allowable cut (in some cases as much as six times the original allowance), which had been customarily granted to the Tree Farm Licences and quota holders, be returned to the government over a period of three to ten years. Instead, the Forests Act of 1978 made this "grant" virtually permanent.

The major change in tenure came from what was known as the Small Business Program. This was designed to provide Timber Sales to registered small logging and milling operations, which were later defined as "firms which are independently owned, which have not developed the managerial structure typical of large, mature corporations, and are not dominant in their field of operation."[14] The aim was to reserve a portion of the allowable annual cut in each Timber Supply Area for the small business sector. Initially, Waterland proposed that this portion be 15 per cent of the cut. His suggestion was greeted with howls of outrage, and he quickly raised it to 25 per cent.

Since its announcement, the Small Business Program has become the most controversial part of the new Act. Its objective is to define a sphere of activity within which only certain kinds of firms can operate. It specifically excludes the holders of any other form of tenure. All the timber allocated under the program is to be sold on a competitive basis, by public auction or sealed tender. And it designates two categories of operations, those with sawmills and those without. Many operators had their spouses, sons, daughters, girl friends and third cousins register as small business applicants. The general feeling among small loggers was that competition could become fierce, particularly if log prices were high, and it was only prudent to gain every possible advantage.

The big companies have kept a fairly low profile on the program. They were far from ecstatic to find that as much as one-quarter of the timber supply had been removed from their grasp. Over the past thirty years, they had come to look upon all Crown timber as theirs, available through a variety of licences and leases that effectively eliminated any competition.

But apparently it is impolitic to object to the program, at least publicly. As much as half of the small business timber could wind up in their hands anyhow, since loggers without mills must sell on the open market. It will be interesting to see whether the big companies agree not to compete against each other for this timber and what measures they take to support those loggers who sell to them and destroy those who do not.

Waterland's initial position on this program was very strong. Basically, he took a stance similiar to Williams's, that there must be some form of tenure available for small, independent and innovative logging and milling operations. He portrayed the timber supply reductions that might affect the big companies as the price they must pay for the security of tenure they are receiving on the licences they already have. But, as is so often the case, policy and practice failed to coincide. The drop in log prices which began in 1980 helped create conditions which, by early 1984, were devastating the small operator sector. In practically none of the TSAs had timber allocations to the Small Business Program reached the 25 per cent level, and independent operators across the province were having difficulty obtaining cutting rights. A wave of protest emerged from the small operators, such as had not been seen since the 1950s — most of it directed at the Social Credit government.

The Small Business Program also includes a new form of tenure, the Woodlot Licences. The simplest way of describing the Woodlot Licence is as a miniature Tree Farm Licence, with a maximum size of 400 ha (988 acres). One of its main purposes is to directly involve a substantial number of provincial residents in "forestry" on Crown lands, and through this policy, to enhance the "understanding of, and goodwill towards forestry."[15]

The idea of the Woodlot Licence came to British Columbia from those parts of the world where a significant portion of the forest industry is based on small land holdings managed for timber production by families, individuals or small companies — as in Europe, eastern Canada, and the eastern and southeastern United States. The practice never became established in British Columbia for a variety of reasons — logging, until recently, has been a harvesting industry; there is little private forest land, and what is available is controlled by a few large companies. The Woodlot Licence is a concept of forest tenure that is in contradiction to the Fernow doctrine of large state- or corporate-managed sustained yield units.

The idea of Crown land becoming available for small woodlot operations surfaced in British Columbia as early as the second Sloan Commission. Oddly, its main proponents at that time were the executive officers of a few of the large companies. H. S. Foley of the Powell River Company told Sloan that if an individual could get access to Crown land "and grow trees and sell them, he becomes a better citizen, he becomes interested in forestry, he is an owner; in my judgement it would be the most wonderful thing that could happen to British Columbia."[16] Others in similar positions within the industry supported Foley's view, underlining the importance of preventing these tenures from falling into the hands of the big companies.

The 1948 amendments to the Forest Act had also established a Farm Woodlot tenure, but these tenures never amounted to much, largely because they were restricted to individuals already owning farms. During the Pearse Commission, a number of submissions once again supported the woodlot concept. The most significant of these proposals came from Jim Collins, a prominent Vancouver consulting forester. He argued that the elimination of competitive timber sales had effectively denied individuals access to participation in the industry except as employees. A woodlot tenure would encourage the growth and development of silvicultural skills as well as open up new ways for people to work in the forests. Pearse agreed, and devoted an entire chapter of his report to small-scale forestry. His proposal, almost identical to Collins's brief, was included in the new legislation by Waterland. More recent policy decisions have included woodlots in the Small Business Program, with an initial allocation of 1 per cent of the allowable annual cut.

The main difference between woodlots and Tree Farm Licences, apart from their size, is that woodlots will be acquired through competitive bidding. They differ from other forms of tenure (except TFLS) in that they provide the right to use Crown land for the purpose of growing, rather than merely harvesting, timber.

There are, however, weaknesses in the new approach which will undoubtedly keep the tenure issue alive for many years to come. One of these lies in the fact that about 85 per cent of the Crown timber will continue to be allocated to the major companies, while the remainder will be fought over by the independent sector in the process of competitive bidding. As one disgruntled observer put it, the independent companies have been given a small fraction of the timber supply, over which they can spend the next twenty years cutting each others' throats.

In the long run, the major weakness of the government's new tenure policy may be the limited means of obtaining forest land for the purpose of growing commercial forest crops. At present, there is no form of tenure that falls between the small woodlots and the large Tree Farm Licences. If the future of forestry in British Columbia lies with our ability to grow trees rather than just cut and process them, then there would seem to be a need for more diverse forms of tenure with which to accomplish that task. Only if we support a diversity of approaches and operations will we be able to discover the best ways to grow the trees of the future. Or, as Peter Pearse has put it: "One of the problems in B. C. is that so much of our land is owned and administered by a single level of government. As a result you tend to get uniform regulations over a wide range of conditions, instead of regulations best suited to the circumstances of particular forest sites."

FIVE

What Is Our Timber Worth?

AS THE HISTORY of Peter Pearse and his Royal Commission indicates, economists have had their effect on the forest industry. They have asked some difficult and penetrating new questions; they have caused some old questions to be examined from new points of view. But economics is not an exact science, and economists are often better at asking questions than at answering them. Although asking the right question is halfway to the answer, in some areas halfway is as far as we get.

One area where we need answers is the matter of "economic rent." This is a fundamental concept in resource economics. Most simply put, economic rent is the true value, in dollars, of any given resource. In the forest industry, it is usually seen as the real worth of the standing trees, the price the owner should charge for them. If the owner charges too much, no buyers will be attracted, or the buyer will find it difficult to be competitive in the marketplace, or the owner will attract buyers who have some unusual advantage, such as particularly efficient processing techniques or an existing operation conveniently located nearby. Generally speaking, however, it would be extremely disadvantageous for the purchaser to pay more than the economic rent. Similarly, it is disadvantageous for the seller to accept less than the economic rent. If that seller happens to be a government, the shortfall must be made up by the taxpayer. The amount of that shortfall will essentially be a subsidy to the purchaser.

Establishing the correct economic rent, therefore, is absolutely fundamental. In theory, this is easy. The trees are simply put up for open bid in a freely competitive market. In almost every case, the selling price will be an entirely satisfactory, practical approximation of the economic rent.

In calculating the amount of this bid, the would-be purchaser must first consider the market in which he must sell his own finished product, whether that product be pulp chips, logs, two-by-fours or what have you. He must judge what a competitive price will be when he has finished processing the trees he is bidding on. From that selling price he will first deduct his own processing costs, then he must deduct a competitive profit for himself — competitive in two ways: it must be high enough to satisfy present investors and attract new ones when needed, and it must be low enough to give his bid a reasonable chance of success. Thus, both the product market and the money market are factors in his bidding calculations. Having judged his selling price and deducted processing costs and profit, he knows how much he can bid for his raw material, the standing trees. Yet that bid must be as high as he can make it because without the raw material to process and sell, all is for naught. There is considerable pressure on him to run a lean operation with efficient processing techniques and the minimum attractive profit.

This, at least, is the theory. In reality, only a very small part of North America's publicly owned timber is sold through competitive bidding. (Washington and Oregon are among the few areas where competitive bidding is the norm.) In British Columbia, certainly, there is virtually no open market for the province's timber resources. Since the introduction of competitive bidding for Small Business Timber Sale Licences, the amount of B. C. timber sold on the open market is in the neighbourhood of 10 per cent of the allowable annual cut. However, even this system is far removed from the classic free-market model because the market is restricted to certain recognized bidders. Here in British Columbia, where the major industry is forestry, the beautifully constructed models of resource economics break down. As a result, no one quite knows how much a B. C. tree is worth.

It is also on this very point — competitive bidding for the standing timber — that the traditional left-wing-versus-right-wing categories of B. C. politics break down. Most politicians of the right and almost all big businessmen in the province actively oppose competitive bidding for Crown timber; many politicians of the left and most small businessmen strongly favour it. Mason Gaffney, an economic advisor to former NDP minister of forests Bob Williams, was forced to conclude:

> . . . There is nothing essentially right wing about the free market. In fact the free market is one of the most radical things there is, which is why big businesses don't really like it . . . and nowhere is this better exemplified than in the relationship between the big forest giants and the [B. C.] Crown in their leases on Crown lands which they like to hold without competitive bidding . . .
>
> Nor is the idea of a government collecting economic rent necessarily a left wing notion. . . . The position that the income of natural resources should be taken for public purposes . . . isn't a socialist position . . . [it's] simply saying that taxation socializes whatever it taxes (and I'm saying you should tax "A" instead of "B," "A" being natural resources and "B" being human beings). When you tax the income of workers, you are socializing the human being. When you tax the resources, you are socializing resources through the tax system.[1]

British Columbia's forest tenure policies also confound the standard left-right arguments over free enterprise. In British Columbia, the privilege to buy timber is restricted to a few buyers, or even to a single buyer, by means of Tree Farm Licences, quota systems and Timber Sale Licences. Sustained yield policies further compromise the free market. Restricting yearly harvests to an allowable cut in a particular sustained yield unit means that there is a point above which the supply cannot be increased no matter what price buyers are willing to pay. In practice, this figure is not quite absolute since higher prices will make some of the inaccessible and low-quality stands worth harvesting while encouraging more complete use of trees previously harvested. A good example of this is to be found in European forests where even roots and branches are converted to pulp and paper. Yet in spite of this marginal flexibility, sustained yield practice is generally considered one of the major obstacles to the working of a free market economy and is especially so considered by economists such as Gaffney:

> The shorter the period of time between planting a tree and cutting it, the more labour is used in adding value to the final products and the less capital . . . and the less land is tied up per worker.
>
> Publicly owned forests are not administered economically. They are administered by foresters who have this drilled out of them in forestry school. [When you looked closely] you discovered that a degree in forestry is a licence to stop thinking and that our forests both in B. C. and the U. S. are administered by people with a very rigid ideology which goes by the name of "even-flow sustained yield," which causes them to hold timber much too long before they cut it [and] to carry an excess inventory of timber at very low productivity, and causes them to develop an ideology which is entirely geared to justifying and supporting this way of doing things.[2]

All these departures from the free-market economy are rationalized on the same basis as sustained yield policy: they are supposed to enable the provincial government to direct and control regional economic development and stability. However, as Mason Gaffney points out, this rationalization is questionable:

> If you look at this argument about employment stability and look at the rate of turnover that occurs in the labour force anyway, you'll find the rate of turnover is extremely high. So what you are subsidizing in a meaningful sense is not really jobs in a particular place — especially way up north, because people come and go very fast anyway — what you are stabilizing is the return on the capital that people have invested there.[3]

In a system of competitive bidding for standing timber, the timber's economic rent is a result of the market for the processed product, the money market, and harvesting and processing costs. However, in the absence of competitive bidding, it should still be possible to determine the economic rent through a system of appraisal. Given an open and active market for the product, one could simply work backward from the selling price to appraise the value of the uncut timber. To use a simple example: a logger believes he can sell and deliver a fir log to a buyer for $50; if the cost of cutting down, hauling out and delivering that log, including an allowance for profit, is $40, the economic rent for the log as standing timber would be $10 and the logger should pay no more and no less than that. The process could be complicated a bit by extending the cost calculation through the manufacturing stage and working backward from lumber or pulp prices. In that instance, the costs and profit allowances for milling or chipping would also be taken into account; but theoretically, the figure for economic rent would be the same.

In British Columbia, this apparently simple process has become an elaborate, little understood and, at times, highly contentious system, partly because there is almost no open market within the province for either finished forest products or standing timber. Most of British Columbia's forest products are exported to the United States where they must sell at a price that is competitive with the home product. This means that to arrive at an economic rent for B. C. timber, economists would have to work backward from prices on the American market. This, in turn, would imply that the value of B. C. timber depends on the value, or economic rent, of American timber. This conclusion is so upsetting to B. C. economists that some of them refuse to acknowledge it.

In the absence of a competitive log market in British Columbia, economists and bureaucrats alike have abandoned the concept of economic rent in favour of a system called "stumpage," which is simply the price a logger pays for access to the trees. Stumpage dates back to 1884, when the B. C. legislature passed an act allowing for a levy of fifteen cents for each tree felled and twenty cents for every thousand feet of lumber scaled at the mill. Prior to this, the government obtained its forest revenues from the outright sale of forest land or, after 1880, from the sale of timber lease rentals. In 1888 the levy on trees was replaced with a royalty system which charged fifty cents for every thousand board feet measure of timber cut on Crown lands. Receipts in the first year of royalty payments totalled $13,286.

In 1914, following the invasion of British Columbia by American lumbermen during the first decade of this century, the Timber Royalty Act was passed which allowed the government to adjust royalty rates in relation to the selling price of lumber. By this time, annual revenues were about $2.5 million from royalties.[4] The 1912 Forest Act also included provisions for selling standing timber by public competition. Bids were in the form of sealed tenders and were expressed as the amount the buyer was willing to pay above a minimal, or "upset," stumpage rate. The upset rate was determined by subtracting the exploitation costs from the selling price, with allowances for profits, carrying charges, interest and risk. The prices and costs used would represent "normal" conditions and were calculated for each timber stand by a Forest Service appraiser who based his calculations on personal knowledge and experience.

Stumpage in its modern form developed after World War II with the adoption of the Rothery System of appraisal in 1948. Currently used by both the U. S. and B. C. forest services, though to somewhat different ends, the great virtue of the Rothery System was the establishment of a uniform method of calculating operating costs and selling prices and relating them to each other. During the 1950s, most of the timber sold in British Columbia was priced by a combined appraisal and bidding system. The appraisal was used to establish the minimum, or upset, rate, below which the timber would not be sold. Competing buyers bid on an additional amount, or bonus, they were willing to pay above that upset price. The timber boom in the 1950s resulted in some very high bidding on timber sales, and out of fear that a drop in the market would bankrupt the loggers holding these high-priced cutting contracts, the government adopted a sliding stumpage scale that allowed for adjustments in the stumpage rates according to changing market values.

Many in the industry look on this era as the golden age of free enterprise. The postwar building boom was in full swing, and a large number of independent operators were competing for timber. Supposedly, the efficient survived and the provincial treasury reaped the benefits in the form of high stumpage rates. Reality was somewhat different, however. All loggers were buying from a single seller, the government, and they had a collective interest in keeping the stumpage rates low. Thus, in the normal course of events, they worked out a sort of gentlemen's agreement, not bidding up the price on another's application. Whenever spirited bidding did occur, it was usually from a newcomer trying to establish himself, with existing operators driving up the stumpage to discourage him. Other means were available to shrink the government's perception of true economic rents: prospective bidders at auctions might be offered a cash payment to refrain from bidding; a larger firm could offer a small one a lucrative logging contract in exchange for its withdrawal from bidding; bankers and other lenders could influence the amount of competition by granting or withholding credit to prospective bidders. Everyone except the government had a vested interest in keeping stumpage rates down.[5]

In recent years, the lack of an active timber market in British Columbia has further obscured the true value of the province's forest resource. Theoretically, stumpage should equal economic rent. However, the appraisal system for determining stumpage assumes the presence of a market in order to arrive at a number of its essential figures. Since no such market exists in the province, stumpage is based on pretence. Consequently, the system of stumpage has become a potentially explosive forest policy issue.

The basic question in determining the price of a publicly owned resource is whether the price is fair to both the buyer and the seller. But is stumpage fair? The forest industry looks upon stumpage as a royalty or even as a tax. Economists and many others still consider stumpage to be a form of economic rent, but critics of the appraisal system declare that the rent is too low. Increasingly, public policy is tending towards collecting the full economic rent, defined as everything remaining after operating costs, allowances for profit and certain risks are deducted from the final selling price. However, this formula works better in words than in practice. Despite numerous academic studies and official enquiries, no one has ever come up with widely accepted figures for any of the variables in the equations used to determine stumpage. The result is that comparisons of appraised stumpage rates with returns derived from the few existing open timber auctions are of considerable amusement to those with a sardonic sense of humour.

One indication of the way the appraisal system undervalues timber is the black market value of "quota." The quota system arose in 1948 with the passage of sustained yield legislation, according to which the large amounts of timber allocated in Tree Farm Licences were priced according to the appraisal system. In the Public Sustained Yield Units, however, timber was still sold at auction, but with a limit on the amount that could be cut annually in each unit. To this, by administrative fiat, was added a quota system which parcelled out the annual cut in each PSYU according to an operator's historical production level and performance record. Existing quota holders were allowed to match any offer on timber they had requested, with the losers in the quota sale forfeiting a bidding deposit of 10 per cent of the estimated stumpage.

At first, quota was not considered a salable commodity, for the transfer of timber cutting rights required the approval of the minister of forests. Under minister Ray Williston, however, the sale of quota became a common, though unofficial practice. One justification for this was that it encouraged small, inefficient operators to get out of the business by selling their timber rights, along with their worn-out equipment, to a more efficient operator. The value they received was considered a reward for having persevered and having helped build up the industry. Although the fact was rarely discussed openly, by the mid-1970s quota sales had become the most common means of acquiring additional timber rights for expansion. Since then, it has been widely recognized in the industry that the real profits are to be made when a company sells out.

Since the unofficial market value of quota can be roughly established by these sales, critics of the appraisal system have argued that quota sales provide a way of measuring the amount of the economic rent the government is losing on the sale of public timber. The value of the timber rights sold can be determined by subtracting the value of the operating equipment and other assets from the selling price of the company. A survey conducted in early 1981 concluded that the usual price paid for quota in British Columbia over the previous couple of years ranged from about \$25 per m^3 (\$71 per cunit) in the Interior to \$30 per m^3 (\$86 per cunit) on the coast.[6]

According to the critics, the money a company receives by selling its future rights to cut timber is an unearned revenue which properly belongs to the public. They say that it is the timber, not the rights, that should have value and that, if the timber had been properly valued in the first place, the future cutting rights would be of relatively insignificant value. They also argue that if buyers can afford to pay another company for those rights, then they could afford to pay higher stumpage rates instead. They see the black market value of quota as a direct measure of the extent to which the appraisal system undervalues timber.

While this argument has some merit, it would be unwise to accept too hastily a dollar-for-dollar measurement which implies a four- or fivefold shortfall in stumpage rates. In 1980 the average stumpage price on all species logged in PSYUs throughout British Columbia was $5.54 per m³ ($16 per cunit).[7] At the same time, quota was valued from $25 to $30 per m³ ($71 to $86 per cunit). Yet apples are not being compared with apples here, because quota confers the right to cut a specified amount of timber each year for an indefinite period. That time element itself has a value. Yet again, even if the government were realizing a full economic rent from timber sales, as long as there is an upper limit on the volume to be cut each year, quota will have an additional value. However, as the rules work now, the only revenue the government realizes from quota values is a light tax on the capital gains when a company sells its quota.

In 1980 the B.C. Ministry of Forests issued a discussion paper on appraisals which stated that the principal objective of timber pricing is "to enhance the management and use of the forest resource for the maximum long term socio-economic benefits of the province."[8] Secondary objectives were that the appraisal system be adaptable to rises and falls in forest product markets; that it be able to collect the full value of the resources being harvested; that it allow for an equitable charge upon timber coming from widely divergent logging conditions and changing economic factors; that it encourage an internationally competitive timber processing industry; that it be applicable to a wide variety of changing management objectives, and that it be as simple a system as possible.

The Rothery appraisal system used in British Columbia calculates stumpage as the value remaining after operating costs and a profit and risk allowance are subtracted from the selling price. The difficulty lies in determining realistic values for each of these factors for a particular stand of timber. The general approach of the Forest Service is to appraise to the value of the end product at the first point in the production process where (a) the quality of the timber can be taken into account, (b) a free market price can be determined and (c) the production costs of the end product can be isolated from other costs. To this end, the province is divided into two zones, the coast, where the end product is logs, and the Interior, where lumber and pulp chips are produced. The explanation for this is that on the coast, where logs can move easily and cheaply by water, there is — in theory — a log market, known as the Vancouver Log Market. In the Interior there is no log market because of the high cost of transporting logs, so the point of appraisal has been moved along the production process to the point where a market theoretically does exist — the production of lumber and chips. Because there is a great deal of variation in the percentage of lumber or chips that can be recovered from logs of different species, size and grade, it is necessary to apply lumber recovery factors to Interior timber stands.

On the coast, the problem is that the Vancouver Log Market is more myth than reality. Twenty or thirty years ago, when there was a significant number of independent loggers and mill owners, a large volume of logs was bought and sold on the open market. The subsequent concentration of the industry in the hands of a few large, integrated companies means that most of the log transactions on the coast now consist of trades between the big companies.

Log market data are collected by the Council of Forest Industries (COFI), which accounts for about 95 per cent of the timber harvested in the province. And while it has never been seriously suggested that COFI alters the figures it receives from its members, it is widely believed that the dollar values assigned by the companies to the trading transactions — particularly transactions involving higher grades of logs — do not reflect the true value of the logs. This suspicion appears to be borne out by comparing prices paid by some of the smaller independent mills in the southern coastal area with the published Vancouver Log Market prices. Obviously, it is in the best interests of the companies to keep these dollar values as low as possible, and the Forest Service has no way of checking the individual transactions. If Company A trades a boom of medium-grade cedar saw logs with Company B for a boom of medium-grade fir saw logs and reports the transaction as such, there is nothing to prevent Company A from sorting out the best of the fir and using it to make plywood, which would give it a much larger return in processing. Or, because the market is largely a trading operation, if a mill owner is willing to pay \$60 per m^3 (\$171 per cunit) for a certain grade of saw log, but has no logs to offer in exchange for them, he will be unable to obtain the logs he needs even though their trading value might be listed as low as \$40 per m^3 (\$115 per cunit) in transactions conducted by the larger companies.

One of the chief weaknesses of the coastal system is that logs are no longer a representative end product and the market for them is now very restricted. This was one justification for creating the Small Business Program — the government's desire to re-establish an independent and competitive logging sector which would inject new life into the Vancouver Log Market. Another approach, long seriously considered, might be to put the coastal appraisal system on the same end-product basis as the Interior's — lumber and chips. While this makes some sense — because it would preclude the possibility of companies trading "cheap" logs and increasing their revenues in the stumpage-free conversion process — it would be a much more complex system, containing its own weaknesses.

The initial difficulty with the Interior system lies in establishing recovery factors. In making its calculations, the Forest Service does not measure a stand of timber before it is harvested and then tally the volume of lumber and chips produced from that stand. Instead, it bases its calculations on what it thinks the "average efficient operator" will be able to recover from the various sizes, grades and species of logs. Two problems are involved here. The average efficient operator is a figment of the Forest Service imagination. He is not the statistical average of all operators, but is an operator "using methods, men and equipment that are efficient for the task to be done in the light of the prevailing state of technological development."[9]

There are a lot of jokes, few of them printable, about the average efficient operator. Since very few members of the Forest Service have had any direct experience logging or milling, the only source of information is industry itself, and it is only recently that the government has had access to company books. And because it is in the best interests of the companies for the Forest Service estimation of the average efficient operator's productive abilities to be as low as possible, the method tends to create some bizarre circumstances. An operator who knows his performance is being evaluated for the purpose of establishing production standards is naturally going to become rather lethargic. Any suggestion by Forest Service personnel that operators are working below average efficiency is apt to produce a flood of caustic remarks regarding efficiency of the Forest Service — considered by many of its own members to be a bureaucratic nightmare.

The main problem, however, lies with the enormous technical difficulty of establishing recovery factors and then applying those factors to an actual stand of timber and the conversion process it passes through to create lumber and chips. The conversion factors themselves have been derived from almost 100,000 trees felled and measured. When an actual stand is being considered, a small percentage of it is sampled and the results applied to the whole stand. Without actually cutting the tree, the cruiser is expected to calculate the gross volume of the tree (excluding the stump and unusable top), the volume of decay, the volume of recoverable soundwood to within 2.5 cm (1 inch) of decayed wood in the tree, the volume of unrecoverable soundwood that will be left on the logging site in logs that are more than 50 per cent defective, and the volume of soundwood that will be broken during falling and yarding and, as a result, left in the woods — all this within a 15 per cent margin of error.

The next step is to calculate the volume of lumber which can be obtained from the soundwood available in the stand. The factors used in this stage make allowance for a host of items including the amount of wood turned into sawdust during sawing, edging and planing, the volume lost in kiln drying, irregular log shapes and so on.

The object of this exercise is to come up with figures for the lumber and chip volumes on which stumpage will be charged. If the operator feels, over time, that he is obtaining less volume than the Forest Service is billing him for, he will complain about the inaccuracy of the calculations. If he gets more, he might still complain for appearance' sake, but he is unlikely to volunteer the information that the estimates are low.

The problem is that the measurements taken, and the decay and recovery estimates made during the cruise, must all be accurate if the appraisal is to be at all valid. Many of the participants — including several members of the Forest Service — feel there is considerable error throughout the process. For just one example, consider the world of the timber cruiser, which is not the world of executives, bureaucrats, economists or beer commercials. It is near the end of the day; it has been cold, with rain and snow. The truck is parked a kilometre away, and the timber cruiser is wet to his skin and chilled to the marrow. Yet he is still measuring the timber stand, trying to be accurate within 15 per cent, though he feels scarcely 15 per cent alive. He will make errors.

Even if he does not err, the standard methods of processing his findings are likely to be quite inadequate. Once the volume calculations for a stand have been obtained and processed, they are matched with lumber and chip prices provided each month by the mills. These prices are calculated at the point when the products are loaded on railcars for shipment and are averaged over whichever of four Interior pricing zones the timber comes from.

As might be expected, there are many arguments concerning the technical aspects of this stage of the appraisal process. But probably more important is the determination of what constitutes a real selling price. Most Interior lumber is sold in eastern Canada and the United States. Much of it is logged, milled and sold by integrated companies. Many of them own or work through marketing companies which occasionally extend to the retail level.

It is one matter for Joe Littleman's Sawmill of Prince George, B. C., to sell a carload of two-by-fours to the Neighborhood Lumberyard in Wichita, Kansas, for $150 a thousand board feet and to report this sale to the Forest Service. But it is quite a different matter for International Consolidated Enterprises, of the same city, to sell four carloads of similar quality two-by-fours to its subsidiary marketing company, International Consolidated Lumber Brokers, also of Wichita, for $100 a thousand board feet — and report that sale to the Forest Service. If those were the only sales in the zone for that month, the average selling price to be used for stumpage calculations would be $110 per thousand board feet.

The "average efficient operator" concept mentioned earlier is used to determine operating costs. These costs include logging expenses on the coast and logging plus milling costs in the Interior. Because operating costs normally exceed stumpage rates many times over, a small percentage of error in cost calculations results in a large percentage of error in stumpage.

In calculating logging costs, the appraiser's task is to estimate what the costs will be to the average efficient operator to log a particular cutting block. Again, it is not an average cost calculation but the appraiser's estimate of what an average logger, using the most efficient and suitable logging technique, will spend getting out the timber. If the operator can do it at a lower cost, so much the better for him; if not, he is the loser.

The Forest Service obtains its cost information from a number of sources: contractual labour rates; time-motion study data; information supplied by logging companies, and the prices charged by logging contractors working for other timber companies. These contractor prices are considered the most reliable guide: contractors are recognized as the most efficient loggers; there are few circumstances under which it is beneficial to the company holding the timber rights to pay inflated contract costs, and contract costs reflect capital as well as operating expenses.

As with other facets of the appraisal process, cost determination is subject to a lot of criticism and is a matter of ongoing negotiation and conflict between industry and government. Industry usually considers the Forest Service estimation of the mythical operator's ability to be too high. But critics, including market loggers who bid for their timber, look on the average efficient operator as an unproductive dolt who would soon starve in a free and open timber market.

The allowances for production costs create a curious situation in an industry which, in the final analysis, must compete in the international forest product market. It is in the timber companies' best interests to see these allowances established at the highest possible level. The more evidence they can provide to support higher costs, the lower their stumpage will be. To some degree there is a disincentive to be efficient. Why bother to keep costs down if efficiency would lead to lower cost allowances during the appraisal process, and thus higher stumpage? Yet to boost profits and compete on the selling market, efficient operations are a decided advantage. The trick can be turned by keeping costs as low as possible while attempting to hide these real costs from the Forest Service.

At this point in our study, we enter the strange world of the resource accountants. These great but unrecognized geniuses have created an environment as arcane, as obscure as laws and regulations will allow — and tax laws and resource regulations allow plenty of obscurity. The result is a surreal landscape bestrewn with sinking funds, deferred charges, accelerated depreciation, depletion allowances, reserves, offsets and other figments of the double-entry imagination — all to paint a picture of desperately high costs and desperately low profits, resulting in compassionately low stumpage rates. These resource accountants are artists who make Dali seem a dilettante, for they paint on a canvas as large as the entire forest area of British Columbia. To the extent that they succeed in their endeavours and gain lower stumpage rates, to that same extent all B. C. taxpayers become unwitting patrons of their art. So surreal and obscure is the result that today no one knows what it really costs to cut a tree in British Columbia.[10]

The price of labour is yet another controversial component of logging and milling costs. Many critics argue that the timber companies have no incentive to take a tough stance when negotiating contracts with the forest industry unions because increased labour costs will automatically be passed through the appraisal process, probably with a healthy markup, and end up as reduced stumpage revenue to the public, thus costing the companies nothing. In effect, the argument goes, the public is subsidizing wages in the forest industry. Union and management spokesmen vigorously deny this argument. But in other contexts, the industry is quick to attribute British Columbia's relatively low stumpage rates in large part to the high costs of labour.

The lack of incentive to keep costs down is further reflected in the final stage of the appraisal process, the application of profit and risk allowances. The object of these allowances is to encourage the maintenance and growth of the provincial forest industry by insuring a sufficient return on investment to attract capital. There are several components: the profit margin is set at 10 per cent on the coast and 12 per cent in the Interior, and there are many risk categories that operate on a sliding scale, depending on economic circumstances at a given time and the financial hazards involved in harvesting and milling timber from particular stands. Although in theory a risk allowance could be as high as 18 per cent, it is normally much lower.

An anomaly of the profit and risk factor is that while its objectives are tied up with ensuring investment, it does not relate to the investment involved in a particular operation. Instead, it is expressed as a percentage of operating costs and appraised stumpage. The implications of assessing profit and risk against operating costs and stumpage were not lost upon competitive timber buyers when the appraisal system was first introduced to calculate stumpage rates for Tree Farm Licences in the late 1940s. One of the central arguments against non-competitive timber sales was that such a system would put the forest industry on a cost-plus operating basis. Inasmuch as this is true, it makes profits a function of operating costs — the higher the cost, the higher the profits.

In reality, the profit and risk allowance ends up as a percentage of selling price. Although this is now common practice in most industries, economists insist that profit should properly be considered in terms of the investment involved in making that profit. Yet in the forest industry, "ultimately, profit and risk allowances hinge on the selling prices of end products, and therein lies the basic weakness of the method, for there is no consistent relationship between sales values of end products and the investment underlying production."[11] But while the deficiencies in the present system are widely recognized, and several alternative methods have been proposed over the years, the system is retained because of its "simplicity."[12]

Once profit and risk allowances and operating costs have been deducted from the selling price, what remains is the appraised stumpage. This is the basic rate applied against non-competitive timber sales and is the upset price, above which buyers bid in competitive sales. It is not, however, the final stumpage rate. There is a minimum upset rate — 3 per cent of lumber and chip prices in the Interior and either 6 or 8 per cent of log prices on the coast, depending on the area in which the logging occurs. The rationale for this stipulation is to establish a stumpage price below which the government will not sell timber. Above that price, the government and the operator share the proceeds.

Revisions in a number of appraisal factors are made periodically. Allowances for logging costs are revised annually and milling costs monthly. Stumpage rates are also adjusted monthly in response to changes in selling prices on the basis of the latest three-month averages. In addition, a company with a considerable portion of its timber supply in Old Tenures which carry a very low stumpage rate (such as MacMillan Bloedel, with about half its timber supply so arranged) can simply switch to cutting on these Old Tenure lands when normal stumpage rates are high. Later, it can cut on its regular TFLs in more depressed times, when normal stumpage rates are lower.

Further, Section 88 of the Forest Act allows operators to receive a credit against stumpage for certain tasks performed on public lands which are commonly accepted as being the responsibility of the landowner, that is, the Crown. These include the construction of logging access roads and reforestation or other silvicultural treatments. These expenditures must be approved in advance if credit is to be received and are calculated on the basis of actual costs. In effect, the licence holder is undertaking this work on a cost-plus basis as a contractor to the government, on lands over which he has tenure.

At this point, a quiet word of reminder: all the foregoing, the labour factors, the operating costs, the risk write-offs, the profit allowances, the average efficient operators, the inflated and deflated selling prices and the rest; all the argument, conniving, fiddling, analyzing, conferring, manipulating; all that effort is expended for just one reason — because there is no open competitive bidding for standing Crown timber in British Columbia.

This description of the timber pricing system used in British Columbia is necessarily sketchy. Moreover, the system is subject to constant change. Pearse's 1974 task force report on Crown timber disposals filled almost two hundred pages and, according to many, still failed to explain how the system works.

In addition, the technical details of the procedure are constantly being altered in day-to-day negotiations between the government and the timber companies.

The important question, however, is the end result — the revenue collected from the sale of publicly owned resources. When the figures are tallied up at the end of each year, the pros and cons of the pricing system are usually the subject of a hot, though not necessarily informed, debate. Part of the problem during this phase of the debate is that there is no such thing as a typical year in the forest industry. Market demand and prices for forest products fluctuate dramatically, as do stumpage rates, making comparison difficult and risky.

During 1979, the B. C. forest industry produced a record harvest, logging 76 000 000 m^3 (26.8 billion cubic feet) of timber.[13] The value of this timber, before processing, was estimated at $3.2 billion — or almost $42 per m^3 ($120 per cunit).[14] Stumpage payments on this timber were $9.75 per m^3 ($28 per cunit) on Tree Farm Licences and $7.57 per m^3 ($22 per cunit) on Timber Sale Harvesting Licences and Timber Sales.[15] Almost $417 million was collected in stumpage that year, along with an additional $43 million for rentals, royalties, fees and other charges on industry.[16] (See appendices for 1980 data.)

The matter at issue is whether this stumpage revenue collected by the government constitutes the full economic rent. The answer to this question requires, among other things, a realistic appraisal of the market value of timber. Because there is no reliable timber market in British Columbia, comparisons are often made with prices and stumpage rates obtained in Washington and Oregon, where most public timber is sold at public auctions. While great caution must be used, such comparisons are useful because both areas sell in the same international markets and because the forests and terrain are similar, as are logging techniques.

A study published in 1980 by David Haley, a forestry economist from the University of British Columbia, has brought out some rather startling results.[17] According to Haley's calculations, average stumpage for public timber in Washington and Oregon in 1978 was $39.11 per m^3 ($112 per cunit) or more than eight and a half times British Columbia's stumpage of $4.58 per m^3 ($13 per cunit).

Between 1963 and 1978, stumpage revenues in Washington and Oregon have risen at a real rate of 11 per cent a year — over 478 per cent — after discounting inflation. Over the same period, they did not rise at all in British Columbia. Indeed, in the vital Vancouver District, they fell by 2 per cent in real terms, despite the fact that while in Washington and Oregon the allowable cut increased by only 13 per cent during that time, in British Columbia it rose by over 336 per cent.

Haley further calculated that in 1977 log prices in Washington, where timber sold on a competitive basis, were more than double the prices in comparable situations in British Columbia — \$59.03 per m^3 (\$169 per cunit) for Douglas-fir, compared to a B. C. price of \$28.82 per m^3 (\$82 per cunit) for Douglas-fir logged in the Quadra PSYU. Although logging costs and profit allowances were slightly lower in British Columbia, the Washington risk allowances were substantially higher. Using the prevailing selling price and operating costs, the B. C. Forest Service appraisal system indicated a stumpage rate of \$0.17 per m^3 (\$1 per cunit), with the upset, or minimal, rate being \$2.72 per m^3 (\$8 per cunit). In the comparable Washington situation, the indicated stumpage rate was \$18.96 per m^3 (\$54 per cunit) and the average stumpage price under competitive bidding of Douglas-fir that year in the National Forest under examination was \$59.22 per m^3 (\$169 per cunit).

The obvious question arises: why does the same species of tree, logged under roughly comparable circumstances at approximately equivalent costs and sold on the same markets, produce almost twenty-two times the revenue for the U. S. Forest Service than for its counterpart in British Columbia? If these comparative figures are applied to the 1979 B. C. harvest of 76 000 000 m^3 (26.8 billion cubic feet), the magnitude of the issue is staggering and suggests that B. C. public coffers are being shortchanged by several billion dollars a year.

Naturally, the forest industry has a whole raft of explanations.[18] One of the most legitimate involves the higher quality timber found in Washington and Oregon. Haley made an allowance for such differences in his study, which increased the B. C. appraised stumpage price from \$0.17 per m^3 (\$1 per cunit) to \$7.13 per m^3 (\$20 per cunit), still only 38 per cent of the appraised price in Washington.

A further argument accounts for an unmeasurable part of the difference between the appraised price usually charged on timber in British Columbia and the bid price in the United States. During periods of rising demand for timber — as in 1977 — buyers at open timber auctions are willing to pay more than the actual value of timber because they are speculating that prices will rise even farther by the time the trees are logged. Evidence of this argument was to be found during 1981 and 1982, when U. S. loggers were clamouring for relief from high stumpage rates during a period of depressed markets. But it is impossible to compute what portion of the $59.22 bid for Douglas-fir in Washington during 1977 could be called speculative. One indication is that even during the worst of the 1982 recession, stumpage rates in the U. S. did not substantially decline.

It is during a period of depressed markets that the issue of comparative stumpage rates becomes particularly contentious. Traditionally, in such a situation, U. S. Pacific Northwest loggers complain bitterly about the low-stumpage B. C. lumber flowing south across the border to compete against their high-stumpage timber. They argue that in effect B. C. forest products are being subsidized, and they usually end up calling for trade restrictions. It was for good reasons that in 1982 the U. S. government trade agency ruled in Portland that these low stumpage rates amount to a subsidy of Canadian lumber and that Canadian lumber therefore deserves a tariff when entering the United States. This would have the U. S. government, rather than the B. C. government, collecting the economic rent on B. C. timber. (Following the Portland ruling, the Pacific Northwest lumbermen called for a 60 per cent tariff on Canadian softwood lumber entering the United States, but their application to the U. S. Commerce Department was turned down in 1983 — much to the relief of the Canadian forest industry.) At such times, the B. C. industry, speaking through the Council of Forest Industries (COFI), goes to great lengths to refute the arguments that B. C. lumber is subsidized.

The COFI report on this issue, published in 1981, is an intriguing document. For the most part it merely explains differences in the appraisal system used in the two jurisdictions. Its chief documented argument rests on the higher labour costs found in the B. C. industry. The main thrust of the COFI position appears to be that the entire situation can be traced back to the unreasonable demands of the B. C. forest unions.[19] The report concludes by stating that "U. S. stumpage rates clearly could not be applied in B. C. as the stumpage alone could exceed the end product value. Obviously the numerous differences between these two areas preclude direct comparison. The effects of these differences unfortunately cannot be quantified."[20]

With so many variables at work, no one with any detailed knowledge of timber pricing would try to put a precise dollar figure on revenues lost to the public. However, if Haley's figures are crudely applied, it appears that somewhere between zero and $4.25 billion a year in economic rent is not being collected by the B. C. government. Where, then, does this money go? What happens to the revenues, generated by sales on the international timber markets, but which in British Columbia do not end up as stumpage payments? If U. S. loggers are paying ten times the stumpage that B. C. loggers are paying, what happens to the differences in British Columbia?

The COFI report argues that if stumpage rates in British Columbia were lower than they should be, the difference would be reflected in excessive profits — which, COFI states, is not the case. However, there are many ways of disposing of money within a large timber corporation besides listing it as profit on the annual financial statement. One way, mentioned earlier, is to siphon it out of the province or the country via a marketing subsidiary. This, in fact, has been alleged in cases such as FABCO exporting wood chips at below market prices to its company in Japan and B. C. Forest Products' MacKenzie mill selling its products at below market value to its Japanese company. In the years before it was taken over by the B. C. government, Columbia Cellulose consistently sold its products to its U. S. parent at below market value.

Perhaps an even more significant area worth investigating is the amount of money companies spend on expansion. Part of this involves investment in logging equipment and processing mills. But over the past decade or two, the largest amount of expansion dollars has probably been spent on the acquisition of additional timber rights. These might cost as little as the \$25 to \$30 per m^3 (\$71 to \$86 per cunit) for quota in a PSYU, referred to earlier in this chapter. Or, as one analyst calculated, the price might go as high as \$140 per m^3 (\$400 per cunit) in the case of the purchase of the Rayonier Tree Farm Licences by Western Forest Products, or \$310 per m^3 (\$886 per cunit) for the B. C. Forest Products purchase of timberland from Scott Paper and Crown Zellerbach.[21] When it is recognized that over the past couple of decades something like 85 per cent of the province's cutting rights has been acquired by a handful of large companies, and that most of the money received by the vendors of these cutting rights has been taken out of the industry and, quite likely, out of the province and the country, it is easier to understand where at least a portion of the unpaid economic rent has gone. The major companies have not only escaped paying the full rent on a publicly owned resource, but have used the "unearned increment" to increase their control of the industry.

At the working level of the forest industry, the most common explanation for the low stumpage rates paid in British Columbia involves a process of dissipation. The money is simply wasted and is reflected in the cost allowances of the appraisal process or the actual cost allowances which are deducted from stumpage.

The major forest companies are notorious for their inefficiencies. In theory, the "average efficient operator" concept should weed out inefficient operators. In reality, the establishing of cost allowances is a process of perpetual negotiation, with the companies constantly pressing for higher cost allowances and the Forest Service gradually giving way.

It is commonly understood in the industry that a gyppo or contract logger, or a silvicultural contractor, can produce up to twice as much as a company-managed crew at equivalent cost. Given the same equipment on the same ground, independent loggers or contractors can put twice as many logs on the landing in a day as company crews. Independent silvicultural crews can plant twice as many trees per man day and space twice as many hectares. Defenders of the companies might occasionally argue that their own crews do a better job of planting, for example, but since all planting is monitored by the Forest

Service and certain standards must be met before the companies are paid for this work, it is rare to hear company spokesmen making this claim in the presence of Forest Service personnel.

To understand how vast amounts of money simply disappear in a corporate logging operation, it is only necessary to appear at a marshalling point at the start of a day's work and count the number of pickup trucks, each containing one "supervisor." Among loggers, MacMillan Bloedel is the most notorious for this sort of thing; it employs a vast army of supervisory personnel, each equipped with a $12,000 vehicle. During 1981 and 1982, MB laid off about five hundred head-office staff, without any noticeable decline in efficiency; of course, the costs of these redundant positions had been factored into the appraisal process for years.

Corporate spokesmen habitually blame union workers for the low levels of productivity in the industry. Curiously, when stumpage rates are being discussed, they boast about the efficiency of the industry. But a subject that is never discussed, except among those at the working level, is the enormous inefficiencies created by the bureaucracies that have developed within all the major companies. And although it may be true that unionized workers directly employed by a major company are not particularly productive, this does not explain why members of the same union, working for a contractor or an independent logger, work more efficiently. The explanation most frequently encountered in the bush or at the mill is that the big companies have created work situations in which there is no incentive to be productive: the jobs are specialized and boring, and bureaucratic management decisions undermine productivity.

In certain types of work — primarily construction of access roads and silvicultural work — the companies receive credit against stumpage for the actual costs incurred. In theory, the Forest Service carefully monitors these expenditures before approving them; in reality, the Forest Service has neither the staff nor the knowledge to do so. The situation which has developed under this system is illustrated when a consultant undertakes a specified task, such as laying out an access road. His costs are $150 per man day worked. He charges the major company $300 a day. The company submits a cost of $450 a day for approval by the Forest Service — and, after some negotiation, gets it. Thereafter, the Forest Service routinely accepts a cost of $450 a day for this kind of work. In addition, the company receives a profit and risk allowance on top of the supervisory costs it was allowed to write off against such work.

In one way or another, all of these escalated costs end up coming out of stumpage, either as a credit against stumpage or through the appraisal process. They are yet another indication of the difficulty of calculating the amount of money lost to the public. Haley's analysis may be as close as we can ever get.

There is no simple answer to the basic economic question of who gets what out of the B. C. forests. Undoubtedly some — the major corporations — get more than others. That vague entity known as "the public," the residents of the province — or to be more exact, some of them — have, over the past few decades, reaped enormous benefits through the forest revenues collected by government. The relatively high standard of living, the large public bureaucracies and costly infrastructures that cover the province have for the most part been funded by the forests.

If corporate profits and government revenues, beyond the costs of harvesting, processing and managing a fat and complacent forest industry, are lumped together, it appears that in one admittedly good year, 1979, something in the order of $2.5 billion was siphoned out of the woods. This examination of the appraisal system used to price publicly owned forest resources and the comparisons with industry operating under similar conditions elsewhere indicate that perhaps an equal amount was hidden or dissipated somewhere between the mountainside and the lumberyard.

SIX

Will the Supply Last?

SINCE THE LAST CENTURY, there have been many prophets of an impending timber famine in North America. There is a monotonous similarity to these predictions: if demand for wood products continues to increase at its present rate, and if the timber harvest is allowed to meet these demands, then by such-and-such a year there will be no trees left to cut. That year is usually about twenty years beyond the time the prediction is being voiced. The idea of the timber famine is the reverse of the belief that loggers could never cut all the trees, that forests grow faster than they can be harvested. And, like most other concepts basic to forestry, the famine scenario is European in origin. European foresters have long believed that a timber famine is the inevitable consequence of a failure to practise sustained yield forestry.

During the first decade of this century, such predictions led to the formation of the Fulton Commission in British Columbia. Fulton concluded that things were not quite as bad as the doomsayers believed; he estimated that the province contained 6 070 500 ha (15 million acres) of commercial forest land, enough to postpone disaster for a while. However, a 1911 report out of Seattle predicted that by 1929 all U. S. timber outside of the federal forest reserves would be gone.

Contemporary timber faminists see the year 2000 as the time when the world will experience severe timber shortages. In 1980, A. J. Leslie, director of the United Nations Food and Agriculture Organization's forestry department, told the Canadian Forest Congress:

> . . . [because of] the failure of so many timber famines to materialize, you could well be justified in discounting this new warning

> as just another instance of calling "wolf." Perhaps it is, but if you remember the fable, then you will recall that the last time the boy called "wolf," the wolf was really there. This could well be the case with wood.[1]

Leslie did not say the world was going to run out of wood by the year 2000, only that projected demand would exceed the available supply if certain measures were not taken. Elaborating on this theme, Jack Munro, president of the International Woodworkers of America for western Canada, told the congress, "We will lose 100,000 jobs in the next twenty years. . . . Thousands of loggers and mill workers who are under forty will be uprooted and forced to relocate in other occupations."[2] British Columbia's deputy minister of forests, Mike Apsey, offered a similar message: there will be "local shortages in every region of the province within the next twenty years."[3]

Considering that none of the past timber famine predictions have occurred, that annual timber harvests throughout North America, including British Columbia, have steadily increased, and that the disaster point is constantly pushed ahead to some future date, one is inclined to wonder about the causes of these gloomy prophesies. In most cases a good part of the answer lies in the vested interest of the prophet. R. B. Forster, chief economist with the Canadian Forestry Service, said in 1979, "The timber famine is a convenient scenario which foresters use to aggrandize their own importance. We are the only saviours in a world hell-bent for self-destruction."[4]

Famine theory is used to support a variety of arguments about the forests and their use. Conservationists use it to argue for reductions in annual harvests. The timber industry uses it, at various times, to justify increased harvests of old-growth forests to make way for faster growing plantation forests, or to resist the creation of parks and wilderness areas, or to pressure government into spending more public funds on forest management. Government agencies and politicians use the same theories to justify reducing annual cuts and charging higher stumpage rates. And professional foresters habitually use famine predictions as an argument for the hiring of more foresters. It seems to be in everyone's best interest for the world to believe that its forests are about to vanish.

Determining the actual timber supply is a difficult task because it largely depends on definitions. In a strict economic sense a shortage is not possible. According to Forster, the prediction of timber famines is a function of mistaken notions about supply and demand. The famine theory, he says, is based upon a

> projected demand which will cross an assumed supply at some specific year in the future. The gap between supply and demand after the year of disaster is the gap that foresters have the obligation to fill. . . . Demand in these models is a projection of current consumption or perhaps one step up the ladder of sophistication, a function of Gross National Product and population. Supply is the allowable cut minus the trend in timber land allocations for other purposes. But what has your economics taught you about supply and demand? They are schedules of production and consumption at a continuum of prices. At any point in time, at some price supply will equal demand. If you believe this, there will never be a timber shortage. There will never be a timber famine. There will never be a gap to fill. Forest products may become more expensive and allocated to higher uses but we will never run out.[5]

It is also difficult to reconcile famine predictions with the ongoing insistence of government and industry — in British Columbia as well as in other areas of North America where timber is harvested from public lands — that rigorous sustained yield policies are and have been conscientiously applied. Either the allowable annual cuts of the province, the country and the continent are within the limits of the sustainable yield or they are not. If they are not and the cut in the past has been too high, it is a curious feature of the industry that the same people who assured the public that harvest levels could be safely increased can in the next breath warn the public of an impending disaster.

The real concern of those predicting shortages of timber is not that the timber supply will decrease, but that the forest industry will not be able to maintain an equal or increased share of world markets. Their fear is not that timber production will decline, though this is frequently stated or implied, but rather that British Columbia's or Canada's share of global timber production will fall off. For the most part, the faminist outlook stems from the realization that the almost unrestricted expansion of the timber industry during the past century is beginning to reach its limits.

For decades the financial structure, the corporate strategies and the basic psychology of the industry have been rooted in the concept of unlimited growth. Both industry and government have considered a growing share of an expanding world market to be a God-given right. This perception is slow to die.

There is a distinct difference between being able to sustain a certain level of forest products output and being able to expand that output in response to anticipated growth in demand. An inability to perform in the first instance could be considered a crisis, depending on the circumstances. But it is somewhat deceitful to cry "Famine!" if the forest industry should prove unable to respond instantly to increased use of wood products in Japan or Europe.

In fact, the very notion of increased demand is suspect. The forementioned FAO study, itself the basis of most current discussion of timber supply, "was largely built up from the industries' views of the way they felt demand would develop."[6] Many have a vested interest in convincing the public that world demand for timber products is going to increase dramatically. This belief attracts investment, it increases the value of the harvesting rights held by forest corporations, it strengthens the forest industry's position in disputes over the use to which forest land will be put, and it justifies increases in the price of forest products.

According to the FAO report, world consumption of timber is expected to increase by 50 per cent between 1980 and 2000. The 1980 world consumption was calculated at 1.26 billion m^3 (444.8 billion cubic feet).[7] After assessing demand predictions, the B. C. Forest Service in 1980 concluded that in order to meet this expanded market, the provincial harvest would have to increase from 75 000 000 m^3 (26.5 billion cubic feet) in 1980 to 91 000 000 m^3 (32.1 billion cubic feet) in 2000 — more than 20 per cent.[8] This is what would be needed for British Columbia to continue supplying between 8 and 9 per cent of the world's timber consumption.

Figure 1

Available Timber Volumes, in millions of cubic metres *(billions of cubic feet)*

	From TSAs	From TFLs	Private Land	Total Annual Harvest for B. C.
LEVEL 1 (long-run sustainable yield)	24.6 *(8.7)*	19.5 *(7.0)*	7.2 *(2.5)*	51.5 *(18.2)*
LEVEL 2 (equal to 1977 allowable cut)	46.7 *(16.5)*	10.5 *(3.8)*	7.2 *(2.5)*	73.6 *(26.0)*
LEVEL 3 (cut required to maintain province's share of projected world demand)	60.8 *(22.5)*	19.5 *(7.0)*	7.2 *(2.5)*	87.7 *(31.0)*

Figure 2

B. C. Timber Production, in millions of cubic metres *(billions of cubic feet)*

1912	6.7	*2.4*	1972	56.5	*20.0*
1920	9.9	*3.5*	1973	70.1	*24.8*
1930	12.7	*4.5*	1975	50.1	*17.7*
1940	17.6	*6.2*	1976	69.5	*24.6*
1950	22.0	*7.8*	1977	70.0	*24.8*
1955	29.3	*10.3*	1978	75.2	*26.6*
1960	34.0	*12.0*	1979[1]	76.2	*26.9*
1965	43.4	*15.3*	1980[1]	72.6	*25.6*
1970	54.7[2]	*19.3*			

1 Source: *Forest and Range Resource Analysis Technical Report* (Victoria: B. C. Ministry of Forests, 1980), B. C. Forest Service, *Annual Reports: 1979, 1980.*

2 Passes British Columbia's long-run sustainable yield of 51 500 000 m³ (18.2 billion cubic feet)

In 1980 the Forest Service published an extensive analysis of the provincial timber supply, the Forest and Range Resource Analysis Technical Report. Actually, the report was only a compilation of the existing inventory data and, as such, is subject to all the limitations of those data — much of them incomplete, inaccurate and of questionable relevance. But these data are the only information available. The report also assessed the timber supply relative to three levels of harvesting in order to predict where and when timber shortages might occur.

The first level represents a harvest equal to the long-run sustainable yield (LRSY). This is defined as the timber volume that can be taken perpetually from the productive and accessible forest sites. This level depends upon only minimal silvicultural treatments — planting denuded areas. It takes into account anticipated reductions in the forest land base and is calculated on the basis of present utilization levels. It includes only species now used commercially, and assumes existing levels of protection against fire, disease and insects. The calculations include only those lands within the Timber Supply Areas; they do not include private timber lands or Tree Farm Licences, though it was noted that the harvest levels in most of the TFLS are presently above the long-run sustainable yield.

The second harvest level projects an annual cut equal to the volume of wood the Forest Service had contracted to supply during 1977. The third level projects a harvest rate roughly equivalent to the increase in world demand over the next ten to twenty years, levelling off thereafter. This level assumes a harvest that will maintain the B. C. share of world timber production in the 8 to 9 per cent range.

If these figures are taken at face value, their implications are quite alarming. In the first place, they indicate that since 1970 the timber harvest has been considerably above the province's long-run sustainable yield of 51 500 000 m^3 (18.2 billion cubic feet). In 1980, the annual harvest for the following five years was set at a figure slightly above the Level 2 projection — 75 000 000 m^3 (26.5 billion cubic feet). They also indicate that if British Columbia is to retain its share of future expanded world timber markets and log accordingly, the harvest would be well beyond the capacity of the long-run sustainable yield.

Figure 3
Years Until Forecasted Timber Shortage Begins

REGION	LEVEL 1	LEVEL 2	LEVEL 3
Bulkley-Northwest	40	40	30
Cariboo	100+	100+	60
Kamloops	60	30	20
Nelson	100+	70	50
Peace River	100+	100+	100+
Prince George	100+	60	40
Prince Rupert	100+	80	40
Vancouver	60	50	40

Source: *Forest and Range Resource Analysis Technical Report* (Victoria: B. C. Ministry of Forests, 1980), p. 783.

The three harvest level projections were compared with the timber available from each Timber Supply Area in the eight regions of the province in order to predict when shortages could be expected to occur (see Figure 3).

These are regional averages. Within each region there are Timber Supply Areas where forecasted shortages will occur much earlier — within five to twenty years for at least one TSA in each region. The authors of the report concluded that "maintenance of present harvest rates over the long term may not be feasible in most regions. Raising harvest rates appreciably will only serve to advance the onset of wood falldowns and increase their size."

Publication of this report touched off a widespread hue and cry concerning the impending timber famine. The Forest Service maintained, as usual, that its estimates were realistic and that the future looked grim. The province's chief forester, Bill Young, issued a series of statements warning against the removal of more land from the commercial forest classification. Both industry and union spokesmen called for immediate and large increases in government silvicultural budgets. Conservationists and nonindustrial forest users called for immediate and drastic reductions in the timber harvest, and opposition members of the legislature made a great deal of noise about the incompetence of the government.

Yet also in 1980, when the Forest Service produced its five-year program for the management of the province's forests, the annual harvest levels for the following five years were set at a figure slightly above the 1977 commitment — in other words, the Level 2 harvest. "Pending detailed examinations of the province's forest resources and the implications of alternative harvesting rates at the Timber Supply Area level," the Forest Service explained, "the average overall timber harvesting program will be continued at about the present level from 1980 through 1985. Approximately 166 000 hectares will be logged each year to produce about 75 million cubic metres of wood. Additional commitments may be possible in some areas."[9]

Why would the government and the Forest Service approve annual timber harvests which are about 50 per cent higher than the long-run sustainable yield of the forests? And why, in the face of the timber shortages predicted in the Forest Service's own 1980 forest analysis, have drastic steps not been taken to bring the annual harvest into line with the timber supply? These questions are easily answered. It is one thing to use these figures to stake out a political position, but to bet money on them is quite another matter. To hazard capital, to risk jobs, to establish policy — no one, not even the Forest Service, takes the data seriously enough to use them as a basis for any action that involves actual dollars. Specifically, no one in a decision-making position is likely to reduce the annual harvest to a level equal to the long-run sustainable yield. That would eliminate about thirty thousand jobs and lower provincial revenues by about $200 million a year. Mills would shut down, another fifty thousand or so indirect jobs would disappear and the provincial economy would be destroyed.

Even if it were unanimously agreed that the projections are 100 per cent accurate, it is doubtful that any government would suddenly or even slowly reduce the annual cut. At most, it would disallow further increases in the harvest while trying to find some way to increase the available supply. Which is more or less what happened. The five-year program of 1980 included increased spending for silviculture and forest protection. Although there was a great deal of ballyhoo accompanying the unveiling of these budget increases and it was implied that they would significantly reduce the predicted timber deficit, the fine print in the Forest Service documents says otherwise. That gross deficit is about 24 000 000 m^3 (84.8 billion cubic feet) a year — the difference between the LRSY of 51 500 000 m³ (18.2 billion cubic feet) and the planned harvest of 75 000 000 m³ (26.5 billion cubic feet).

There are two kinds of silvicultural expenditure by the Forest Service: basic and intensive. Basic silviculture is the simplest stewardship of the forest. It maintains the forest's productivity, essentially by planting after logging. During the 1980–85 period, basic silvicultural expenditures were projected at $60.8 million a year. This money will not produce any additional timber; it is only maintenance money — what must be spent to maintain the timber supply at the level of the long-run sustained yield.

Then what of the deficit, the overcut of 24 000 000 m³? Intensive silviculture aims beyond maintenance to actual enhancement of forest yields. It involves such practices as spacing, fertilizing, catching up with planting not done in the past and improving growing sites. The five-year program calls for expenditures on intensive silviculture of $31 million a year and these are expected to increase future wood supplies by about 3 400 000 m³ (1.2 billion cubic feet) per year.

By increasing its expenditures on fire protection an additional $5 million a year, the Forest Service estimates that fire losses will be reduced by 11 000 ha (27,180 acres) a year. Based on the average volume cut per hectare during 1980, this expenditure would make available another 4 250 000 m³ (1.5 billion cubic feet). A further $4.5 million in the annual budget for combatting insects and disease is calculated to reduce losses by another 1 600 000 m³ (565 million cubic feet).

In total, the Forest Service plans to produce an addition 9 250 000 m³ (3.3 billion cubic feet) — only about 38 per cent of the amount by which the long-run sustained yield is being overcut. This alone is going to cost $40.5 million a year, about $4.38 per m³ ($13 per cunit). By this reckoning, to bring that 38 per cent up to 100 per cent — in other words, to balance the overcut entirely with new growth — would cost another $70 million, totalling about $110 million in intensive silviculture each year. This would maintain the industry at just above its 1977 production level. That is to say, it would if those gains in timber volume were fully realized. But that is a large assumption, which will be explored in chapter eight. Another large assumption is that there will indeed be a market for the additional timber nearly a century from now. Some very big money is riding on two very large assumptions.

If our aim is to balance the overcut with the sustainable yield, we need not risk such huge sums of money to do it. Other ways exist to increase the wood supply. These alternatives do not require such heavy investment, do not depend on century-long guesses, can be quantified very quickly and can be estimated even now.

The most rewarding approach is to use the existing stands more intensively. The gains possible in this area can be seen by a rough comparison of Canadian practice with utilization levels achieved in the Scandinavian countries. Norway, Sweden and Finland, with a productive forest area about one-quarter that of Canada's, obtain an annual harvest equal to two-thirds of the Canadian yearly cut. The major portion of the Scandinavian gains are due to better utilization.

There are several facets to the concept of improved utilization. The Forest Service's use of the term "utilization standard" refers to the wood that loggers are required to take out of the woods during harvesting. There are two standards of utilization in British Columbia: "intermediate" and "close." At present the general requirement is close utilization, and the forest inventory figures pertaining to available timber volumes are calculated to this standard (see p. 49). Logging to close utilization standards makes use of about 55 per cent of the weight of a tree; another 22 per cent is found in branches, needles and bark, and the remaining 23 per cent is in the top, stump and roots. It is this last category that offers an increased source of supply. The forest industry in many European countries has learned how to use most of this wood for pulp and has developed techniques for harvesting stumps and even roots.

In addition, there are a lot of trees in many stands which fall below the 18.0 to 23.1 cm (7.1 or 9.1 inch) diameter class. At present they are left behind during a logging operation. Also disdained are logs less than 3.0 m (9.8 feet) long, most of them the result of breakage during logging. It is remarkably difficult to calculate the volume of usable wood that never gets out of the logging site. The best information comes from the United States and Europe, where extensive studies and experience have resulted in tantalizing data. It is risky to make a direct application of these findings to the B. C. situation; nevertheless, they provide some indication of the potential for increasing the wood supply.

A Pacific Northwestern U. S. study examined the portion of logging residues tied up in cull logs in western Washington and Oregon. Culls are logs left in the forest because of a wide range of defects which are taken into account by U. S. National Forest utilization standards. "Cull log volume left after logging in western Washington and western Oregon amounts to, at most, 10 per cent of the log volume consumed by the lumber industry in the two states," the report concluded.[10] A major Swedish study on whole tree utilization conducted between 1974 and 1977 determined that stumpwood, undersized trees and other residues normally left behind could provide 17 per cent more wood fibre.[11]

Along the B. C. coast many logs are lost during sorting, booming, towing and barging operations. A Council of Forest Industries study concluded that 827 000 m^3 (29.2 million cubic feet) are lost annually, of which only 40 per cent is recovered by log salvagers. The other 500 000 m^3 (17.7 million cubic feet) either sink (35 per cent of the total initially lost) or end up on the beaches (25 per cent). The 200 000 m^3 (7.0 million cubic feet) that pile up on the beaches each year are not used because they become imbedded with sand and rocks. No mills are presently equipped to handle these contaminated logs.[12]

Once the logs have safely arrived at the processing mills, there are other improvements in efficiency and utilization that could increase the wood supply. In 1978 the Canadian Forest Service's Western Forest Products laboratory published figures indicating that wood supply could be increased about 27 per cent by increasing efficiency in the mills. Gains could be made in sawmilling by improved techniques of log bucking and sawing control, and by reducing saw-tooth widths. Plywood output could be increased with improved maintenance of lathes and better control of the peeling process. Glued lumber products could be made from short lengths and low-grade lumber items presently regarded as waste. The report concluded that "it is apparent that impending pressure on timber supply could be relieved much more quickly from increased efficiency than from more intensive forest management, which, however, should not be neglected."[13]

The volume of wood available from all these sources has never been seriously calculated in British Columbia. Nor have the costs of utilizing this wood been worked out. Forest inventories include only wood considered merchantable under close utilization standards; waste assessments conducted after logging are concerned only with determining the volume of merchantable wood left on the ground.

The standard response from industry is that the costs of utilizing waste, both in the woods and at the mills, are more than the wood is worth on the market. At the present time this is true, thanks mainly to low stumpage rates. But if demand increases over the next few decades, then it seems quite possible that higher prices will make this wood worth processing.

There are good reasons for being skeptical about the major companies' aversion to better utilization. Operators have historically claimed economic inability to log and process wood smaller than that to which they are accustomed. At one time, they could only make a profit by highgrading the first-growth Douglas-fir which was more than 61 cm (24 inches) in diameter. A decade or so ago, the integrated coastal forest corporations claimed that there was no money to be made in milling lumber out of logs less than 30.5 cm (12.0 inches) in diameter, so they put them through their whole log chippers and turned them into pulp. A number of smaller operators came along — notably Whonnock and Doman — and built small-log sawmills. They bought small saw logs at pulp log prices and made fortunes, forcing the entire industry to a higher level of utilization. The history of the industry, particularly during the past twenty to thirty years, leads to the conclusion that the established companies, in claiming their inability to use the wood now being wasted, are really confessing to entrepreneurial tired blood.

Events associated with the depressed timber markets of the early 1980s further underline the unwillingness or inability of industry to make use of the available timber. During 1983 and 1984, coastal logging operations had all but abandoned close utilization standards. Enormous volumes of small-diameter logs were left to rot, with only the best and most profitable logs removed for processing. Faced with the threat of shutdowns and layoffs, the Forest Service simply neglected to enforce utilization standards during this period. The famine had turned into a glut.

When the timber supply of British Columbia is being discussed and the volumes calculated, only certain "commercial" species are included. The only woods generally used by the forest industry in this province are the coniferous, or softwood, species — fir, spruce, cedar, pine, hemlock, balsam, larch and cypress. But there are also vast stands of deciduous, or hardwood, trees. They are, in order of magnitude, aspen, cottonwood, birch, alder and maple; they account for about 3 per cent of the mature timber volumes in the province. These non-commercial species take up about 4 per cent — about 2 000 000 ha (5 million acres) — of the productive forest land. But in 1979 the hardwood species made up only three-tenths of 1 per cent of the timber harvest.

The simple explanation for the relatively small hardwood harvest in British Columbia is that there is no market for these species. At first glance this seems true. If a logger were to harvest half a million cubic metres of any of the deciduous species and try to sell them, he would soon be bankrupt. Apart from a limited amount of cottonwood used in soft tissue paper, there is no historical market for these woods. Few of the mills in western North America are equipped to process them into lumber or pulp and paper on any significant scale. The lumber and pulp from hardwood behaves differently from that from softwood, and it is put to different uses. The hardwood industries have traditionally been centred in the eastern part of the continent. The western states and provinces have generally treated these trees as weeds.

Yet at various times, certain softwoods have also been so regarded. For example, until World War II, hemlock was not wanted. Loggers in British Columbia considered it a weed, much as they now regard alder or aspen. But during the war, the Koerner brothers, who had been active in the European forest industry, realized there were two main obstacles to the marketing of hemlock: it needed special drying and seasoning methods, and its name had unfavourable associations in Europe. They developed appropriate procedures for handling hemlock and began marketing it as Alaska pine. It has been a moneymaker ever since.

As there is nothing inherently inferior about any of the major hardwood species found in British Columbia, it seems reasonable to expect that they will one day become merchantable. This possibility is enhanced by some of the points brought to light by the FAO study. During the next twenty years, world demand for hardwoods is expected to increase much more rapidly than the demand for softwoods. At the same time, tropical hardwood forests, which have for decades supplied much of the world's hardwoods, are being depleted, and few of these forests are being managed for future production. All of these factors combine to make British Columbia's hardwood stands potentially valuable.

Additional timber now excluded from supply calculations and projections includes wood that can be obtained from immature stands at certain stages of their growth. These "thinnings," as they are generally called, represent an additional volume of wood quite apart from the calculated volume of the stands at the end of their rotation. To a certain extent, thinnings include wood that would otherwise be lost in the normal growth of the forest — diseased or damaged trees, or those that would be crowded out and eventually die.

The theory behind thinning is that once immature trees have reached a useful size, a portion of the stand can be periodically removed without affecting the ultimate volume of the stand at culmination. Consequently, thinning does not impinge upon the allowable cut calculations undertaken as part of sustained yield forestry. Thinning salvages natural mortality. Properly practised, it can increase the value of the forest well beyond what it would otherwise be worth at culmination.

For a whole host of reasons, thinning has never been practised in British Columbia on any significant scale. In the first place, only recently have accessible second-growth forests existed in sufficient quantity and quality to make thinning worthwhile. Until the past few years, there has been no serious incentive to consider this wood part of the timber supply; there have always been untouched, mature forests to harvest, and the entire industry is biased towards them. Further, the skills and technology have never evolved in British Columbia to thin immature forests properly without damaging the trees left behind to grow. And although various types of selective logging have been done in the past, a great deal of it has in fact consisted of highgrading, taking the best trees and leaving a legacy of diseased, damaged and commercially worthless forests. Consequently, many foresters are highly suspicious of the very concept of thinning. Nevertheless, there are enormous volumes of merchantable wood in the province's second-growth forests. It is entirely possible that as much as half of this timber could be harvested in thinning operations without affecting long-term yields or commitments already made to other licencees.

An indication of the amounts of wood involved in thinning can be obtained from a 1977 Forest Service study of the Sayward forest. The Sayward is part of the Quadra Timber Supply Area of the Vancouver Forest Region. With 186 920 ha (461,873 acres) of forest land, the Sayward makes up about 14 per cent of the Quadra TSA. The present annual cut of the Quadra area is 2 000 000 m^3 (70.6 million cubic feet); it is probably the most overcut TSA in the province and, according to the Forest Service, will experience serious timber shortages within five to ten years.

About two-thirds of the Sayward forest is covered with immature timber stands, much of it in Douglas-fir that was planted during World War II. According to the report, most of these stands are too dense to maintain their potential rate of growth, to enhance wildlife populations and to make the forests useful for recreation.

> The drastic reduction in density necessary to restore vigorous growth in these overstocked stands will require an approximate 50 per cent volume removal by thinning. This will produce a total volume in the order of 150 million cubic feet [4 240 000 m^3]. With a stand upgrading program spread over ten years, an annual yield of 15 million cubic feet [425 000 m^3] can be expected from a complete program.[14]

In other words, the immature stands in the Sayward forest, just 10 per cent of the Quadra TSA land area, are capable of producing about 425 000 m^3 of wood a year, or 21 per cent of the present annual cut of the entire TSA. None of this volume is currently considered in timber supply calculations — and it is only a portion of the immature stands within the TSA that can be thinned.

On a provincial scale, a rough indicator of the thinning volumes available was contained in a submission to the Pearse Commission. Working from Forest Service inventory figures, Jim Collins, a Vancouver forestry consultant, calculated that there are about 4 700 000 ha (11.6 million acres) of medium- and good-growing site coniferous stands on easily accessible Crown-managed lands (excluding Tree Farm Licences) between the ages of 40 and 120 years — the generally acceptable range for thinning operations.[15]

It is a bit hazardous to make a direct comparison of these lands with those of the Sayward, which has some of the most productive forest land in the province; the growth rate there is probably double that of most areas in the Interior. Thinning medium site lands in the Sayward has produced about 210 m^3 per ha (30 cunits per acre). If — and this is a very hypothetical if — we assume that 4.7 ha (11.6 acres) in the rest of the province can be thinned at one-third the rate of the Sayward, we suddenly find a great deal of new timber: about 330 000 000 m^3 (11.7 billion cubic feet), or more than four years of harvesting at current rates.

Without trying to estimate accurately the timber volumes available by thinning, it nevertheless appears that large amounts of merchantable timber are available which have not been included in the timber supply projections which have touched off the latest predictions of famine. Nor, it should be repeated, can we attach accurate volume figures to any of the other potential sources of supply listed in this chapter but currently excluded from conventional quantifications of the timber supply. In most cases, the basic data for acceptable estimates do not exist. It remains an open question whether these additional volumes would bridge the gap between the long-run sustainable yield and the predicted demand, or even current harvest levels, over the next twenty years. A great deal of research and inventory work is required to come up with the answer. It is clear, however, that proponents of the current timber famine scenario are ignoring some significant factors.

A clue to the motives of the faminists may be found in the current debate over reductions in the commercial forest land base. The Forest Service's long-term timber supply analysis of 1980 incorporated potential reductions in the area of land that would be available for timber production. One of the more curious features of this part of the analysis was the way these projected reductions were presented. It was suggested that during the next twenty years, the province's productive forest land base would shrink by about 25 per cent, mainly to provide land for urban expansion and environmental allowances.[16] There was an immediate and widespread outcry focussed primarily on that 25 per cent. The opposition chorus included industry, unions and Forest Service spokesmen who all united around one point: the industry, and hence the economy, could not afford further withdrawals from the commercial forest land base for environmental, recreational, ecological, agricultural or any other use not immediately related to timber production.

In the first place, the Forest Service produced no supporting evidence to justify these projected reductions. Close to half the hypothetical reductions in the land base are areas that are considered economically inaccessible during the next twenty years. In other words, they are too expensive to log, so have never actually been part of the productive forest land base. They were included in the 1980 timber supply analysis only to be excluded again as part of the 25 per cent reduction. After the year 2000, the bulk of these lands may become economically accessible because of increased timber values or cost-cutting technological advances or both. But until then, these inaccessible areas should be excluded from the Forest Service's projected reductions. In that case, the projected land base shrinkage during the next twenty years would actually amount to slightly less than 15 per cent.

The questionable handling of the reductions issue and the dubious debate over timber supply suggest that the projected timber shortages may have more to do with a struggle for control of land and resources than with any real problem over timber supply. If this is true, the Great Timber Famine might be no more than a propaganda tool employed by the timber processing industry in its continuing battle against other users of British Columbia's forests. A similar note of skepticism can be detected in this comment from an unnamed industry manager quoted in one of the trade newsletters:

> As long as I've been in the business, all I've heard is that we are going to run out of timber. It's just not true. The industry is already harvesting substantially large amounts of second growth and it will continue to be phased in with the mature timber. I can bore you with figures, but in my opinion this timber shortage is being used as it has been since the turn of the century by people wanting to get more. There's no doubt we must manage the resource better and that's the route for increased supply.[17]

There is really very little firm evidence of timber shortage in British Columbia or, for that matter, in Canada. The most interesting possibilities for this country, and this province, are the economic opportunities afforded by the anticipated increases in consumption around the world. It is quite clear where the wood will have to come from if those opportunities are to be realized: it must come from better utilization, increased efficiency and the development of silvicultural skills.

The other possibility is that the projected, or the hoped-for, increases in wood consumption will not occur. Foresters and industry associates have often been criticized for a blind faith that the future will merely repeat the past. These people assume that a constantly expanding world population will demand an ever-increasing amount of forest products. Any departure from this tendency is considered abnormal and unlikely to last. However, the North American pattern of residential housing may be undergoing a permanent change. It may be that single family residences will continue to decline against apartment, condominium and townhouse development. If so, the impact on wood consumption will be profound; apartment buildings use a lot less wood than detached houses. As another example, the widespread use of electronic information and communications systems could, as many predict, lead to decreased consumption of newsprint.

Although the industry is psychologically and structurally incapable of considering the possibility of a static, or even declining, timber market, that possibility is real and must be taken into account when considering timber supply policy. To do so is not easy for an industry that has become conditioned to thinking of timber as a scarce commodity. A timber surplus, like a timber famine, conjures up images of unemployed loggers, idle processing mills and a depressed economy. The main difference between surplus and famine would be the reaction of the industry. When faced with the prospect of declining consumption, most conventional forest managers would cease to concern themselves with improving utilization standards or developing their silvicultural capabilities. However, that would be a totally inappropriate response and a grave error in judgement.

No one knows what the demand for forest products will be one hundred, fifty or even twenty years hence. For this reason, it is absurd to base current decisions — supply commitments, forest land allocations or silvicultural expenditures, for instance — on any particular assumption of future timber demand. This is the basic fallacy underlying the scare tactics used by proponents of the timber famine. It is quite possible that their view of the future is wrong. If so, they have seriously undermined some of the broader reasons for using our timber supplies wisely, for enhancing the growth of the forests and for conserving the forest land base.

There are good reasons for managing the forests that go beyond the needs of the forest industry. It would be easy enough a century from now to clear land of trees if the wood is in great demand or the land needed for other purposes. But if we do not now plant and tend the land, that choice will not exist. Further, forests provide benefits other than timber. They are important for watershed protection, fish and wildlife habitat, oxygen source, air pollution control and simply as a soothing balm to the harassed soul. For these ancillary reasons alone, it makes sense to cherish and tend our forests. An abundant timber supply, should it be needed, might be viewed as an additional benefit rather than as a matter of utmost necessity.

The real danger of the alarmist vision is that it warps judgements and distorts priorities. Predictions of a timber famine create a climate of crisis and encourage desperate reactions. To a certain extent, predicting timber shortages is little more than an attempt to intimidate people into committing a larger proportion of the forest resources to the exclusive use of the timber industry and larger amounts of money in frantic and ill-considered silvicultural programs when cheaper and more effective alternatives may exist.

To have adequate timber reserves in British Columbia a century from now, whether or not they are needed by the forest industry at that time, would benefit everyone in the province. But to spend money which is sorely needed elsewhere in order to prevent a fictitious timber famine would be folly. Furthermore, it would be a mistake to neglect the nontimber values of the forests and to devote all our silvicultural efforts to the future production of commercial timber. There are other priorities with a legitimate claim on silvicultural expenditures. Forests can enhance fish, wildlife and water resources, as well as supply timber. Unless we develop silvicultural policies which address all these needs, we will never resolve the continuing conflicts over appropriate uses of our forest resource.

SEVEN

Do We Have a Plan?

ONE OF THE BASIC articles of faith in resource management is a profound belief in the value of planning. This is particularly true when the resources are publicly owned. A corollary of this belief is that resource-use conflicts are a result of poor or inadequate planning. The assumption is that planning leads to a sensible allocation of resources and the avoidance of conflict. Good planning is seen essentially as a technical problem: if trained personnel pool their objective, scientific knowledge, they will, as a matter of course, make the right decision. What is missing in this creed is the recognition that in the resource field, most "objective, scientific knowledge" rests upon a series of assumptions that may not be valid. The best planning will not correct faulty assumptions. For decades, as an example, forest planning has been derived from the assumption of a growing demand and rising prices for forest products. Because this growth has occurred in the past, it is assumed that it will continue in the future.

To a large extent, the resolution of resource-use conflicts has been seen as the reconciliation of contradictory objectives held by resource users or agencies. The main emphasis in British Columbia in recent years has been to devise means whereby the perceived conflicts between, say, the timber industries and the Forest Service on the one hand, and the Fisheries Service, the Fish and Wildlife Branch, the commercial fishing industry and recreationists on the other, be resolved by mutually agreeable plans concerning the use of specific areas and their resources. Thus, the public agencies, the corporate bodies and, more recently, the voluntary associations of vested interest groups all have developed a planning function. Now a small army of resource planners expends a great deal of time, effort and money in an attempt to come up with integrated resource management plans acceptable to all. The fact that resource-use conflicts do not seem to be declining is at least one indication that all this time, effort and money is not being very well spent.

A likely conclusion is that the real conflict over resource use does not occur between the various government agencies, corporate resource users or voluntary associations. For the most part, these various bodies are staffed and represented by people who have all received the same type of technical training, who are all paid to participate in the planning process and who all reside and work in urban areas, well away from the forests. Most resource conflicts appear to arise between these people or the agencies for which they work on the one side, and individual citizens or businesses who are excluded from the planning process on the other. Looked at from this perspective, the major resource controversies in British Columbia are really power struggles between urban bureaucrats and rural residents whose lives and livelihoods are being directly affected by the integrated planning establishment.

As an example, a rather minor dispute arose between MacMillan Bloedel's Estevan division and a number of citizens from the small west coast Vancouver Island community of Kyuquot over the planned logging of part of nearby Tashish Inlet. The dispute soon developed into years of integrated resource planning. Dozens of meetings were held involving scores of bureaucrats from industry and government, salaried experts from environmental organizations and a token representation from the local population. Funds were provided from the public treasury for research projects, reports were prepared and presented, and hardline positions were taken and abandoned. The purpose was to produce a plan for the edification of the Environment and Land Use Committee which, meeting in a committee room of the Parliament Buildings in Victoria, far from the Tashish, would make the final decisions regarding the inlet's resources. The Kyuquot population observed from the sidelines, alternately bemused and exasperated.

This conflict between urban bureaucrats and rural citizens is not a new feature of B. C. politics; it has been a fundamental issue since this part of the world was a colony. During the early decades of the last century, when the Hudson's Bay Company administered what is now British Columbia, a bitter dispute developed between the two chief officers of the company. John McLoughlin, the chief factor, pursued a policy of encouraging settlement and developing an established population throughout the territory. On the other hand, Governor George Simpson looked upon the country as a storehouse of resources which could be most efficiently extracted by the use of trading posts and ships, with all settlement discouraged. Neither view prevailed but both survived, creating one of the essential tensions of B. C. politics. The province was settled, but ownership and control of almost all the land and resources was retained by a central authority — the provincial government. Consequently, there has always been a tendency for resource decision-making to occur in the urban centres of Victoria and Vancouver. In recent times, as University of British Columbia professor Alan Chambers has pointed out, the North American trend towards urbanization has further aggravated the situation.

> The metropolitan appetite for energy and materials is enormous and growing at a rate larger than the rate of population growth in these centres. The urban based organizations required to feed this gargantuan appetite are necessarily insensitive, or at least unresponsive to symptoms of hinterland malaise, be it social, economic or ecological.
>
> Secondly, control of resources and markets is rapidly flowing from the hands of hinterland businessmen and into the hands of urban bureaucracies, both public and private. Control of agricultural soils and marketing quotas are being sequestered by agribusiness. Forest harvesting rights are concentrated and held by fewer and fewer forestry giants. Even ocean fisheries have now become a private property, resources controlled by fewer and fewer licence holders and their bureaucratic, government counterparts. The result is a population of alienated, disenfranchised and bitter hinterland people.[1]

One of the major causes of resource-use or environmental conflict is the organizational structure encompassing both public and private sectors. The most common structural pattern in

North America is for private institutions — from individual proprietorships to multinational corporations — to utilize a single resource, and for the government agencies to be responsible for a single resource value. Thus, when a corporation such as MacMillan Bloedel obtains a quarter-million-hectare Tree Farm Licence, the terms of the licence restrict the company to growing and harvesting timber. The company is not allowed to utilize any of the other resources found within the confines of the licence area — fish, minerals, wildlife, water power and so on.

Similarly, public agencies controlling the resources are equally narrowly focussed. To continue the above example, the agency responsible for the administration of MB's Tree Farm Licence, the Forest Service, has no jurisdiction over any of the resources found on the land other than forest cover and range land. A host of other public agencies become involved in the same piece of land with powers and authority not always proportional to the resources found there. The federal Fisheries Service has jurisdiction over the anadromous fish, primarily salmon; the Fish and Wildlife Branch over the remaining fish and the wildlife; the Mines Department over the minerals; the Highways Department over the public roads running through the area — and so it goes.

The relationship between the government agencies and the private sector is one of mistrust. Yet the private sector, which includes landowners as well as resource licencees such as Tree Farm Licence operators — essentially anyone commercially exploiting the woods who is not on the public payroll — must necessarily find a way to co-operate with the public agencies. Mistrust is thus tempered by practical considerations, yet it remains paramount. This sort of relationship can create situations which are ecologically inefficient as well as economically unsound.

For example, a MacMillan Bloedel Tree Farm Licence on Vancouver Island includes the land of the Eve River drainage basin. The river has been a highly productive salmon spawning area, with annual returns to the river of up to 200,000 pink salmon. The returns are subject to some variation owing to the nature of the river. The Eve River runs through a steep, mountainous area of north Vancouver Island with almost 250 cm

(100 inches) of rainfall a year. Occasionally there are storms, during which the river level rises dramatically. Large trees are swept into the river with their enormous root systems intact, and they drag along the river bottom until they are hung up on a gravel bar or swept out into Johnson Strait. There are a number of huge log jams in the river, but virtually none of the logs show a saw mark. They are not in the river as the result of a logging operation; they are part of the river's ecology. During a major storm, these log jams are swept downstream, dramatically altering the course of the river, particularly in its lower reaches. When this happens, a significant part of the salmon hatch which has been deposited in the gravel is destroyed. Two years later, the returns might be less than one-tenth of the peak — a mere ten thousand to twenty thousand salmon, as in 1982.

In the late 1970s the Eve River division of MacMillan Bloedel proposed to remove all logs from the river. The motive behind this proposal was not entirely one of profit. Many of the 150 MacMillan Bloedel employees who work in the valley feel highly protective of its resources; they can become quite indignant when they see commercial fishermen and so-called sports fishermen violating not only the fishing regulations but simple ecological common sense. A lot of people who work in the valley also use the area for their recreation, and at least a few of them understand the ecology of the river more intimately than the majority of experts employed by the Fisheries Service and the Fish and Wildlife Branch.

In addition, the Eve River division possesses several million dollars' worth of the most sophisticated logging equipment in the world, including machinery that is capable of lifting fallen trees out of the river, roots and all. The operators of these machines are highly skilled. The obvious course of action, as seen by the MB divisional staff and supported by the resident Fisheries officer, would be to carefully remove the trees from the river to lessen further damage to spawning grounds, and ship the trees to MB mills to pay for the costs of the operation.

Given the nature of resource administration in British Columbia, it is not surprising that the proposal got nowhere. One reason is that there are no legislative or regulatory provisions whereby MacMillan Bloedel or any other private entity could remove those logs, either for profit or out of goodness of heart. The entire administrative apparatus of the resource agencies concerned with fish is directed towards protecting fish and fish habitat from a wide variety of resource users. There are no tenure provisions concerning the managment of fish resources on the Eve or any other B. C. river. In the case of the Eve River, fish management is almost nonexistent — merely a set of protective regulations. As the administrative apparatus currently works, the only entity in a legal position to manage the resource — the federal Fisheries Service — has neither the funds nor the technical capability to undertake the work. Essentially, the fisheries agencies, particularly at the federal level, are police forces: they enforce fisheries laws. Because what happens in the Eve River is essentially a natural phenomenon and has not been caused by an individual or a corporate body, there is nothing for the fisheries agencies to do — there is no one to arrest or force into repairing the damage to the salmon resource. They have no way to approve the MacMillan Bloedel proposal; they can only prosecute the company should it proceed with its attempt to protect the fish.

In their dealings with each other as opposed to the private sector, the various public agencies are usually antagonistic. As Professor Chambers points out,

> At best it is covert rivalry. Individual agencies compete for individual parcels of land from which one resource is to be extracted. . . . The behaviour of government agencies towards the territory under their jurisdiction parallels that [behaviour] sometimes found in the private sector, and resembles that of seagulls defending their breeding territories.[2]

There have been many attempts within the public sector to deal with interagency conflict and confusion. At times, multi-agency agencies have been created, such as departments of the environment charged with the administration of a number of individual resource agencies. Other bodies such as the Environment and Land Use Committee, its secretariat, a variety of task forces and regional resource management committees have been established from time to time. None of them are particularly useful because the administrative structure of an area is derived not from the ecology of the area but from needs perceived in the centres of administrative power — essentially, a few urban areas.

Some of the most important public agencies involved in resource management never appear at resource planning meetings at all. These are the tax or revenue agencies, whose function is to raise money for government. These government charges come in the guise of stumpage on timber harvested, land taxes or payroll deductions on wages earned, and they all have an enormous effect on the physical environment of a resource-rich province or state. The land tax system which assesses the value of privately owned forest land in British Columbia on the basis of the value of its mature timber encourages some of the worst silvicultural practices in the world. Until recently, logging practices extremely destructive to nontimber resources were encouraged by the Forest Service as part of a policy aimed at maximizing revenues from the sale of timber. For instance, appraised stumpage has normally been calculated and logging methods prescribed in order to maximize stumpage rather than protect the environment.

Over the past three to four decades, more and more of the public revenues raised in the hinterlands are being spent in the cities. The fact that millions of hectares of productive forest land in British Columbia have not been satisfactorily restocked with trees is a function of provincial taxation and spending priorities. This backlog of unproductive public forest land is not, as is widely assumed, the result of corporate mismanagement. The forest companies do not directly provide the funds for reforestation; the government as owner of the land does so, from revenues received from the companies. Political parties of all stripes gain and retain power by extracting money from the resource-bearing lands of the hinterlands and in providing services to the areas where the majority of voters now live — the cities.

Ironically, the most visible resource-use conflicts over the past decade or so have involved clashes between the urban-based public and private resource institutions on the one side, and the urban-based environmental organizations such as the Sierra Club, Greenpeace and the B. C. Wildlife Federation on the other. "The 'ecofreak'," Chambers has observed,

> is essentially an urban phenomenon; the result of an incredible naive view of the natural world, heightened sensitivity to social and ecological malaise and mistrust of the institutions which appear to generate the disease. While many such individuals fill the ranks of the environmental protest movements, others migrate to the countryside as urban refugees to find that Mother Nature is not quite so kind and loving as Walt Disney told them she was. Together these people have conditioned the political environment of elected decision-makers to a very significant degree.[3]

Until perhaps fifteen years ago, resource managers accepted the notion that multiple use would resolve resource conflicts; with a little give and take and a lot of "scientific" planning and management, everyone could get what they wanted in the way of natural resources. This was an attractive concept which was bolstered by a large body of literature and a great deal of enthusiasm for the prospect of the multiple-use forest. The typical image envisioned a forested mountain valley with a hydroelectric dam near the top end providing an abundant supply of energy and feeding a steady flow of sparkling water into the river below. In addition to being well-stocked with trout, the river would provide a contented population with adequate supplies of pure, clear water for domestic and irrigation purposes. The fertile valley bottom would be devoted to agriculture, while the lower slopes of the towering mountains would support magnificent stands of timber from which an annual harvest could be taken perpetually without unduly disturbing the large populations of resident wildlife, the slow and steady trickle of groundwater or the aesthetic sensibilities of the people living below. The steep upper slopes and the alpine meadows would provide a home for the grizzly bear and the bald eagle and recreation for occasional hikers from the valley below. A healthy, tanned, vigorous people would be secure in the wealth of their resources and the benevolence of the land they inhabited.

However, things did not work out that way. The multiple-use forest was a dream founded upon false expectations. It was not compatible with a society and an age that believed in infinite progress based upon constant industrial development and perpetual economic expansion. The history of resource management in British Columbia reveals that multiple-use and scientific planning have never had as much influence on decisions about resource use as economic, political and bureaucratic considerations.

For the first half of this century, there were few restrictions on logging practices in British Columbia. Existing controls and planning policies were aimed mainly at avoiding high concentrations of inflammable logging slash and providing for higher levels of natural regeneration. But little thought was given to the impact that a particular logging operation might have on other forest resources, nor were allowances made for the interests of other resource users. Similarly, hydroelectric dams were built and their reservoirs filled with scant consideration for the timber being flooded, the fish and wildlife habitat eliminated or the farmland inundated. Whenever they were forced out of one area, the various vested interest groups looked elsewhere for the particular resource they wanted.

Until the 1960s, resource planning was practically nonexistent. In theory, the forest management units established during the previous decade — Public Sustained Yield Units and Tree Farm Licences — required a sustained yield plan. But the plan emphasized timber production; other forest resources were given short shrift. And in any event, the Social Credit government of that era saw unhindered industrial development as the primary consideration. Companies holding Tree Farm Licences were expected to do their own planning with the approval of the Forest Service, which was also expected to manage the Public Sustained Yield Units. Since the main interest of the Tree Farm Licence operators was to harvest timber and the main concern of the government of the day was to fatten the provincial treasury, the only planning undertaken involved the rate and pattern of logging.

During the late 1950s and early 1960s, a number of factors combined to create the beginnings of widespread conflict over the use of forest resources. Technological advances in the design of logging equipment made large-scale clearcutting the most practical and profitable method of logging. The existence of large, long-term forms of tenure, particularly Tree Farm Licences, made the financing of this expensive equipment feasible. Artificial reforestation — tree planting — became a widespread practice with the establishment of nurseries, thereby eliminating the necessity of restricting clearcutting to small blocks of land in order to assist in natural reseeding. And as a final incentive, the world timber market was steadily growing. The annual harvest was constantly expanding and the increasingly favoured logging method was "progressive clearcutting" — starting at one end of a valley and working to the other, cutting everything in sight.

The first serious conflicts to arise out of this situation involved the salmon spawning streams in the areas being logged. A major area of conflict was that salmon, by law, came under the jurisdiction of the federal government, while forestry is a provincial concern; thus, the obvious physical resource conflict was further complicated by a bureaucratic and political one. Resolving the logs-versus-fish question was not, therefore, simply a matter of common sense. It became enmeshed in the posturing of politicians, the machinations of various public bureaucracies and the perpetual propaganda campaign that lies at the heart of federal-provincial relations in this country.

An additional complication arose because salmon are a federal responsibility, while all other species of fish, as well as all the wildlife in the province, are under the jurisdiction of the provincial Fish and Wildlife Branch. During this period of emerging conflict, there was little interest from any quarter in British Columbia in enhancing the influence of this branch of the provincial government, or of any other agency of the government that would conflict with the forest industry. So while the Fish and Wildlife Branch had the legal authority to moderate some of the excesses of the forest industry, it lacked the administrative capacity to act effectively or even sensibly. As a consequence, in the dawning of opposition to indiscriminate logging, the issue of salmon protection took centre stage.

During this era, a widespread popular conception developed which assumed that fish and logging are incompatible. As timber harvesting expanded, so did the market for fish and the technical ability to catch them. Consequently, concern increased over the depletion of the coastal salmon populations. Yet there are many reasons for the decline in salmon stocks.

While it is true that many salmon spawning streams have been damaged or destroyed by logging, it is also true that the salmon runs in many streams have been wiped out in an evening by a single set of a seine boat. This kind of fishing can completely clean out a bay full of salmon that are waiting for high water to run up a creek to spawn. Loggers have no monopoly on greed.

Nevertheless, the Fisheries Service blamed the forest industry for the salmon decline. These bureaucrats liked to present themselves as the virtuous protectors of the beleaguered salmon while conveniently ignoring their inability to restrict the excesses of rapacious fishermen, not to mention their own policy blunders. The idea became widely accepted that logging was an unqualified disaster for fish and, by extension, for all other wildlife.

In 1956, in an attempt to alleviate this timber-fish conflict, the Forest Service devised a referral system. Applications from forest companies for cutting permits near salmon streams were forwarded to the Fisheries Service, which then offered advice which the Forest Service could incorporate as a restriction on the logging operation. In 1970 much the same procedure was extended to the B. C. Fish and Wildlife Branch in an attempt to protect fish and wildlife species under provincial jurisdiction.

The referral system is a good idea, but it does not work. With perhaps two thousand applications for cutting permits in British Columbia every year, it has been simply impossible for either the Fisheries Service or the Fish and Wildlife Branch to process them with appropriate care. A typical logging application might go through a process similar to this: a logging company submits its application for a cutting permit to the Forest Service; the application passes through various levels of that bureaucracy and at some point is sent off to one or more other government departments at both the federal and provincial levels; these departments refer it back to their regional and field offices where files and maps (quite likely out of date) are checked; complicated arrangements may then be made to visit the site, and eventually a recommendation is formulated; it is sent back up the chain of command — during which the suggested course of action will probably be altered — and eventually is passed back to the Forest Service; in their own time, the appropriate forms find their way into the hands of the Forest Service officer responsible for the final disposition of the application, who may or may not include the recommendations of the other departments or branches. During this process, which lasts a year or two, many of the civil servants will have quit, been fired, promoted, or transferred to another part of the province. It is virtually unheard of for officials of the various government agencies with final authority on the matter to visit the proposed logging site with a representative of the logging company and decide, then and there, how the timber should be harvested in order to protect or even enhance the nontimber resources of that particular section of forest. The system has been, and remains, a bureaucratic nightmare which satisfied few of the participants that forest values of any kind have been protected. Rather than reducing the fish-timber conflict, the referral process has exacerbated it, further isolating the respective interest groups into hostile camps.

Under pressure from an aroused public and their political representatives, the Forest Service in 1972 introduced another complication — a series of logging guidelines which were to apply on all coastal logging operations. These were general rules of thumb aimed at protecting nontimber forest resources. Specifically, they determined the maximum size of individual cutting areas, or "cut-blocks," the width of strips to be left along streams, the construction of forest roads and similar blanket measures.

The guidelines sprang from political considerations rather than ecological reality. In many instances, their application probably did more harm than good. For instance, when a 9 m (30 foot) strip of mature timber was left along each side of a creek running through the middle of an 81 ha (200 acre) clearcut — with the intention of protecting the stream — the most likely result was that the first major storm would blow down the remaining exposed trees. Most of them would end up in the creek, possibly doing more damage to the water resource than if the entire area had been clearcut. In addition, the timber company would have "lost" the value of the trees left behind while enduring the higher harvesting costs involved in adhering to the guidelines. But the guidelines gave the public the impression that something was being done to protect nontimber forest values. Again, the guideline approach excluded the option of intelligent, practical on-site decision-making. In this case of the hypothetical creek running through the clear-cut, the process would exclude the option of the responsible fisheries biologist, the Forest Service officer and the local logging manager getting together to decide which trees to cut and which to leave, where to build the roads and how to reforest the area. Instead, they were bound by the blanket restrictions and directives of the guidelines, which were not a creation of the resource managers but something which had been imposed upon them by the public and the politicians.

As the guidelines were coming into effect, resource managers were developing their own response to the growing resource-use conflict. In 1973 the Forest Service introduced what was called the Resource Folio Planning System. This system has an underlying assumption: if, in a given area — usually a watershed — all data relevant to all the resources were brought together, a resource plan could be drawn up which would satisfy all users or interest groups. Logging could be conducted in such a way as to protect, or even enhance, the fish and wildlife populations and water and recreation resources.

Physically, the folio system consists of a series of maps printed on transparent plastic sheets, each map containing all the available data for a particular resource — forest cover, soils, fish, wildlife, recreation potential, agricultural capabilities, roads and so on. These maps are laid one on top of the other to indicate at a glance areas of potential resource use, co-ordination or conflict. From the folio the Forest Service, in co-operation with the timber companies, can draw up a five-year operation harvesting plan to harmonize with the objectives of other resource agencies.

Again, the folio system is a nice idea that does not work. Part of the system's failure is found in one of the central assumptions upon which it is based — that adequate centralized planning can satisfy all interests. The map overlays tend to highlight areas of argument rather than ensure harmony. For example, the fisheries people often do not limit their sensitive areas to the streams in which the fish live, but expand them to include large portions of watersheds where most of the timber is to be found. At best the folio system indicates where choices have to be made; it does not provide an acceptable means for making the choices.

A further problem: for the system to work properly, the resource maps would have to contain all data for the relevant resources. Fish and wildlife species and populations have to be known, as do the use they make of different parts of the planning area. The forest cover has to be known in detail, as well as soil types and geological formations. Many of these factors are in a state of constant change: deer move from one area to another for reasons unknown to wildlife biologists; creeks and rivers change course; fish populations can be drastically altered by factors occurring outside the management area. To gather and keep the essential data up to date would require an army of highly trained specialists, and British Columbia is a very large province. The folio system was the beginning of integrated resource planning in the province, the first serious attempt by the public resource bureaucracies to co-ordinate their activities. The process is dominated by the Forest Service, which initiated it, co-ordinates it and is ultimately responsible for final decisions.

At about the same time as the folio system was being implemented, attempts were being made to organize resource planning into more formal structures. In 1971 the Environment and Land Use Committee (ELUC) was established. Composed of certain members of the provincial cabinet, this committee became the ultimate political decision-making body on resource matters short of the legislature itself. This was a significant departure from the procedure that had prevailed for decades, whereby the province's major forest resource policies were established only by the minister of forests and the premier.

In 1972, with the NDP in office in Victoria, Regional Resource Management Committees were set up in some parts of the province. These comprised representatives of various resource management agencies who met on a regular basis to co-ordinate planning for timber and other resource development. When ELUC acquired a secretariat in 1973, the plan was to appoint regional resource managers as regional representatives of the secretariat. Thus, the structure taking shape in the early 1970s was that of a central decision-making body

(ELUC) with its own bureaucracy (the secretariat) which dominated the regional planning bodies (the Resource Management Committees).

Since the change of government in 1975 and the promulgation of the new Ministry of Forests Act in 1978, a somewhat different approach has evolved in British Columbia for dealing with resource-use conflicts. Section 5(c) of the Ministry of Forests Act instructs the Forest Service to

> plan the use of the forest and range resources of the Crown, so that the production of timber and forage, the harvesting of timber, the grazing of livestock and the realization of fisheries, wildlife, water, outdoor recreation and other natural resource values are co-ordinated and integrated, in consultation and co-operation with other ministries and agencies of the Crown and with the private sector.

When this is translated into government policy, the basis of current forest resource planning procedures being used in British Columbia becomes clear. The policy was laid down at a resource management conference in 1978 by Premier Bill Bennett and Deputy Minister of Forests Mike Apsey, commonly acknowledged to be the major resource decision-maker in the Socred government. The catch phrase used to describe the B. C. approach is "Integrated Management of Resources" — IMR. At the 1978 conference, as on many occasions since, Apsey spelled out government policy:

> The Forest Service must manage forest and range resources, but it must reconcile its production goals with the goals of other natural resource sectors. Success at this will depend on how well other resource agencies can adapt to the IMR principles contained in the Ministry of Forests Act. Although IMR is stressed, the Forest Service is not given responsibility for anything other than timber, forage and forest recreation. IMR is a requirement rather than a mandate.[4]

The B. C. Forest Service was also given a planning function in the new act. Every ten years after 1979, the Forest Service must provide an analysis of the province's forest and range resources. This analysis must include a description of the forest inventory and a listing of logged lands which have not been restocked with trees or which are producing timber at a rate lower than their potential. It must also describe the programs being undertaken by the ministry regarding forest management, protection, conservation, inventory and research, and as well it must provide a forecast of supply and demand for timber and forest products. The legislation also requires the Forest Service to provide, every five years, a resource program containing a series of alternative management programs for restocking forest land, increasing the productivity of the land and otherwise improving the resource. Also required are estimates of the economic and social benefits and costs of each alternative. Finally, the Forest Service is to recommend which program is to be implemented during the following five years. Both the ten-year analysis and the five-year program are submitted to the cabinet, which in turn must present them to the provincial legislature. In effect, then, the final decision on resource planning lies in the hands of the cabinet. In practical terms, the cabinet's decisions are made by ELUC. In contrast, on National Forest lands in the United States, much of this responsibility is vested in the hands of the Forest Service. These changes in British Columbia's bureaucratic structure culminated in the abolition of ELUC's secretariat in 1981. The action was a bureaucratic convenience and was consistent with the shape of the 1978 Ministry of Forests Act, with its reassignment of responsibility for data gathering and decision making.

Public participation in the planning process is not even mentioned in the B. C. legislation. In the Ministry of Forests Act, the primary responsibility for resource planning is in the hands of the various government agencies; "the private sector" is almost an afterthought. Apsey later defined "the private sector" to include the public, a semantic convolution that is significant because it lumps together everyone not part of a government resource bureaucracy — forest industry corporations, environmental groups, fishermen, recreationists and ordinary, unaffiliated citizens. Nevertheless, since the Ministry of Forests Act was passed, the Forest Service has gone through a radical transformation of its relationship with other resource users and the public. This is partly owing to the redefinition of the agency's function and concern. But much of the change is also a result of the government's instructions to provide the public with information. In the past, it was difficult to get information on Tree Farm Licences, timber allocations or anything else from most offices of the Forest Service. The unstated policy seemed to be that the business conducted by the Forest Service was a secret, particularly from the public, which was regarded as the enemy. Now the policy is for employees to provide the public with answers so long as the questions are within the employee's area of competence.

The recent changes in resource administration, legislation and revised administrative procedures all indicate that the concept of multiple use is being abandoned in British Columbia. It was once widely held that with the proper application of technical skills and knowledge, a wide variety of uses could be accommodated on a single tract of land. This view no longer has much currency. It has been replaced with the belief that in most areas, irreconcilable conflicts between resource users are apt to arise and that choices will have to be made. An attempt is being made to shift the responsibility for resolving such conflicts from the technical-bureaucratic sphere to the political. As Mike Apsey has explained,

> It is important for elected officials to recognize that resource allocation cannot be passed off as a technical problem that will take care of itself. I would go so far as saying that resource allocation may soon become the most important political issue facing any politician in British Columbia.[5]

In this instance, Mr. Apsey was speaking from hindsight. For a number of years, there had been a particular and highly visible conflict over allocating the resources of the Tsitika River. This issue had attracted a host of corporate and government bureaucrats, consultants, scientists and politicians, all concerned about which interest groups would get what out of the Tsitika River watershed. The river drains a 39 490 ha, 42 km (97,576 acre, 26 mile) long valley on northeastern Vancouver Island, carrying more than 250 cm (100 inches) of rain a year into the sea at Robson Bight. The productive forest lands in the valley, according to the principles of sustained yield forestry, were capable of maintaining a harvest of 82,000 cunits of timber a year, or 232 000 m³ (8.2 million cubic feet). After a complex series of calculations, this translates into 1274 jobs. The river, one of the most diverse in fish species on Vancouver Island, contains all the species of salmon as well as steelhead, cutthroat, Dolly Varden and rainbow trout. Between 2500 and 3000 deer live in the valley. The valley has no resident human population.

Until the early 1970s, the Tsitika valley was considered to be primarily a timber-producing area, though provisions had been included in the Tree Farm Licence contracts, held by three separate forest companies, to withdraw cutting rights in favour of other resource allocations, primarily recreation. An informal coalition of recreational interests such as federal and provincial government agencies, conservation groups, sport hunters and fishermen and commercial fishermen, began a campaign to have the Tsitika valley and a surrounding area reallocated as a park, a wilderness area, an ecological reserve — almost anything except its designated use as commercial forest land. Pressure was applied at the political level and in 1973 a moratorium was placed on any development. Public meetings were convened, technical studies undertaken, committees struck and, eventually, ELUC made the political decision to designate part of the area as parkland and the Tsitika watershed as timberland. The Tsitika would be developed according to an integrated resource management program to be devised by the Tsitika Planning Committee. However, during its deliberations, this body worked itself into a deadlock between the forestry-oriented groups and the recreationists. Specifically, the Forest Service refused to go along with the Fish and Wildlife Branch's demands regarding the preservation of mature timber stands deemed essential to maintain the existing deer population. The matter was referred to ELUC, which in turn passed it along to a committee consisting of the ministers of forests and recreation, Tom Waterland and Sam Bawlf. The two ministers supported the Forest Service decision. The uproar which followed ended the cabinet career of Mr. Bawlf and, it was widely believed, his future as a member of the provincial legislature.

In the end, the Tsitika Planning Committee sided with Fish and Wildlife; it recommended a plan to remove 1750 ha (4324 acres) of productive forest land from the Tsitika's allowable annual cut calculations for a period of 150 years. The annual cut was reduced by 3729 cunits which, the committee stated, meant forgoing forty-two direct, indirect and induced jobs each year.

The allocation was a victory for the sport hunting arm of the recreation industry. Although it was possible to estimate the negative economic consequence of reductions in timber allocations, the planning committee admitted that it was more difficult to assign an offsetting positive value to a resource such as deer; it only stated: "This resource will have a significant financial value in terms of expenditures associated with hunting."[6] Industry foresters had no difficulty in calculating one measure of the annual deer harvest being protected in the valley. They merely multiplied the number of lost jobs by the average industrial wage and benefit cost; this figure was divided by the sustainable annual deer harvest, and again by the average weight of deer bagged in the valley. This calculation determined that deer in the Tsitika watershed would be worth $54.00 per kg ($24.50 per lb.) on the hoof.[7]

The Tsitika incident was an early indication of one of the key features of the integrated resource management concept: essentially, it centralizes power over resource allocations. The pattern that institutions have evolved over the last decade to resolve resource-use conflicts in British Columbia is quite clear. In areas of real or potential conflict, a structure is established by the Environment and Land Use Committee to organize or co-ordinate all the public and private interest groups that are, or might be, concerned with the issues involved. These structures, known variously as "study groups," "planning committees," "task forces" and so on, are not permanent bodies. The decision to abolish the ELUC secretariat was in large part a political decision to eliminate a potentially powerful permanent technical-bureaucratic institution, located uncomfortably close to the centres of power in the province. The alternative temporary bodies established by ELUC from time to time are normally instructed to recommend a course of action for allocating the resources of a specific area. The reports from these groups are only recommendations, not decisions. ELUC makes the final decisions: it accepts, rejects or modifies the recommendations or, as in the Tsitika case, resolves deadlocks between the participants. The techniques of integrated resource management are, as presently constituted, powerful instruments at the disposal of the government for the determination of social and economic policies throughout the province.

There is a substantial body of opposition to this shift in the centres of power within the resource establishment. Professional resource technicians, particularly those involved in the utilization of publicly owned resources, have traditionally had a built-in opposition to any land-use decisions that flout conventional professional dogma. Professionals generally consider politics to be an unworthy occupation, but this opinion, justified or not, fails to grapple with the real difficulty in British Columbia's resource politics. The political process is the only mechanism we have whereby all citizens can establish the relevant legal agreements. What many resource scientists and technicians find hard to accept is that in politics, feelings and emotions play just as legitimate a role as the hard, technical data of objective reality.

The major problem is not that certain kinds of resource decisions have been taken from the hands of the "experts" and are being made by the political establishment, but that these decisions are being made at provincial and federal levels of the political apparatus which are far removed from the geographical locations being affected. The danger is not only that the handful of decision-makers who sit on ELUC have the authority to make foolish decisions concerning areas of the province with which they are only vaguely familiar. It is that the political arena in which this process is conducted is the Victoria-Vancouver urban axis. The process tends to be dominated by the citizens who live in these centres or gather there to take a more active part in the process. As Peter Pearse wrote in the preface to his Royal Commission report on forest resources,

> It is probably safe to say that only a small fraction of the province's population has ever set foot in the northern half of British Columbia — that vast territory north of Prince George larger than the states of Washington and Oregon combined — or have more than a vague impression of what it contains. The same is true of the huge region west of the central Interior. This gives

> rise to difficulties in public policy formation, because natural resource policies, particularly, must be sensitive to the full range of conditions they govern.[8]

Whether by bureaucrats, corporate managers, politicians or environmental activists, centralized decision-making in determining natural resource policies is bound at times to be ecologically inefficient. In the long or the short run, it can destroy the ecological systems to which it is applied, as well as the local economies, the social structures and the local political institutions which it dominates.

For a very long time it has been obvious that there are many structural weaknesses in the mechanisms of resource planning. The concept and the practices of integrated resource management which have been introduced to solve some of those problems are in limited ways successful — the managers of different resources at least confer with each other. But the gains made in this area over the past decade or more may be more than offset to the extent by which integrated resource management practices and procedures can be and are being used by the centres of corporate, bureaucratic and political power to make relatively detailed resource-use decisions which affect the lives of people in the most remote areas of their jurisdiction.

EIGHT

Can Silviculture Solve our Problems?

HISTORY PROVIDES some spectacular examples of intensive forest management. It is said that some two to three thousand years ago, the Greeks planted trees that were not expected to reach maturity for at least half a millennium. Such a sense of time and future is difficult to understand today. It is not likely that the ancient Greeks undertook these plantings lightly. Then, as today, tree planting was hard, expensive work when done on a major scale. They must have had sound cultural and economic reasons for planting those trees and for choosing the particular species that they did.

Four and five centuries ago, British foresters developed highly sophisticated silvicultural techniques for the production of ship-building timbers. They would plant oaks with a planned rotation of 150 to 200 years. Around the oaks would be planted protective, light-shielding beech trees, which would be felled at certain times in order that the oaks would grow with a certain desired curve or sweep in their trunks, making them suitable for use as keels. As well, large rocks would be buried in the ground beneath the oak seedlings to shape their roots for the production of ship knees.

Almost two centuries ago, Danish foresters had developed techniques of thinning immature forest stands. They also used remarkably sophisticated cost-benefit formulae for calculating the economic factors involved in such operations.[1] Essentially the same financial calculations are used today in the rare cases where foresters are required to demonstrate that the silvicultural treatments they propose to implement are economically sound.

The Chinese have several thousand years of silviculture behind them. In recent decades, they have been engaged in a series of five-hundred-year projects to surround and contain their northern deserts with trees in order to raise the subterranean water table, thereby making some form of agriculture possible.[2]

All these projects have been carried out for purposes which dictated, according to the prevailing knowledge of the time, the species and strains to be planted and the techniques to be used in caring for them. This is no less true of forest management in the Pacific Northwest. Those who today advocate massive expenditures of public money on intensive forest management hope, first and foremost, to provide enough timber to sustain, and perhaps even expand, the existing forest industry. It was to this end that in 1980 the B. C. government considered spending $1.4 billion over a five-year period. While there are other, incidental benefits anticipated from such a massive injection of cash into the forests — the enhancement of water resources, the improvement of fish and wildlife habitat and improved recreational facilities, for instance — the basic justification for this scale of spending is to increase the future volume of timber beyond that which could be expected if forestry operations were limited to harvesting — cutting and getting out.

No one really knows whether this amount, or indeed any amount, of money will actually produce the desired increase in timber supply. The silvicultural techniques which are currently in vogue and those which are likely to be in vogue in the future are relatively untried in areas like the Pacific Northwest's coastal rainforest. They are based as much on faith as on pragmatism. As silviculturalists we are — literally — babes in the woods.

Pacific Northwest silviculture is an infant science. We know less about it than we know about the basic principles of horticulture. We know more about chrysanthemums than we do about Douglas-fir. Yet there is strong and increasing pressure on government from all sides — from industry, the Forest Service and the public — to apply what we do know about silviculture in wide-ranging and expensive programs. There are also attempts to convince governments that we know enough about silviculture to achieve significant results from the application of intensive forest management in a comprehensive manner. The advocates of intensive forest management reason that the larger the program, the greater the results. The major element in these proposals is money, and since this is public money, our money, we would do well to look closely at some of the technical ingredients of the silvicultural solution.

The catalogue of silvicultural techniques upon which such hopes rest is rather small. In a managed forest, there are but four general types of silvicultural treatment: harvesting, establishment of new crops, stand tending, and protection. In practice, these are usually quite interdependent and are not easily divided into neat categories. For instance, twenty years ago it was usual to log an area and then worry about establishing the subsequent crop. Today, most logging strategy takes into account certain site-specific factors. The logging can be scheduled to take advantage of a good cone crop for natural regeneration. A dry site may be prelogged — removing some trees and leaving others — so that natural regeneration can become well established in the shade of the remaining trees, which will then be harvested in a second operation. In order to change the species growing on a site or to eliminate disease or insects, fallers will be required to cut all trees, merchantable or not.

Planning the new crop should begin before the site is logged. The decision must be made whether to plant seedlings or to rely on natural regeneration. Once the choice has been made, the harvesting techniques are planned accordingly, and carried out.

The next step is site preparation. This can involve measures to deal with logging debris, unwanted vegetation and unsuitable soil conditions. Logging debris — slash — can create a number of problems: it is a fire hazard; it makes planting difficult; it can hinder the growth of young trees, and its physical appearance has a tendency to outrage large numbers of the public. The most effective and common way to dispose of slash is to burn it, usually in the spring or fall when the fires are more easily controlled. Although ground crews used to burn the slash, today the most popular method is to drop napalm from helicopters. While there are certain advantages to burning slash, there are also some drawbacks: fire can destroy many soil nutrients; it can lead to erosion and, like the slash itself, fire can provoke the antagonism of the public. An interesting argument in favour of slash burning is that it mirrors nature — the forest fire.

To some extent, brush, weeds and unwanted tree species can also be eliminated or controlled by fire, but fire is a fairly crude instrument for this purpose. Increasingly, herbicide is sprayed from aircraft or applied to specific plants by hand. Although many foresters are convinced of the effectiveness and economy of herbicide, evidence is mounting of unwanted side-effects. Opposition to herbicide use in certain areas is strengthening to the point where obtaining approval to use it is often worth neither the bother nor the delay.

Both vegetation control and slash disposal can be accomplished, with varying degrees of success, by scarification — mixing or agitating the soil, primarily to bring mineral soils (sand, gravel, clay) up to the surface to aid in the survival and growth of seedlings. Scarification is done by heavy machines, usually bulldozers, and if not done carefully or in the right sites, can create more problems than it solves, such as erosion, soil compaction and removal of some nutrients.

In the Pacific Northwest, plantation forestry is almost entirely done by transplanting seedlings rather than planting seeds. Seeds of certain species and strains are collected from preselected regions, sites and elevations in an attempt to match the seedling requirements that were determined during the prelogging assessments. Thus, planting involves a lead time of two to five years. A series of genetic manipulations is performed on these seeds which at its simplest involves selecting seeds from the best trees, or "supertrees." However, the process also includes everything from the establishment of seed orchards to the application of techniques from the frontiers of biological engineering. Some industry people like to joke that the ultimate or perfect tree will be one which grows quickly to the dimensions of a two-by-four, then increases in height only until it is harvested.

In British Columbia the aim — only recently achieved — is to plant 100 million seedlings a year. To produce this quantity the government maintains, either directly or by stumpage offsets to private industry, about a dozen enormous nurseries throughout the province. These grow the cheaper but more vulnerable bare-root seedlings rather than plug stock, which is a seedling with its roots encased in a growth medium. In the spring, or sometimes the fall, seedlings are shipped to the planting sites in cardboard cartons. Depending on the circumstances of their storage and journey, they may be a fine dark green, or yellow from light deprivation, or brown from dehydration, or moldy from too much water and too little ventilation. Regardless of their condition, they will be planted.

Planting is almost invariably done by hand or, more correctly, by hand, mattock and boot. Down with the mattock in one hand, making a hole for the seedling in one stroke; with the other hand, the seedling is taken from a sack slung around the waist and put into the hole; then mattock or boot refills the hole, and boot firms the loose soil. This unique, exhausting ballet is performed a thousand or more times a day by a temporary, migrant labour force hired by tree planting contractors who have their contracts from the Forest Service or the licencees and who are supervised by foresters. The quality of the planting depends on a number of factors: the commitment of the planter, the weather, the size of the mosquitoes, the steepness of the site, the amount of slash cover or the temperature of the coffee at breakfast. It can be exhilarating and rewarding or tedious and backbreaking, but never is it leisurely. Planters are paid on a piecework basis — about a dime a seedling — and to make a reasonable wage a planter must be fast.

In bad terrain he must be even faster. A friend recently told me of a day he would rather forget. It was raining and cold, with the stiff breeze often found on a mountainside. Not only was this site steep but the slash was particularly dense. The day began, as usual, by packing the cartons of seedlings one at a time up the mountain. Only after two hours of this could be begin to plant, yet so thick were the slash, stumps and brush that he could find few planting spots. In ten miserable hours of work he had planted 175 trees and made a dazzling $17.50.

Various conditions can cause bad blood between planter, contractor and Forest Service. The planter is concerned about his count, the contractor is concerned about time and overhead, and the Forest Service is concerned about the quality of the job. When there is strife, the survival rate of the seedlings is liable to suffer. Planters will dispute this, arguing that they are doing a job which they feel is worthwhile and that they enjoy the satisfaction of doing it right. Contractors also protest, pointing to elaborate contractual requirements which they must fulfil. The Forest Service likewise insists that its foresters have a lifelong career interest in the well-being of the forest. All these arguments are true and should not be belittled. Yet planting bad seedlings can be dispiriting to a planter, a bad site can be ruinous to planter and contractor alike, and a forester who insists on too close adherence to the contractual requirements can hurt the entire project. No two planting situations are precisely the same. No matter how detailed the regulations that go with a planting contract, they cannot cover all the possible conditions that actually exist on the planting site. The survival even of good seedlings ultimately depends on the willingness of all parties to adapt to the conditions of each site and their skill in doing so. The trees can be doomed simply by planting to contract. The results may not be apparent for two, three or four years, long after planter and contractor are gone, but they can be so drastic as to require a completely new planting operation.

Spacing, or the distance between seedlings, is an important factor in planting. In theory, there is an optimum number of trees for any given area, a certain density that will permit root systems and the crowns, or tops, of the trees to occupy all the available area without crowding each other and restricting growth. This initial spacing is usually about 2.4 m^2 (8 square feet), but it is feasible to alter the spacing to obtain certain results. For instance, if the objective is to grow trees for timber production, emphasizing saw logs rather than pulp wood, the area would be planted more densely. This would encourage the growth of taller trees with less taper; it would also encourage the lower branches to die and fall off at a relatively early age, producing a higher proportion of clear lumber.

Some critics of the forest industry condemn the alternative of natural regeneration, arguing that a tree should be planted for every tree cut. They overlook the point that natural stands are usually extremely dense and consequently, the trees there are relatively tall, straight and clear. Widely spaced trees, particularly those in well-spaced plantations, have larger diameters at eye level, but taper more quickly; they are less valuable for lumber because the highest lumber recovery rates are achieved with logs that are near-perfect cylinders. A good illustration of this comes from comparing British Columbia's first timber exports, the Douglas-fir trees of 1861, with the Douglas-fir planted 1.8 m (6 feet) apart during World War II. The spars Capt. Edward Stamp shipped to England from the Alberni Inlet were 61 cm (24 inches) at the butt, tapering to 28 cm (11 inches) at 55 m (180 feet) in length. These trees were probably two hundred years old, and perhaps older. In the Sayward forest, there are forty-year-old firs that are also 61 cm (24 inches) at the butt, but they have tapered to 28 cm (11 inches) at 12 or 15 m (40 or 50 feet).

Once a plantation has been established there is still a series of stand-tending techniques which can be applied to influence the forest's character. Most of these practices are concerned with increasing a site's timber volume.

Juvenile spacing has been one of the major preoccupations in the commercial forests of the Pacific Northwest. This is the practice of regulating the spacing of trees in a plantation's early stages, before the trees are big enough to be of any commercial value. In British Columbia, this technique is applied predominantly to lodgepole pine, Douglas-fir and western hemlock. Although a variety of spacing techniques have been tried — herbicides, bulldozers, explosives — the usual method is simply to chainsaw all the undesired trees, leaving them to rot on the forest floor. Normally the trees are spaced from 4.6 to 6.1 m (15 to 20 feet) apart when they are about twenty years old. The composition of the stand can be influenced during the operation by favouring one species over another. Diseased or deformed trees can be removed from the forest entirely.

Most juvenile spacing in British Columbia is done by small, migrant contracting companies. As with planting, contracts are let by the Forest Service and allocated on the basis of competitive bids. Others which are under the control of the forest companies are on a less competitive basis. And again, as with planting, spacing is a highly competitive business. Bidding between the contracting companies if often intense, particularly in times of high unemployment. Workers are usually paid by piecework — so much per tree for planting, or so much per hectare or acre for spacing — and the injury rate of workers is relatively high. For the most part, the work force is very unstable. And just as the Forest Service's contractual requirements can be detrimental to good tree planting, so can the biological demands of specific sites be overridden by the terms of the standard-form spacing contract.

There are a number of theoretical objectives involved in spacing, one of them being to increase the yield of the stand. Within limits, this growth will be achieved regardless of the stand's density. In certain situations, however, growth rates can slow because the trees grow too closely together; in this instance spacing will increase growth. Another effect of spacing can be to concentrate growth in fewer but larger trees. A major benefit of this is lower harvest costs at some point in the future: it costs less to harvest 100 m^3 from ten trees than from one hundred trees of 1 m^3 each.

When the trees removed during a thinning operation are used in some way, such as for lumber, pulp or firewood, the operation is called "commercial thinning." Most of the same objectives involved in juvenile spacing apply, but commercial thinning also contributes to the industrial wood supply, providing revenue to defray the cost of the treatment or, in some cases, even produce a profit. An important aspect of commercial thinning is that it is a blend of traditional logging practice and the relatively new techniques of silviculture. The job requires a great deal of skill to remove the thinnings from the stand without damaging the remaining crop trees. The amount of commercial thinning in British Columbia is miniscule — 31 ha (77 acres) during the 1980–81 fiscal year.

Widespread thinning has been rejected mainly for bureaucratic reasons, though there are also economic and technical factors involved. As mentioned, one of the virtues of commercial thinning is its blend of logging and silvicultural techniques. However, that same blend produces some regrettable legal and administrative tangles. The Forest Service's Timber Administration Branch is responsible for all forms of timber harvesting, while the Silviculture Branch is responsible for silvicultural practice on Crown lands. Because commercial thinning is considered a form of harvesting, it falls within the jurisdiction of the Timber Administration Branch rather than the Silviculture Branch. By provincial law, the Timber Administration Branch can only allocate timber through some form of tenure. But the Silviculture Branch feels that the existing forms of tenure do not allow enough control over the spacing operation with its sensitive techniques. Therefore, the Silviculture Branch is reluctant to allow anyone to bid in open auction for the commercial thinning operations; it feels that these operations cannot be properly controlled.

Underlying this bickering is a factor that reveals more about the nature of the bureaucratic beast than it does about the pros and cons of commercial thinning. The limited experience gained from thinning operations indicates that during periods of moderate to good markets, the stumpage value of thinnings is about $5.00 per m^3 ($14 per cunit). According to the Forest Service's own 1977 estimates, 4 250 000 m^3 (150 million cubic feet) would be available from commercial thinning in the Sayward forest.[3] This suggests that thinnings from the Sayward could return about $21 million to the public treasury. During the early 1980s, the question of the use to which those stumpage revenues should be put was the subject of heated and fundamental debate between the Timber Administration and the Silvicultural branches of the Forest Service. Administration took the position that, according to practice and legislation, the funds should go into general provincial revenues. Silviculture maintained that in order to control the quality of the thinning, it was necessary to have the work done on a contract basis, with the Forest Service keeping title to the timber and selling it on the open market. This arrangement would not involve any form of tenure; the Silviculture Branch could therefore maintain close quality control over the operation and the profit would go, not to general revenue, but to the Silviculture Branch to be put back into intensive forest management. The result of the debate was that, in 1981, commercial thinning operations were suspended in the Sayward forest. Meanwhile, private contractors had invested large amounts of money in thinning equipment on the strength of the potential thinnings and the Forest Service's initial encouragement. They were left holding the bag.

Some stands in the Sayward forest, containing timber considered merchantable by Forest Service standards, have been spaced rather than thinned. The trees that were cut to provide room for the crop trees have been left on the ground to rot. One reason for this is an intensive forest management agreement between the federal and provincial governments. The five-year agreement involves a program to juvenile space 66 000 ha (163,000 acres) annually by 1986. The logistics of launching a program of this size are enormous; even the basic task of finding young stands that would benefit from spacing is often beyond the capacity of the Forest Service. Consequently, at various times in a number of forest districts, in order to "spend the budget," the simple solution has been to space older, more accessible stands containing merchantable timber. Further, the federal-provincial program does not include commercial thinning. The triumph of bureaucratic convenience over economic common sense is an increasingly frequent phenomenon in the forest industry, as elsewhere.

A similar situation can exist when deciduous trees are involved in the thinning treatment. In most parts of the province, fast-growing deciduous trees compete with and often dominate young coniferous stands, whether they are plantations or naturally regenerated. On the coast, red alder is the conifer's most common competitor, while in the Interior it is aspen. These deciduous species are considered undesirable weed trees because no marketing structure for them has traditionally existed. In 1980–81 almost 2700 ha (6670 acres) of such stands were treated, all in the Vancouver Forest Region. These conifer release treatments, designed to encourage the growth of the more valuable coniferous species, are accomplished mechanically with chain saws or chemically either by hand application or aerial spraying of herbicide.

The deciduous trees eliminated during these treatments are usually valueless, but on some sites, particularly some of the coastal sites containing red alder, they are large enough for industrial use. Yet coastal loggers who have begun to find markets for alder have had great difficulty getting the rights to harvest it. Once again, the reasons are primarily bureaucratic. Merchantable alder volumes are not included in allowable annual cut calculations, so their harvest does not interfere with existing timber supply calculations and allocations; however, because alder is not part of the allowable annual cut, no convenient procedure yet exists for allocating harvest rights for this species. The result, at least until very recently, is that very little alder has been harvested from Crown-managed lands; much of the alder lumber used in British Columbia is imported from Washington and Oregon states.

Another stand improvement practice is fertilization, almost all of it in the coastal Vancouver Forest Region. The main fertilizer used is nitrogen, applied in pellet form from helicopters. A fertilization program of this sort must be repeated at regular intervals, as the effects are only temporary. Because of increases in the price of the natural gas used to make the fertilizer, considerable research is underway into the potential of seeding stands with nitrogen-fixing plants such as alder, vetch and lupins. Most fertilization projects are applied to stands that have previously been juvenile spaced because it has been found that there is a synergistic increase in the growth of stands that have had both treatments, this increase being greater than merely the sum of the growth factors of each treatment applied separately.

Although pruning is common in some parts of the world, it is rarely practised in publicly owned forests in the Pacific Northwest. The chief purpose of pruning is to remove the lower branches of a tree, so that as the tree grows in diameter it will produce high-grade, clear wood which can be used for lumber or plywood. The greatest economic gains are made by pruning trees on which dead branches remain for long periods. Douglas-fir is a good example; its branches take twenty-five to thirty years to fall after dying. During this period, the tree continues to grow around these decomposing branches. When these trees are eventually harvested and milled into lumber or peeled into veneer, the knots created by these branches will probably be loose, causing the timber to be graded and valued at lower rates than tight-knot or clear wood. If the branches are pruned at an early age, perhaps during juvenile spacing or commercial thinning, the wood will grow over the wounds rather quickly, and from that point on, that section of the tree will grow clear wood. In European forests, pruning is done with a variety of tools — handsaws, axes, even clubs. In some Scandinavian forests, it is common to prune with a chain saw to a height of 2.1 or

2.4 m (7 or 8 feet) while spacing or thinning. Chain saw attachments have been developed which allows the saw to "climb" up the tree, cutting branches as it goes and then returning, but they are not commonly used.

Pruning has not become a popular silvicultural practice in the Pacific Northwest partly due to the process of calculating annual cuts in sustained yield forests. In a narrow accounting sense, the most valuable silvicultural investments are often those designed to increase growth, and hence to provide an immediate increase in annual cuts — the allowable cut effect mentioned in chapter three. Because pruning does not increase yield, but rather improves quality, it is not favoured as a silvicultural investment, even though it may realize higher economic returns in the long run than many of the yield enhancement practices currently in vogue.

Forest protection, the safeguarding of forests against fire, desease and insects, is a facet of forestry which predates silviculture. When the B. C. Forest Service was created in 1912, protection was one of its major responsibilities; indeed, it provided much of the justification for the service's very creation and cost. The idea of protection — of fighting fires, combatting insect infestations and preventing disease — was adopted along with the earliest concepts of sustained yield forestry. For a long time, the common image of the forester has been as a protector of the forests. And it is during the most dramatic of protection activities, such as fighting an out-of-control forest fire, that the profession, the industry and anyone else with an interest in the forest abandon their usual antagonisms and concentrate on a single object — eliminating the threat to the forest. A forest under attack by any agent of destruction is generally agreed to be worth everyone's best efforts.

This was not always the case in North America. As late as the turn of the century, it was considered legitimate in some areas to start wildfires and let them burn out of control. Indians were reputed to do so in order to increase game populations. Large forested areas in the East were burned by white settlers to clear the land for agriculture. In the West, fire was often used to denude large areas for mining operations. It was in opposition to this attitude and these practices that the concepts of forestry and forest management were developed.

The evolution of silviculture and the recent widespread application of certain intensive management practices has brought about some basic changes in attitude towards protection. One aspect of the change is that a greater need for protection is now acknowledged; by the time a site has been prepared, planted, spaced and fertilized, anywhere from $1,000 to $2,000 may have been invested in each hectare. That is a lot of money to go up in smoke or be eaten by bugs.

Silvicultural treatments and protection practices should not be independent of each other, but they often are. Some of the first plantations of Douglas-fir on Vancouver Island were planted during World War II in areas infected with a number of root rot diseases, including one to which fir is particularly susceptible, *Phellinus weirii,* or Gilbertson root rot. At the time of planting, the disease was active in some fir stumps in areas that had been logged or burned by wildfire. The organism can live for a century or more in such a stump. It moves from the stumps into the young fir plantation via the roots of the trees. As the roots of the growing plantation extend and begin to intertwine, the rot spreads in all directions from the centres of infection, at a rate of 20 to 40 cm (8 to 16 inches) a year. An estimated 2 000 000 m^3 (70.6 million cubic feet) of timber are lost in this way each year in the Pacific Northwest, much of it in pure Douglas-fir plantations.[4] It is within these same forests that a large portion of funds allocated for juvenile spacing and fertilization have been spent. Yet it is a melancholy fact that to date, virtually no funds have been spent on protecting these stands from root rot. The habits of Gilbertson root rot have long been known. Its potential for destruction in young stands has been understood since the 1920s, but an economical way of treating it has yet to be found. The only known method is to isolate the infection by removing the host Douglas-fir trees and physically uprooting the diseased stumps. Then other species may be planted on the site.

Protecting a Douglas-fir forest from root rot is clearly an expensive proposition. What is most remarkable about this particular situation is, first, that Douglas-fir was planted at all in these infected areas, and second, that large amounts of money are still being spent on intensive management practices in these same stands while the infections continue to spread.

There are occasions when silvicultural treatments create protection problems. One example involves juvenile spacing. A standard protection practice is to burn the slash in logged-over areas in order to eliminate the inflammable debris in a controlled manner. Spacing creates large amounts of slash which, in most situations, cannot be so eliminated and which constitutes a major fire hazard for several years. Consequently, for protection reasons, there are limits to the amount of spacing that can be done in any forest. The large amount of spacing done in the Sayward forest during the late 1970s, for example, increased the danger of fire in that area so much that special firefighting crews had to be stationed there during the summer season at a cost of about $1 million a year.

Protection issues become even more complicated when other users of the forest are taken into account. The intensively managed Sayward forest, for example, is a prime recreational area. It contains dozens of lakes and streams; it is covered with a network of old trails, ideal for hiking; it has large populations of fish and wildlife, and in the summer it is heavily used by campers. During times of extreme fire hazard, the most common-sense protection measure in those parts of the forest containing high concentrations of spacing slash would be to exclude people altogether. This would help prevent fires, since almost 10 per cent of forest fires are caused by recreationists. But a much greater concern is that a major fire, however caused, can spread at incredibly high speed. Then the forest is a dangerous place to be in. Yet attempts to close off these areas, even during extremely hazardous conditions, often meet with stiff opposition from the recreation industry.

The most contentious protection issues of all are connected with the battle against major insect infestation. The annual loss of growth from disease and insects is an estimated 16 000 000 m^3 (565 million cubic feet) in British Columbia alone. The major pest problems in the province are mountain pine beetles, spruce and Douglas-fir bark beetles, and spruce budworms. There is a complex arsenal of insect control techniques — biological, silvicultural, mechanical and chemical — none of which is very successful against insect attacks. The controversy arises almost exclusively when forest managers and ministers of forests attempt to launch wholesale chemical attacks on the insects. Advocates of spraying programs see these as cheap solutions to an enormous, if narrowly defined, problem. To their opponents, the programs are ecological catastrophies.

Aerial spraying of insecticides involves many of the same issues as the silvicultural use of herbicides. The basic conflict is between maintaining or enhancing the commercial timber supply and the undesirable effects, real or imagined, that spraying programs may have on other resources, resource users and the entire ecological well-being of the forest. Ultimately, this conflict concerns the price we are willing to pay for the benefits of managed forests. The aims and objectives of contemporary forest managers, particularly the sometimes extravagant claims of intensive forest management advocates, must be examined in the light of this issue.

In the late 1970s, when the B. C. government announced that it would underwrite massively expanded intensive forest management programs, responsible officials made statements about increases in timber yield the programs would produce. The minister of forests, Tom Waterland, talked confidently of 300 per cent increases in timber volumes over comparable untouched stands. His statements echoed similar claims from a number of other enthusiasts, many of them in the upper levels of the Forest Service's Silviculture Branch. By the time the minister got around to announcing his $1.4 billion intensive management program, he and other proponents of large public budget allocations for silvicultural programs had become much less specific about the yield increases to be expected. During the interval, it had become apparent to anyone looking beneath the surface of silvicultural knowledge that neither experience nor research could justify those initial claims.

Lack of experience with silvicultural programs makes it difficult to support claims about their effectiveness. Whether in British Columbia or the northwestern United States, there is no body of silvicultural experience of long enough duration to provide firm and specific conclusions. The gains predicted by some prognosticators cannot be measured for a century. The first forest plantations in British Columbia are less than half a century old. Most other silvicultural practices have been introduced in the province within only the last ten to twenty years. Conditions are admittedly more advanced in Washington, Oregon and California, but only by perhaps a decade. On either side of the international border, whenever specific yield figures are used, they invariably refer to research projects, most of which originate in the United States; only a very small amount of silvicultural research has taken place in British Columbia. The reports of this research all have one factor in common: they are inconclusive, and this fact reflects more on silviculture's essential nature than on researchers' ability.

Most research reports caution against applying to larger forested areas the data gleaned from small research plots. Research plots are seldom placed in nonproductive forest areas with roads, streams and rock bluffs such as are found in larger regions. The degree of quality control may be quite different in research projects than in actual field practice. A research plot's rate of seedling survival is likely to be higher than in an actual plantation because the time from nursery to transplanting is shorter and the seedlings are handled more carefully. Fertilizer will probably be more carefully and uniformly distributed; in actual practice, when fertilizer is applied from the air, there are significant variations in distribution. Research plots will not normally be placed in steep areas or on sites which have experienced natural damage, unless these factors are part of the research objectives. None of these limitations invalidate research; they merely mean that allowances must be made before research results can be applied to operational situations.

A typically optimistic scenario uses the example of a naturally regenerated, untreated Douglas-fir stand on an average site.[5] At age fifty, one hectare of this forest land is expected to have produced 350 m^3 (49 cunits per acre) of commercial wood on 2500 trees with an average breast-height diameter of 28 cm (11.8 inches). This stand is compared with a hypothetical hectare planted with 1500 seedlings obtained from genetically improved seeds. At fifty years, this managed hectare is projected to produce 560 m^3 (78.4 cunits per acre) of fir, with diameters averaging 38 cm (15 inches) — a 60 per cent increase in yield.

Next, projections are made for a stand of either natural or plantation fir that was spaced to 750 trees per hectare (300 trees per acre) when it was fifteen years old. By age 50, this hypothetical hectare should contain 700 m^3 (98 cunits per acre) of commercial wood — a 100 per cent increase. Theoretically, by applying 225 kg (500 lbs.) of nitrogen fertilizer to the same hectare at age twenty-five, the yield at age fifty can be increased to 840 m^3 (11,760 cubic feet per acre) on 46 cm (18 inch) trees.

Finally, thinning to 370 crop trees at age thirty-five should increase the yield on this fully treated hectare to 1050 m^3 (14,700 cubic feet per acre) of merchantable fir at fifty years — a 300 per cent increase over the natural, untreated stand.

No existing body of empirical knowledge is capable of supporting such a projection. Nowhere in the Pacific Northwest has a stand of Douglas-fir been intensively managed in such a manner. Nor is it possible to arrive at such a conclusion by using the findings from research projects, except by the most liberal application of the data. Most research projects in the Pacific Northwest examine one kind of silvicultural treatment, occasionally two. Although the relatively well financed U. S. Forest Service research institutions have conducted studies for several decades, British Columbia has no comparable research program. The major endeavour in the province is the Canadian Forestry Service's Shawnigan Lake project, begun only in 1970. Early results from this project — an examination of the effects of spacing and fertilizing Douglas-fir — are just beginning to appear. And although these results indicate that spacing and fertilizing do accelerate growth, they by no means support the hypothesis of a 300 per cent increase.

The most important research programs involving intensive management of Douglas-fir have been undertaken by the Pacific Northwest Forest and Range Experiment Stations in Portland, Oregon. The research foresters from the station have published an evaluation of most of the treatments discussed above. In assessing the potential gains from planting genetically improved seedlings, the authors define two main approaches to this technique.

> The first uses seed orchards composed of grafted cuttings from intensively selected parent trees and depends initially on efficiency of selection for its gains. The second is based on collection of wind-pollinated seed from selected trees in the forest. Here, some gain comes from selection but most from progeny

testing aimed at identifying the top quarter of the parentage. A study dating back to 1912 shows this gain to be substantial and sure if the test is long continued.

Under both types of program, a second round of tree improvement has been started using controlled crosses from parents in the present programs. For commercial seed production, ungrafted progeny are grown in orchards from which the poorer three-fourths of the families will be removed, with the remainder expected to provide elite seed in fifteen to twenty-five years. Breeding of the best individuals from controlled crosses is handled as a separate phase of these programs.

The potential improvement in volume growth has been conservatively estimated at 10 per cent for the first round, and at least another 10 per cent when progeny from known crosses becomes available as a seed source.[6]

While the report acknowledges that gains other than volume growth are to be had from genetically altered stock, such as better log form and wood quality, and hardier and healthier trees, the authors also recognize potential hazards. The improved trees may turn out to be less, rather than more, hardy — more susceptible to climatic injury and pests. "Such susceptibility may not be quickly apparent and is far more difficult and costly to correct in forestry than in agriculture."[7]

Over a range of research projects, the response to fertilizer has been quite variable. The greatest gains in volume growth have occurred in situations where a nitrogen deficiency in the soil is the principal cause of limited growth. Thus, major gains can be realized from some of the poorest forest sites, usually much higher gains than from sites that are naturally more productive.

Growth increases following fertilizer application are temporary. Present estimates are that response will generally last at least ten years and that it many be possible to fertilize as many as five times at ten-year intervals without diminishing the response per application.[8]

The authors concluded that increases in volume growth over a ten-year period on medium site land will average approximately 15 per cent. They point out that a combined program of spacing or thinning with fertilizing "in some cases exceed[s] the added effects of either treatment alone."[9]

The gains to be made by controlling stand density are likewise enhanced by combining treatments.

> Commercial thinning alone will produce about a 5 per cent gain in production over a rotation, compared with the normal yield table for well-stocked, (unspaced) natural stands; while the combination of precommercial and commercial thinning will increase total production by about 30 per cent. The relative gain from precommercial thinning is greater on poorer sites, while that from commercial thinning is greater on better sites.[10]

The report notes, however, that seventy-five-year-old intensively managed stands of Douglas-fir in Europe appear to be providing yields greater than these estimates.

The treatments studied in this report are generally the same as those proposed in the B. C. government's management program that was projected to produce a 300 per cent volume increase. But if the most optimistic results for the Pacific Northwestern research plots are combined, the gains over a rotation amount to a mere 65 per cent. An allowance for the synergistic effects of thinning and fertilizing might possibly bring the projected gains up to 75 per cent, but that is still a long, long way from the promised 300 per cent.

Maximum growth rates are biologically possible only in small areas under ideal conditions. Any larger intensive management program is unlikely to achieve equal results. Losses from insect and disease attacks, though controlled by intensive management, will still occur. In some cases, intensive management practices may inadvertently increase such losses. Recent evidence, for example, indicates that the presence of red alder in a Douglas-fir stand inhibits the spread of Gilbertson root rot. If this is the case, then some of the brushing and spacing projects that have removed alder from fir stands will lead to smaller gains, or even to net losses in volume growth.

Any practical management program will also be affected by a wide variety of site-specific factors. Some sites will be too steep for profitable thinning; others will support resource uses that preclude juvenile spacing for aesthetic reasons or to protect wildlife, recreation opportunities and watershed function.

The final point, to be investigated more fully in the following chapter, is that even though these treatments may be biologically sound, there are many situations in which they are not economically feasible. A site which could be biologically capable of achieving a 75 per cent volume increase through intensive management may be so inaccessible that costs of treatment become unreasonably high.

Probably the most significant factor concerning the economic and biological feasibility of these silvicultural treatments involves the manner in which they are carried out. There is a very small margin for error. Each seedling must be supplied to the site in good health and be correctly planted, or it will not grow. Every stand must be spaced or thinned according to the ecological realities of that stand, as well as according to broader economic considerations. What is required is a highly developed sense of judgement by the people doing the work. If the capacity for that kind of judgement is not present, either through a lack of knowledge or for reasons of bureaucratic organization, then it is unlikely that any gains will be realized.

It may be theoretically possible to "triple the yield" of Douglas-fir or any other tree. If enough proper care is lavished on a tree, it can undoubtedly be induced to grow larger and faster than if it were left to its own devices. But so far, there is no evidence that the means exist to create the enormous increases in growth that some people have predicted, and most certainly not on any commercial, profitable scale. Spectacular silvicultural feats may some day be possible. But until such feats are also economically practical, they cannot be counted on as the ultimate salvation of our forest resource.

NINE

What Will the Managed Forest Cost?

PROVINCIAL AND FEDERAL GOVERNMENTS take enormous amounts of money out of the forests, most of it via industry. They return only the merest pittance for forest protection and enhancement. Few statements are easier to prove; the figures speak eloquently. In addition to the $417 million in stumpage the B. C. government collected in 1979, the provincial and federal governments extracted well over another billion dollars from the B. C. forest industry.[1] The biggest chunk of this, $745 million, was in the form of corporate and personal income taxes. An additional $145 million was acquired through various other forms of taxes and import duties. In total, the B. C. government took in $963.7 million and the Canadian government $532.2 million from the forest sector in 1979. In that same year, $210.3 million was spent on all aspects of forest managment in British Columbia, $204.6 million of it by the provincial government. In other words, almost $1.3 billion taken from the forests was spent on other things.[2] Predictably, the largest forest-related expense was administration — $66.1 million. Expenditures on silviculture were $60.3 million.[3]

The last figure is particularly interesting because it represents the amount of money the B. C. government, during the most profitable year on record, was willing to reinvest in the mainstay of the provincial economy. It is only 4 per cent of the total income from forests of both levels of government during that year.

The figures are obvious and damning, but they tell only part of the story. Politicians have no monopoly on greed, incompetence or irresponsibility. During 1979, the B. C. forest industry enjoyed after-tax profits of nearly $1 billion. The industry was willing to spend $343 million buying and repairing equipment (other than processing plants), but only $11.2 million of its own money on silviculture — even on its own privately held land, and even though the costs would be tax-deductible. At least government revenues stay in the province where they can be of some benefit to the citizens who are owners of the forests. In the case of corporate profits, a large but unmeasurable portion of the money earned from B. C. forests is shunted out of the country.

Although it is not a good idea to say so in union halls, forest workers can be as lazy, unproductive and irresponsible as any other part of the industry. If one can use the word "greed" in reference to governments or corporations, why not use the same word about the forest unions? Jack Munro, president of the IWA and cochairman of the 1980 Canadian Forest Congress, certainly sounded greedy as he explained to the congress who should pay for silviculture programs: "You from B. C. have heard me say it many, many times: you, the employers, and you, the government; your role is to give and our role in the unions is to receive. So you can pay!" Nowhere did Munro offer the least hint that his members might contribute some time or money to the silviculture programs designed to employ future generations of union members.

All parts of the industry sing loudly for silviculture, albeit for different reasons. Politicians join in because it is the right issue — the politically expedient, motherhood issue. It would be political suicide to argue against silviculture. Civil servants take up the melody because they sense power; empire-building is fundamental to bureaucracy. Industry harmonizes; it wants to be sure of a supply of raw material. Unions provide the rhythm: "Jobs, jobs, jobs."

Yet for all the apparent harmony, when a sour note is heard, all fingers point to government. When the long-range sustained yield is being overcut by industry and workers, the fault lies with government. Whether money is needed for education or health care, or whether a stadium is really a very fine thing to build during a depression in the construction industry, the government should spend more on the forests. Whether the corporations spend only 1 per cent of their profits on silviculture, or whether the unions offer no help at all, the government should spend more than its present 4 per cent of revenue.

Strangely, the government contributes to its own villainous image. The government owns and insists on controlling 95 per cent of British Columbia's forest land. Furthermore, part of the stumpage the government collects is theoretically earmarked for silviculture. These factors, plus the public nature of government enterprise, support the universal opinion that the government should spend far more on forest protection and enhancement. But should it? If, for a moment, we forgo that delicious warm glow of righteousness that silviculture advocacy brings and look instead at the economics of the enterprise, we may find cause to doubt the conventional wisdom that governments are remiss in their role as stewards of the forests.

An essential and frustrating feature of any financial examination of the costs and benefits of silvicultural treatments is the absence of concrete information of the kind investors normally require before spending large sums of money. The economic analyses and projections customary in the construction of a hydroelectric installation or the establishment of a retail merchandising business are models of empirical precision compared to those available for silviculture. In site-specific, pragmatic, operational terms, it is usually impossible to produce a worthwhile economic analysis of silvicultural programs — which is why such analyses are rarely attempted. What passes for forest economic analysis is, in fact, speculation. Figures derived from a very few research situations are applied to hypothetical forests, producing results that are often more reflective of the motives of the analyst than the effects occurring in an actual forest. There are complex and numerous reasons for this.

One reason is the lack of a silvicultural tradition in most North American forests. We have already seen that there is no experiential evidence for the supposed relationship between cause and effect, treatment and response; there is no body of emperical knowledge which says that if you plant a certain species of tree on a certain piece of land and apply certain treatments to the forest over the next 80 to 150 years, the costs are reasonably likely to be a certain amount and the returns a certain amount, or that the forest will be reasonably certain to increase in health, vigour and productivity, and that its owners and managers may be reasonably sure of a fair return for their efforts.

Other spheres of economic activity enjoy a strength and confidence in their projections that foresters can only regard wistfully. An obvious example lies just a mountain-hop away, where Prairie farmers still work land settled by their great-grandparents. The farmers owe much to academic theorists and results from research plots, to be sure; yet greater by far is the debt they owe to generations of their forebears who yearly calculated the seed and fertilizer needs for each section of land, drawing on knowledge gained from their own successes and failures and those of their parents and neighbours. Year after year, these pragmatic visionaries would cast their sight one season into the future; year after year, their calculations would be proved or disproved within the twelvemonth. From generation to generation, this previous knowledge would be transmitted, to grow into the traditions of agricultural economics so vital to the region today.

No such tradition exists in the forests of the Pacific Northwest. We have no population of third- or even second-generation forest farmers, and there is only a handful of first-generation people skilled in the arts and techniques of growing trees and tending forests. Our crops do not come to fruition for a century; our plans and theories must wait a hundred years to be proved — or disproved.

Other conditions in the forest industry have combined to inhibit the development of traditional knowledge, particularly in those parts of the country where the majority of forest lands are publicly owned. Because of the tenure provisions on public lands, even second-generation loggers are rare. Logging families tend either to lose their timber supply or sell off their rights to well-financed corporations for what may seem at the time large amounts of money. Further, the industry in these areas has been primarily a harvesting industry. We have been cutters rather than growers. The economics of timber harvesting can be calculated with some precision, in no small part because experienced loggers can provide forest economists with accurate data. Forest economists attempting silvicultural analysis have no similar body of knowledge upon which to draw.

A second problem with the financial analysis of silvicultural practice concerns the objectives of the particular program under consideration. Almost all such analysis is expressed in terms of timber production, particularly when attempting to assess the benefits. Yet there is an even wider range of management objectives involved in forest planning. Whatever the silvicultural prescriptions in a particular forest, they will have a profound influence on other forms of life in that forest, as well as on such factors as water flows, visual appearance and the substance of the earth itself. Some of these factors may be enhanced, others inhibited. Part of the explanation for the concentration on timber values lies with a belief that timber has a real, or market, value, whereas most other forest resources do not. If venison could be bought and sold, perhaps there would be a means of assessing, for example, the economics of the management plans for the Tsitika valley. But perhaps not; salmon has a market value, with salmon populations in a fairly well known relationship to the availability of spawning and rearing areas, most of which are found in forest lands. It should be possible to calculate salmon values involved in the management of relevant areas, but this is rarely attempted.

In a province like British Columbia, many people assume that timber resources can legitimately be used to finance a major portion of more diverse public spending. This contrasts with the narrow — almost ideally narrow — view that the monies earned from timber production on a specific site should be used to finance its reforestation. But in practice, the narrower viewpoint is not argued closely. The same principle could apply in evaluating the reforestation of a watershed that had no recoverable timber at all but which had been burned by a fire from a sport fisherman's cigarette. In such a case, a reforestation decision would probably rest solely on the economics of future timber production for the burned-off site. It would be very unlikely to involve a financial analysis of other factors such as wildlife or water production. And even if such an analysis were involved, it is unlikely that even a part of the planting would be financed from budgets for fisheries enhancement, wildlife management or water resources.

At times, it is difficult to ascertain the objectives of intensive management programs. Ostensibly, their purpose is to increase the timber supply. Most financial analysis is directed to that end. But a number of other objectives have become part of the rationale for intensive management expenditures. W. G. Burch, one of the major figures in the forest management establishment, listed the major benefits of a vastly expanded intensive management program: "A reduction in rotation from 100 years (under natural conditions) to 60 years for a managed forest, which would allow us to cut nearly two crops off the same ground in the same period of time. . . ."[4] Burch is not talking here about yield enhancement so much as the enticing prospect of obtaining earlier returns on investment.

Another factor which Burch mentions is increased employment: "Most forestry projects are labour intensive: in fact, it is conceivable that at certain periods of the year, a logging operation practising a full range of intensive forestry projects could employ more people on forestry work than on logging."[5] This is a persistent theme among advocates of increased spending on silviculture, particularly during times of high unemployment. It is part of a belief prevalent among politicians and bureaucrats that jobs can be "created" by allocating funds (usually from the public treasury) to various projects. The unfortunate aspect of most of these "job creation" programs is that their objectives are usually considered to have been achieved once people have been hired and the project is underway. Whether the "job" which has been "created" is productive in a silvicultural sense is irrelevant. Job-creation and make-work projects are notorious for the attitudes they foster among their participants: namely, that the way to fulfil the program objective is to show up for work, collect a paycheque and spend the proceeds, thereby keeping the economy rolling and idle hands from getting into mischief.

"A managed forest," Burch goes on to say, "will provide for more recreational capabilities, better control of water quality, and an increase in most game populations, as compared to an unmanaged forest."[6] It is legitimate to point out that while a managed forest *might* produce these benefits, it could just as well reduce recreational capabilities, pollute the water and lead to a decline in game populations. All of these results can be seen on forest lands managed by the timber corporation for which Mr. Burch serves as a senior executive. Which is not to question the man's integrity, nor the corporate behaviour of his company, B. C. Forest Products. In fact, this company is generally regarded as one of the most environmentally conscientious and silviculturally innovative in Canada. It is merely to observe that forest management projects are primarily designed to enhance timber values. Other objectives are not allowed to interfere with this basic goal. Not only is there no mechanism for a forest land owner or licencee such as B. C. Forest Products to enhance and reap the benefits of nontimber forest resources but, in fact, such undertakings are actively discouraged, even if the company is prepared to undertake them for the timber returns alone. Even though many other resource values may be affected, for better or for worse, by intensive management programs, the only factor used in considering the costs and benefits of those programs is timber values. In the end, this one-sided emphasis grossly distorts the process of economic analysis.

A major analytical problem develops when a forest industry shifts its focus from harvesting an existing resource to growing the timber it harvests. The central feature of a silviculturally oriented industry, in economic terms, is the long period of time involved in producing results. No other economic endeavours which use conventional methods of cost-benefit analysis have to deal with such long-range calculations. If operations such as planting, spacing and fertilizing are considered investments, then the analytical tools normally used to take time into account — interest and discount rates — must be adjusted to the lengthy period of the rotation of the particular forest sites under consideration. In current practice this may range from 50 to 150 years.

One way of dealing with this problem is to consider silvicultural expenditures part of the cost of staying in business, as operating costs rather than capital investment. Few forest economists consider this practice a legitimate method of cost accounting. Nonetheless, in various parts of the world, silvicultural costs are viewed as one of the expenses involved in obtaining timber, expressed in terms of costs per unit of timber volume. Thus, until recently, B. C. Forest Products calculated its intensive management costs at \$1.60 per m^3 (\$5 per cunit).[7]

Putting this calculation in broad terms, the 1979 Canadian timber harvest of 157 000 000 m³ (5.5 billion cubic feet) involved silvicultural costs of $156 million, slightly less than $1 per m³ ($3 per cunit).[8]

The difficulty with this approach is that it provides very little help in deciding how much to spend or where to spend it. On public forest lands, where silvicultural costs are expected to be covered by the landowner (that is, out of public funds) the problem becomes more acute. There is a widespread demand within the Canadian forestry establishment — the private sector and government professionals alike — to increase the expenditures to $2 or even $3 per m³ ($6 to $9 per cunit). The justification for this argument is that public revenues of all types from forest activity are in the order of $20 per m³ ($57 per cunit). Basically, this argument rests on such intangibles as the "fairness" or the "reasonableness" of increased spending, which is of little help to governments under siege by a host of claims on the public purse. In the end, the proponents of large-scale publicly financed intensive forest management programs will have to justify their proposals in more conventional economic terms.

The various economic justifications of silvicultural programs encounter a number of mechanical problems. The measure of value for a particular silvicultural investment is expressed as the stumpage value of the treated stand at the time of harvest, minus the value that would have been produced on that stand had it not been treated. Stumpage is basically a function of selling price and harvesting costs, yet neither of these factors can be determined at the time of investment. Therefore, assumptions must be made. After discounting the effects of inflation, it is known that lumber prices have increased at about 1.8 per cent a year since 1800. Real prices — that is, similarly discounted for inflation — of plywood and pulpwood, have remained constant in the fifty years or so for which there has been a market for them. It is usually assumed that these real price trends will continue, as will the relative amounts consumed of each type of product. This assumption implies that the timber grown in managed stands will be of sufficient quality to produce these various products in constant proportions. Thus, other things being equal, if cultivated timber turns out to be more suitable for pulpwood than lumber, there will be serious economic consequences.

The assumption of rising prices is basic to the whole notion of forest management; it was one of the essential "laws" enunciated by Bernhard Fernow:

> All things in the production of which nature plays the important part have the tendency to rise in price, while those relying principally on labour and capital, sink. That the price of wood is bound to rise is not only a matter of simple philosophy as long as forest area decreases and demand for wood increases, but also of history wherever natural resources have been reduced to the necessity of management.[9]

Harvesting costs will be subjected to a variety of conflicting pressures. On the one hand, they are expected to rise because it costs more to log the smaller trees taken from managed second-growth stands than the larger trees taken from virgin forests. But on the other hand, the silvicultural treatments of spacing and thinning reduce harvesting costs in managed stands compared to unmanaged stands because they concentrate growth in fewer trees. Generally, it is assumed that in constant dollars harvesting costs will remain the same.

Access costs are yet a further example of the complexity of silvicultural economics. In British Columbia, for example, certain road costs incurred during the logging of virgin timber are not charged against operating costs. Like silvicultural costs, roads on Crown lands are paid for by the landowner and are considered investments or land improvements. The roads will be used during the management of the subsequent crop and again when the managed crop is harvested. In calculating the costs and benefits of silvicultural treatments, it is normal to ignore these road costs; in real practice, they are a legitimate factor.

A second problem with financial calculations was discussed in the last chapter: the lack of a known response to various treatments. In the Pacific Northwest, most silvicultural knowledge has been obtained from a relatively few research plots, none of which has been in existence for even one full rotation. In the past few years, this problem has been addressed by the use of computers. A number of programs have been devised which simulate growth response to various silvicultural practices. In large part, the recent flowering of optimistic predictions is due more to developments in computer technology than to increased understanding of what is actually going on in the forest. Partially, one suspects, because of the appearance of precision in their statements, along with the mystique that surrounds any report containing within its appendices a stack of computer printouts, these simulations possess an aura of authority and credibility they rarely deserve. But a computer program is only as good as the assumptions on which it is based. The stock phrase for this within computer circles is "garbage in, garbage out."

A sophisticated example of the role these simulated projections play in forest planning and financial analysis is a 1980 study of forest management options for the Okanagan Timber Supply Area.[10] When the Forest Service completed its timber supply analysis for the Okanagan TSA, as called for in the revised 1978 Forests Act, it was apparent that "the potential supply deficit . . . is at least 900 000 cubic metres [31.8 million cubic feet] per year or 19 per cent of the present annual consumption of 4 800 000 cubic metres [169.5 million cubic feet]." At the time, 2 900 000 m^3 (102.4 million cubic feet) was coming from Okanagan TSA lands. The other 1 900 000 m^3 (67.1 million cubic feet) was being supplied from other TSAs, private lands, Tree Farm Licences and temporary tenures. The forecast indicated that some of these sources would disappear in the near future and that an additional volume of timber — 900 000 m^3 (31.8 million cubic feet) — would have to be taken from the Okanagan TSA if the mills in the area were to continue operating.

In 1979 a joint task force was established, called the Shuswap Okanagan Forest Association and involving the Planning Branch of the Ministry of Forests and fourteen timber companies operating in the Okanagan TSA. The Forest Service paid Crown Zellerbach $50,000 to organize the task force, draw up its reports and provide the technical expertise, including computer modelling and planning systems.

By August of the following year, Crown Zellerbach had prepared a report that analyzed the timber supply and the various silvicultural treatments which could be appied to the predominantly lodgepole pine forests, projected the yield increases these treatments would provide and calculated the costs of the treatments. The yield responses upon which all these calculations rested were taken from a 1979 Crown Zellerbach research report, *Intensive Management of Lodgepole Pine and Associated Species*.[11] The data for this report had been drawn from three sources: a series of seven U. S. research reports (none of them related to lodgepole pine, and only one, on western hemlock, from the Pacific Northwest); Forest Service inventory data, and reports on two Crown Zellerbach research plots in one Okanagan drainage system that were set up in the 1960s to test the responses to chemical thinning and fertilization. The report noted that extrapolating results from only two areas of one drainage system was questionable. This caution did not deter the Forest Service when, a few months later, it accepted these yield predictions for use on Crown land. And by the time they appeared in the analysis prepared for the task force, all cautions had disappeared and the predictions were presented as a legitimate, acceptable basis for determining the gains to be obtained from spacing and fertilizing throughout the TSA. The report did not cite the source of its projections for gains from other treatments, but concluded that together "the net effect of these improvements across all planning units in the TSA, comparing basic to full intensive management, is a yield increase from 2.07 to 3.55 cubic metres per hectare [29.0 to 49.7 cubic feet per acre] per year." This represents a 71.5 per cent increase in yield.

The report recommended a course of action of which the above analysis was an integral part. The problem was where to find an additional 900 000 m³ (31.8 million cubic feet) of wood a year in order to keep the area's processing mills operating at present levels of production. The solution offered was to increase the annual harvest within the TSA by the required amount, 900 000 m³ — a 30 per cent increase in the allowable annual cut. In addition to keeping the mills supplied, this level of harvest would supply the government with an additional $12 million a year in stumpage revenue. The intensive management program required to offset the long-term timber supply deficit created by such an increase in logging was estimated to cost between $2 million and $5 million more than the $1 million currently being spent on silviculture in the area.

It is difficult to determine which is the more remarkable feature of this proposal: that a future timber shortage could be avoided by logging more trees now, or that such detailed timber yield and financial projections should be extrapolated from such a minute amount of marginally relevant research data. Apparently the Forest Service was not convinced. It established the allowable annual cut at 2 700 000 m^3 (95.4 million cubic feet) — a decrease of about 7 per cent.

A financial analysis of a forestry investment encounters yet a third difficulty in establishing a rate of interest which reflects the return on costs over time. If private silvicultural investments have to compete in the money markets for financing, they must offer returns comparable to those obtained from other investments, currently 3 to 5 per cent after discounting inflation. There are a number of arguments advanced for accepting lower rates from forestry investments: they are safe, the risks from fire and other destructive agents being relatively small; they are long-term, decreasing or eliminating the need for reinvestment at regular intervals; a long-term view of money indicates a worth closer to 2 per cent after inflation, and after a certain point the investments can provide returns from thinnings or partial harvests. But in the Pacific Northwest, and particularly in British Columbia, where there is no history of silviculture and little experience with long-term investment in forestry, it is extremely difficult to raise private capital on the open market for such purposes.

Many involved in forestry consider the matter of interest rates to be largely academic, since most silvicultural expenditures in British Columbia involve treatment of publicly owned land at public expense. At one extreme there are those who argue that society should take a long, broad view and undertake the necessary programs regardless of interest rates. At the other extreme is the argument that the money would be better spent on other programs — education, health, highways — letting the forests look after themselves. Somewhere in the middle are those who suggest that a real long-term rate of between 2 and 3 per cent is reasonable for calculating costs and benefits. Just how academic or irrelevant the interest rate may be can better be judged after one or two examples of cost-benefit analysis.

The B. C. Forest Service's intensive silviculture project for the 1980–85 period, discussed in chapter six, is projected to produce 9 250 000 m^3 (326.7 million cubic feet) a year at rotation, for an expenditure of $40.5 million.For the sake of simplicity, let us accept these figures without quibble — no questions raised about the 3 400 000 m^3 (120 million cubic feet) to be achieved by spacing and fertilizing, no skepticism over the 4 250 000 m^3 (150 million cubic feet) saved by firefighting programs, or the 1 600 000 m^3 (56.5 million cubic feet) found as the result of battling insects and diseases.

Again for simplicity's sake, let us assume a rotation period of precisely seventy-two years. Overall, this is a generous assumption for B. C. forests, but it is useful for purposes of example since capital invested at 1 per cent doubles in seventy-two years; invested at 2 per cent, it will quadruple in that time. Furthermore, the capital will quadruple in real value because the 2 per cent represents a real interest rate, that is, 2 per cent over whatever inflation rates may be during that time. Economists refer to this analytical tool as the "banking alternative," since anyone with a little astuteness and a lot of capital to invest can make just such an arrangement with a bank. Therefore, it represents the true break-even point of an investment: if the investor does not realize 2 per cent over inflation, he should have banked his money instead. Yet another advantage to this kind of analysis is that it expresses everything in terms of the base year — in this case, 1980, the first year of the intensive silvicultural program. Thus future returns can be directly compared with present returns for the same commodity, as we shall see.

A cost-benefit analysis based on these figures tells us that if after seventy-two years the B. C. Forest Service produces 9 250 000 m^3 (326.7 million cubic feet) by spending $40.5 million in 1980 — a cost of $4.38 per m^3 ($13 per cunit) — that wood in 2052 will have to be worth four times the 1980 investment: $162 million, or $17.52 per m^3 ($50 per cunit) in 1980 dollars. Even more to the point, if the government found it worthwhile to invest $4.38 per m^3 on a seventy-two-year investment, it should have been receiving at least $17.52 in stumpage throughout 1980. Only a product worth $17.52 in 1980 can justify a 1980 investment of $4.38 over seventy-two years. If stumpage in 1980 was more than $17.52 ($50 per cunit), the government stands to make a profit on the silviculture project; if less, a loss.

In 1980 the provincial across-the-board stumpage rate was $6.76 per m^3 ($19 per cunit). By this analysis, the investment is obviously a disaster in purely economic terms. If the taxpayer must wait for seventy-two years to get $6.76 for a $4.38 investment, the government should spend part of the money on pocket calculators instead. But what are the alternatives?

The first and most likely alternative is that the government will talk a lot. Specifically, it can point to the ancillary economic benefits of the employment generated by such a labour-intensive program, the indirect employment created by the enhanced economic activity, the reduced welfare rolls, the increased tax base and so on. This sounds good until the other choices are examined.

Another course of action would be total inaction. The government could not only abandon the project but it could also refuse to collect the $40.5 million in taxes. The economic effect of leaving this purchasing power in the hands of the citizenry is unknowable; it would depend on the prevailing mood of the populace at the time, expressed by economists as the "marginal propensity to consume" and the "marginal propensity to save." Consumption has a buoyant effect on the economy, dampened somewhat by purchases of foreign-made goods. (That caveat would apply equally to the newly employed in the silviculture program.) Savings would also be useful, perhaps even more so, depending on the method of investment: whether through insurance companies (it makes a difference whether the companies are Canadian or foreign) or by banking (again it matters whether the money goes into British Columbia or national banks and on the foreign commitments of the banks). Despite these variables, the net effect on the B. C. economy would be substantial. Of course, there would be no enhancement of timber production.

Another interesting option available to the government would be to consider the "banking alternative" as a real option

Figure 4

Economic Analysis of Intensive Forest Management Program

TREATMENT		Years to Harvest (Rotation)	Yield Increase Due to Treatment[1] (m^3 per ha)	Value of Yield Increase at Rotation[2]	Treatment Cost per Hectare	Interest Cost on Interest		Return on Investment (%)
						At 2%	At 5%	
PLANTING	Fir	96	578 m^3	$42,674	$782	$5,234	$84,602	4–4.5%
	Pine	96	208 m^3	$1,270	$782	$5,234	$84,602	0.5%
SPACING	Fir	76	173 m^3	$12,800	$633	$2,851	$25,810	4–4.5%
	Pine	76	62 m^3	$381	$633	$2,851	$25,810	0%
FERTILIZING	Fir	76	15 m^3	$1,110	$142	$640	$5,790	2.5–3%
	Pine	76	5 m^3	$33	$142	$640	$5,790	0%

1 Yield increase is found by multiplying the number of years the stand grows after treatment by the mean annual increment due to the treatment. The figures used for Douglas-fir are a ninety-six-year rotation with a mean annual increment of 6.02 m^3 per ha (84.3 cubic feet per acre), the average for a medium site land in the coastal portions of the Vancouver Forest Region. The lodgepole pine figures are a ninety-six-year rotation with a mean annual increment of 2.17 m^3 per ha (30.4 cubic feet per acre), average for medium site land in the Kamloops Forest Region. Is is assumed that fertilizer is applied to land already spaced, with both treatments undertaken the same year.

2 Value of increased yields is calculated by assuming a 1.8 per cent annual increase in stumpage values over the rotations. Thus, fir stumpage in the Vancouver Region is calculated to increase from the 1980 average of $13.32 per m^3 ($38 per cunit) to $73.84 per m^3 ($211 per cunit) ninety-six years later. Pine in the Kamloops Regions is assumed to increase from $1.10 per m^3 ($3 per cunit) to $6.10 per m^3 ($17 per cunit).

rather than as an economic abstraction. For $40.5 million for seventy-two years, any bank would offer at least 2 per cent over inflation and would agree to use the money solely within the province. In fact, the government could do with the money the very thing it does not do with timber sales — deposit the money with the highest bidder. The bank would not lend that money directly to borrowers. Throughout the western world a different method is used: banks purchase some form of treasury bill from either the central government or the central bank; using this as collateral, they may then lend out as much as ten times that amount to their customers. In other words, depending on the federal banking policies of the moment, that $40.5 million could inject as much as $405 million into the B. C. economy. Some of that would go for consumer credit, but most would finance industrial expansion. Whatever the proportion, the economic effect would completely eclipse that of the silviculture program. But again, no forest enhancement.

Of course, there is one other option open to the government, an option that might make the silviculture investment well worthwhile: that is the simple expedient of collecting the economic rent for the timber. If timber had an economic rent of more than $17.52 per m³ ($50 per cunit), the program becomes economically justifiable and is subject only to the normal hazards of any long-range investment.

A slightly different approach can also serve to illustrate the problems involved in economic analyses of silvicultural expenditures. The following examination of the $50 million intensive forest management program launched in 1979 by the Canadian and B. C. governments is theoretical in that it is not an analysis of particular treatments applied to specific tracts of forest. Figure 4 contains estimates of the volume increases obtained from a number of management practices, the initial costs of these treatments and the accumulated interest charges until the stands are harvested, the value of the increased yields and the financial return on the investment. Unlike the first analysis, this one incorporates an assumption that lumber prices will continue to rise in real terms over the rotation, at the historical rate of 1.8 per cent. The treatment costs used were obtained by averaging the costs encountered in the first two years of the federal-provincial program: 7800 ha (19,273 acres) of backlog reforestation was accomplished at a cost of $6.1 million ($782.05 per ha; $316.50 per acre); 21 000 ha (51,890 acres) were juvenile spaced at a cost of $13.3 million ($633.33 per ha; $256.31 per acre), and 19 700 ha (48,678 acres) were aerial fertilized for $2.8 million ($142.13 per ha; $57.52 per acre).

The table is based on calculations for a hectare of coastal Douglas-fir and a hectare of Interior lodgepole pine, both on medium sites. The rotation and annual growth were obtained from Forest Service inventory statistics and stumpage values from the Forest Service's 1981 annual report. Embodied in the calculations were a number of assumptions about yield responses: the backlog reforestation was done on land containing no established commercial species and would have a 100 per cent survival rate; the spacing would yield a 30 per cent increase in volume, and the fertilization a 2 per cent volume increase. In addition to the historical price rise of a real 1.8 per cent, it was also assumed that all the timber obtained from the stands would be used for lumber, rather than pulp- or plywood.

These calculations include a number of distortions, which in themselves underline the difficulty in obtaining a reasonable financial analysis. It is unlikely, for instance, that such a wide spread would develop between the stumpage values of Douglas-fir and lodgepole pine. To some degree, the present difference in stumpage for these two species reflects their different qualities: Douglas-fir is in greater demand, which pushes its market and stumpage values up in relation to pine. Over the next ninety-six years, however, it would be normal to expect a continuation of this price spread to lead to the substitution of pine for fir, thereby lowering the relative value of fir and increasing that of pine. A further factor is that the managed stands of the two species under consideration will be qualitatively more alike than wood currently available. Second-growth Douglas-fir will not be worth as much per cubic metre as first-growth fir; the difference may not be so marked in the case of pine. If nothing else, these considerations illustrate the difficulty in establishing spending priorities.

In addition, there are a considerable number of financial factors that are not included in these calculations. A variety of costs, not always specific to particular treatments nor always predictable, are usually involved. There are administrative expenses, which in the 1980–81 fiscal year cost the Forest Service more than 10 per cent of its silvicultural budget and a full seven times the amount spent on inventory and research work.[12] These costs are a major and conveniently ignored factor in financial considerations concerning expanded intensive management programs. If history teaches us anything, it is that bureaucracies expand geometrically in proportion to the undertakings they administer. Parkinson's law will be obeyed.

There are some intensive management practices which incur expenses not usually charged to the treatments. Spacing a forest increases the fire hazard for several years until the slash has settled to the forest floor and rotted. This hazard raises costs, either in the form of increased fire losses or accelerated protection costs. Arithmetical increases in spaced hectares lead to geometrical increases in protection costs. Widely scattered stands of spaced forest land constitute one degree of hazard: fire will move through a spaced area many times faster than it will travel in an unspaced forest. From a protection point of view, the untreated forest surrounding an area of young spaced trees is the first line of defence; in times of high fire hazard — every summer — it is considered virtually impossible to extinguish a fire in a spaced slash area for up to five years after the spacing treatment. When a large number of spacing projects are undertaken in one area, the hazard rises to an entirely new plane, as do the costs of providing protection services for the area.

Forestry financial calculations do not usually include a failure factor, but some of the trees planted each year do not survive; not all the areas brushed remain free of unwanted growth; increases in growth do not automatically follow spacing and fertilizing. Statistically, some of these factors are known and predictable but tend to be ignored because they are not considered normal or acceptable. In 1976 a report on plantation survival in the Nelson Forest Region stated that during the previous thirteen years about 50 per cent of the trees put in the ground died. Between 1962 and 1969, a third of the Douglas-fir plantations in the Vancouver Forest Region above the 600 m (1970 foot) elevation level did not survive. Some areas have been planted four and five times.

Yet another financial factor must be included in the calculations: the value of the immediate increase in the allowable annual cut which becomes possible because of expected future increases in yield. This is the "allowable cut effect" referred to in chapter three. It is argued that the effect is a legitimate factor if two conditions prevail: if there is an abundance of mature timber available in the sustained yield unit where the silvicultural treatment is applied, and if there are harvesting constraints aimed at sustaining an even flow of timber throughout the period being analyzed. These conditions exist in almost all parts of British Columbia.

The allowable cut effect is easily explained: the annual cut in an area is equivalent to the annual growth of immature trees plus the amount obtained by dividing the total mature volume in the area by the rotation. If the annual growth rate is increased, then the annual cut can be increased by an equivalent amount without, at some point in the future, reducing the sustainable yield. As indicated in the illustration earlier, spacing a medium site hectare of Douglas-fir in the Vancouver Forest Region at age twenty years will theoretically produce an increased annual growth rate of more than 2 m^3 (70.6 cubic feet). In order to sustain the minimum allowable annual cut for the Timber Supply Area, it is not necessary that the 2 m^3 a year accumulate until the spaced stand is harvested seventy-six years later. Instead, the annual harvest of mature timber in the TSA can be increased by 2 m^3 for every hectare of medium site land spaced within the TSA.

The economics of this approach, without taking into account real increases in stumpage values, are the same as receiving an annual annuity equivalent to the stumpage value of the increased yield — in the above case, $26.64 per year. If the "annuities" over the rotation are evaluated at the same compound interest rates as those used to calculate the interest charges on the silvicultural investment, the returns are altered enormously. In this instance, the accumulated stumpage value of the increased allowable annual cut, evaluated at 5 per cent for seventy-six years, would total $22,251.33. If the returns on the $633.00 per ha ($253.20 per acre) cost of spacing the stand of fir are calculated in this manner, the investment pays interest at 5.4 per cent per year, compared with the 4 or 4.5 per cent indicated earlier. There is, however, an even more lucrative way of calculating the allowable cut effect. Instead of merely increasing the annual harvest of mature timber in the sustained yield unit by 2 m^3 for each hectare spaced, the accumulated yield increase of 173 m^3 (6110 cubic feet) projected for the treatment can be harvested at once. With a stumpage value of $13.32 per m^3 ($38 per cunit) the return is $2,304.36 — an astounding 364 per cent.

This type of analysis is implicit in many of the arguments advanced for increases in silvicultural expenditures. It is essentially the position taken in Crown Zellerbach's Okanagan TSA proposal, rejected by the Forest Service. The risk involved by including the allowable cut effect in allowable cut calculations is that the intensive management practices instituted will not produce the predicted yield increases, and that at some point in the future the annual cut will have to be severely reduced. In practice, the Forest Service has established for each silvicultural treatment a schedule of productivity gains which is quite conservative when compared to many of the more widely held predictions. For inventory purposes, and in calculating annual harvests, gains of 10 per cent are calculated for juvenile spacing, and 1.5 to 5 per cent for fertilization; other treatments are calculated on a site-specific basis.

One of the reasons the allowable cut effect remains a rather obscure theory is that even with the additional returns which this approach provides for expenditures on intensive management, there are still much cheaper ways for industry to obtain additional timber supplies — at least in the short run. As calculated above, an expenditure of $633 on spacing will yield an additional 2 m^3 of timber a year. But, as indicated in chapter four's discussion of the mechanisms of timber allocation, quota can be purchased in the Vancouver Forest Region for $25 to $45 per m^3 ($70 to $130 per cunit) — about a tenth what it costs to grow. Buying and selling quota does not produce any more timber, but if the primary concern is merely to obtain quick timber, the most profitable course for a timber company is to purchase the harvest rights from somebody else rather than spend the money attempting to increase the productivity of forests it already owns or controls. Of course, this does not prevent that same company (and others like it, as well as forest industry unions and some professional foresters) from trying to convince the government that it is perfectly reasonable to spend public funds on programs to increase productivity.

The time spans involved in forest management make the enterprise unique in one other way. When a new forest is established, capital expenditures are locked up throughout the forest's early years; it is not possible to realize any return by liquidating saplings. Eventually, the trees reach a size at which they have some market value, and this market value increases with time. During this stage, some of the fixed capital can be recovered without loss by thinning or harvesting parts of the forest. It is similar to a savings account or term investment, in which the interest can be left to accumulate or can be drawn off at various periods and used elsewhere. But while there are advantages to this type of investment, there is also a danger: at a time of urgent need for money, the forest might be stripped clean for whatever it might bring. It was for this reason that Fernow insisted, ". . . . not only capital, but economic capacity and character and moral strength are required to maintain a systematic forest management and withstand the temptation to realize 'a quick and immediate profit'."[13]

In present practice, economic analysis plays only a small part in determining forest management expenditures on public forest lands. This is true even in cases where the primary consideration is the production of timber and is largely so because of the imprecise nature of the data available and the unique nature of the enterprise. When other, nontimber uses of the forest are being examined, however, economic considerations become important as a negative tool for discouraging action. After observing this phenomenon for many years, Marion Clawson, one of the most respected and thoughtful resource economists in North America, commented:

> As one contemplates the application of economic analysis and the use of the test of economic efficiency for publicly owned forests, the question immediately arises: How far are we willing to abide by the results of such tests? The enthusiasm of forest users for economic analysis applied to a publicly owned forest seems to be highly correlated with their expectation of the results of such analysis. If a group thinks economic analysis will

> show its desired use of the forest as the economically most valuable, then it is likely to support such analysis more enthusiastically than if it suspects that some other use will produce a higher net economic return.[14]

Economic analysis is clearly inadequate as a tool for deciding how forests should be managed. In practical terms, it serves as little more than another weapon in the arsenals of the various interest groups. For this reason, it may be more enlightening to come at the issue from another perspective and consider who should be in charge of forest management decisions.

TEN

Who Runs the Forests?

THE ESSENTIAL ORGANIZATIONAL CHARACTERISTIC of the forest industry can be described with a single word: bureaucracy. Whatever the sector, whether public/government or private; whatever the position, whether professional, managerial or entrepreneurial; whatever the status of the worker, whether union or nonunion; whatever the component, whether operational, research, educational or communicative — hierarchical bureaucratic organizational structures overlie them all. The administrative apparatuses of most phases of the industry parallel each other: the Forest Service bureaucracy is mirrored by the corporate bureaucracies, which are in turn reflected by the labour bureaucracries.

These bureaucracies tend increasingly to dominate the functions for which they were established, not to mention the individuals who work within them. There are few free agents in the forest industry, which is ironic considering it has historically attracted staunch individualists. Yet individuals have become overshadowed; bureaucracies have acquired personalities of their own, behaving like actors or dancers engaged in ritualistic performances. The script changes slowly over time; the roles are constantly recast; but the scenes remain unchanged, as do the essential natures of the organizations.

Insiders, the people who think of themselves as "working in the forest industry," relate to each other in fairly definable ways, in both individual and collective senses. These interrelationships constitute the internal politics of forestry — at least as seen from "outside." One of the characteristic differences between those who work in the industry and those who do not is that insiders do not usually consider their interactions to be political, but rather see them as technical, working relationships. Within the industry, "politics" is generally understood to include all the influences on the industry from the "outside," and is widely considered to be an irrational factor.

The largest component of the industry is the private sector — corporations, companies, individuals, indeed everyone not paid directly out of public revenues. During 1979, there were about 54,000 loggers working in Canada, more than 23,000 of them in British Columbia. These people were working in the forests (as opposed to the processing mills) and for the most part were employed by the private sector. In the same year, another 250,000 Canadians were employed in the processing plants. During the same period in Washington and Oregon, 159,000 people were employed at essentially the same tasks — harvesting and processing timber.

Almost all of the work force employed in this sector is employed by large corporations. These are organized in a fashion that was unknown until recent times. Typically, they are complex structures: they are vertically integrated, in that they perform the various stages of production from growing trees to harvesting, processing and marketing. Increasingly they are, as individual entities, part of a larger corporate structure that may or may not include other forest corporations.

The ultimate justification for forest companies turning themselves into diversified multinational corporations, as did MacMillan Bloedel, or becoming part of larger corporate enterprises, as did most other large timber companies, is that they would acquire the financial stability and strength needed for long-term forest management. This argument was central to Fernow's thesis and underlay many of the explanations proffered during the restructuring of the industry from the 1950s onward.

What actually occurred was a somewhat different matter. The recently published history of MacMillan Bloedel casts an interesting light upon the nature of a modern, integrated, diversified forest corporation.[1] The corporate entity now known as MacMillan Bloedel was put together in the late 1950s, partly in response to the growth and development of other large timber corporations in British Columbia. Essentially, it was a merger of a timber marketing company (H. R.

MacMillan Exports), a lumber company (Bloedel, Stewart and Welch) and a pulp and paper company (Powell River Company). These three companies were among the strongest, most efficient and most capable in the province, with their primary owners, all of whom had grown up in the forest industry, actively participating in their management. The major figure, H. R. MacMillan, a student of Fernow, was the province's first chief forester and one of the main builders of the province's export industry. The new corporation was now the largest operating company and the largest holder of timber rights in the province.

Shortly after the merger, MacMillan did a curious thing: as de facto head of the company, he replaced himself with a complete outsider to the industry, J. V. Clyne. A former justice of the B. C. Supreme Court, Clyne spent fourteen years as chairman of MB, transforming it from a B. C. forest company into a major multinational corporation. MB, said Clyne, "must adopt new and more flexible concepts of corporate management that are tailored to rapid expansion and change."[2] His objectives were organizational or bureaucratic in nature, neither derived from nor necessarily appropriate to forests and the forest industry. "When we think of a multinational, or global, company today, we think of a number of subsidiaries scattered through several countries all reporting to a parent company which is the single profit centre for all of them."[3] Clyne's management style was the sort devised by hired efficiency "experts," combined with a ruthless purging of many management practices and personnel inherited from the parent companies. The locally oriented, low-key traditions of the Powell River Company were especially attacked, the blood-letting becoming so vicious that the company's former owner-managers, the Foleys, publicly withdrew from any participation in MB.

Clyne had managed to use the assets of MB, essentially its timber rights in British Columbia, as leverage to create a global corporation that was able to move from forest-based industries into a number of other activities. It is often argued by critics of the industry, particularly those from the political left, that during this period — the 1960s and early 1970s — the MB expansion with the concomitant bureaucratic growth developed by its management experts was financed by the economic rent it was able to avoid paying the government, as well as the profits that it did not distribute as shareholder dividends.

Among these shareholders was the irrepressible Gordon Gibson. As with many formerly independent forest operators who had cashed in their timber rights, Gibson had invested in MB stock. As the Clyne program gathered momentum, an ever-growing portion of MB ownership fell into the hands of similar corporations, also managed by professionals who thought as Clyne did. During the 1966 annual meeting, Gibson accused Clyne and the MB directors of funding their expansion program out of profits that should have been paid to shareholders and of plundering the corporation's timber assets. Clyne was not impressed. Gibson, along with many others, disposed of his MB shares; control and direction of the company clearly had gone into the hands of the professional corporate managers.

The cracks in the edifice did not begin to show until the mid-1970s, a few years after Clyne retired. MB's transportation needs had always been handled by the subsidiary Canadian Transport Company, which chartered ships to haul MB-produced lumber, pulp and paper around the world. Its sole function was to serve MB's shipping needs. In the early 1970s, its management, with the encouragement of MB management, decided to turn the company into a freewheeling transportation company in its own right, chartering, building or buying ships and competing for general cargoes in addition to those from MB. By 1975, when the international shipping business went into a general decline, Canadian Transport found itself committed to a number of long-term leases on ships, but with no cargoes to carry. During that year, the MB transportation company lost $46 million, while MB itself lost close to $20 million.

These reverses were part of the general economic decline of that year and the beginning of a corporation-wide crisis. While the market rose to record heights during the next four years, MB went through a massive reorganization and a change of direction. Heads rolled at the top of the hierarchy, the head office bureaucracy was drastically thinned and the financial resources of the company were redirected towards modernizing and expanding the physical assets of the corporation's base

— its forest industry operations in British Columbia. However, these alterations should not be mistaken for a shift away from the corporation's monolithic tendencies. Rather, they were a honing of the corporate bureaucracy and a purging of some of the contradictory elements held over from earlier years. Power and control were consolidated, one of the results being yet more mergers and takeover bids. Yet the reconstituted MB was no more able, and was in many ways less able, than most other forest corporations in British Columbia to cope with the market decline of the early 1980s.

It is now rare for such forest corporations to be owned by individuals. The major shareholders are other corporations. Within the past decade in Canada, ownership or control of a number of these corporate entities has even been acquired by provincial governments or paragovernment agencies. This may have had less effect on the nature of the corporations than on that of the governments. The tendency is towards the corporate state rather than a socialized industry.

Another feature of this corporate structure is that it has international scope, though for the most part it is concentrated into a continental framework. Historically, one of the most enduring characteristics of the industry is multinationality. From the very beginning, when the eastern forests were logged to build the European sailing fleets, the industry has been owned, controlled or its products consumed far from the site of the actual forests which make it all possible. What has changed recently is that these corporate entities have become more pervasive — the MacMillan Bloedel insignia is found in the bathroom as well as in the bush, from British Columbia to Brazil.

The result is that a corporation such as MacMillan Bloedel is, paradoxically, an abstraction, almost a nonentity. True, it has many concrete component parts, most of which are involved with trees and the products of trees. The corporation can be broken down into units as basic as a logging division or a tugboat company, and as complex as a global marketing network. A notable characteristic of such a corporation is that it requires, as one of its components, a large central management group or head office to co-ordinate the activities of its operational components. Yet few corporations operating in North American forests are actually autonomous operations. Theoretically, of course, they are: they hold separate timber licences, their trucks are painted different colours and so on. But beyond a certain point most of them are part of a larger, more nebulous supracorporate structure — a vaguely defined, largely unnamed and constantly changing level of organization. The nature of this superstructure is indicated in some of the realignments of corporate connections that occurred between 1978 and 1981.

At the beginning of this period, the largest single shareholder in MacMillan Bloedel was Canadian Pacific, the one-time railway company which became directly involved in the forest industry in 1905, when it purchased the Esquimalt & Nanaimo Railway and its huge landholdings on Vancouver Island. In 1974 CP traded some of this land for shares in MB, after which CP purchased more shares from the MacMillan and Bloedel families.

In 1978 Canada's third largest forest company, Domtar, was one-fifth owned by the Argus Corporation, orginally established by E. P. Taylor. Taylor had established B. C. Forest Products in 1946 and for seven years all its timber was marketed by the H. R. MacMillan Export Company, a parent company of MB. A convoluted series of transfers began in late 1978, with MB obtaining the Argus share of Domtar and making an offer for another 30 per cent of Domtar. At the same time, Domtar's directors made an offer to buy at least 51 per cent of MB shares. To further add to the situation, CP made a public bid for 51 per cent control of MB. At this point, the B. C. government entered the scene and made it clear that, whatever arrangements were being made to restructure the industry, they could not include changes which would cause MB to lose its B. C. identity, whatever that might be. Both Domtar and CP pulled back (the B. C. government threatening to exercise its power to cancel MB's Tree Farm Licences if either took over control) and within a year, MB sold its interest in Domtar. The following year, 1980, CP sold its interest in MB to the B. C. Resources Investment Corporation (BCRIC), a unique corporate entity established and controlled by the B. C. government and involved in the forest industry through its ownership of the various forest operations which the NDP government had bought several years earlier. Within a year, BCRIC (pronounced "brick") and MB proposed to the government that BCRIC turn over to MB the ownership of Canadian Cellulose (one of the ten largest forest companies in British Columbia) in exchange for another 17 per cent of MB shares. Premier Bill Bennett refused to go along with the suggestion. Apparently the government rejection had more to do with MB's acquisition of Canadian Cellulose than BCRIC's takeover of MB, because BCRIC followed up with a public offer for MB shares, which was followed by other corporate manoeuvres.

One of these manoeuvres involved the Alberta Energy Corporation, partly owned by the provincial government. Another was a public offering for MB shares by Noranda Mines. At this point, Noranda owned 28 per cent of B. C. Forest Products and half of Northwood Pulp and Timber, another major B. C. forest company. In the end, the government backed the Noranda bid and BCRIC disposed of its MB interests, giving Noranda 49 per cent of MB. Within a few months, 42 per cent of Noranda was taken over by Brascade Resources. Thirty per cent of Brascade was owned by a quasi-public Quebec agency which manages that province's pension funds and which also happens to be the company to which MB had sold its interest in Domtar. The remainder of Brascade is owned by Brascan, a corporation that shares with MB the ownership of Embrasca, a 121 000 ha (300,000 acre) tree farm in Brazil.

Early in 1980, B. C. Forest Products bought Elk River Timber from Scott Paper and Crown Zellerbach for $151 million. At the time, this was looked upon as an astounding sum — only a year earlier, Elk River Timber management believed the company to be worth $45 to $50 million. B. C. Forest Products was then itself partially owned by Scott Paper — 26 per cent of the shares being held by Brunswick Pulp and Paper, which was jointly owned by Scott Paper and the Mead Corporation. In effect, the purchase was a convenient transfer of capital from B. C. Forest Products to Scott Paper, which then had enough funds to underwrite the costs of a mill expansion that enabled it to obtain, in 1982, a Tree Farm Licence for growing cottonwood on lands in the Fraser Valley, Bute Inlet and Kingcome Inlet.

The foregoing is only a sample of the action occurring on the supracorporate level during the postwar period. The holding companies or conglomerates have been around for a long time, and the only major new feature at this level of organization is the government, or quasi-government, corporate entities such as BCRIC, Alberta Energy or the Spanish goverment agency that shares with MB the ownership of a newsprint mill in New Brunswick.

This is a global network, in which the connections are sometimes obscure, but nevertheless real. When in 1982, after a decade of trying, Crown Zellerbach finally managed to unload its Canadian operations, it had taken the rare step of publicly announcing that the company was for sale. Crown Canada was taken over a few weeks later by Fletcher Challenge, a New Zealand conglomerate formed a year earlier when a number of forest, agricultural, manufacturing, construction, real estate and financial companies joined forces. One of these was Tasman Pulp and Paper, previously owned in part by Reed International and the Bowater Corporation, both of which have owned or shared forest industry operations in eastern Canada.

Ultimately, all these connections rely upon people, the individuals who occupy the key boardroom and executive positions. Increasingly, these people are professional managers, as are the people who staff the administrative or management positions of the forest companies. The changing nature of the corporate structures, essentially the creation of the corporate forest bureaucracies, is a process which has been closely tied to concentration of forest resource ownership, the decline of the competitive timber market and the growing *idea* of forest management.

The major forest companies in North America were almost all formed out of the merging, combining or consolidating of timber harvesting companies and lumber companies that controlled significant amounts of standing timber. In the United States, and to a minor extent in parts of eastern Canada, much of this timber was found on private land. In most of Canada, particularly in British Columbia and to a lesser degree in the western and northwestern United States, this control took the form of leases on publicly owned land. Some companies, like Weyerhaeuser, have grown from small operations that usually own timberland and mills into much larger integrated corporations. Others, like B. C. Forest Products, were created suddenly with large amounts of "outside" capital that was used to buy up a number of companies along with their timber rights, usually on public land. It is this latter group that has tended to develop the most complex and sophisticated — but not necessarily productive — bureaucracies.

By and large, the companies that went into the making of corporations such as MacMillan Bloedel, Western Forest Products, B. C. Forest Products or any one of a dozen others, were efficient, well-managed operations. In the 1940s and 1950s, when many of these corporations were formed, the logging and lumbering companies then controlling much of the timber supply were the survivors of a depression and a war. To a much greater extent than today, they had been forced to compete for their timber. Characteristically, the managers, including the senior managers and the owners, were people who had gained their knowledge of the forest industry, from bush to balance sheet, from first-hand experience. A typical logging operation would be managed by someone who had started out, years before, setting chokers; a mill by someone who had worked on the greenchain. If that person happened to be the offspring of the company owner, it was almost essential that he legitimize his position in the management structure by spending a certain amount of time employed in the lower decks of the operation, learning the forest business from the "roots" up.

Over the past twenty years or so, virtually the entire management structure of the forest corporations has been taken over by a class of professional managers. The hierarchy of managers, superintendents and foremen that managed most logging operations even a decade or two ago, and whose authority was derived from experience, has been replaced by a group of engineers and foresters whose qualifications lie in the arcane knowledge they have acquired in formal, academic settings. This evolution has had some significant consequences.

One result has been the creation of a fairly rigid class structure within the forest companies. There is a labour group of wage earners and a salaried management group. Both have affiliations outside the particular corporation that employs them; the managers belong to professional associations, the workers to labour unions — essentially one union, the International Woodworkers of America (IWA). There is practically no mobility between these two groups; in fact, there are many rules and conventions prohibiting such mobility. A logging engineer operating a machine is enough to provoke a full-scale union walkout in most logging camps. By the same token, a faller who decided not to cut certain trees, for environmental or other reasons, would most likely be packing his gear the same day.

In most logging shows, the only place where the two groups mix is at the foreman level. These people have worked up through the ranks and their experiential knowledge puts them in a position to mediate between the professional managers and the relatively uneducated work force. It is rare for any of them to move up through the management ranks, so in a sense they are in dead-end jobs — a barrier of professional qualifications has been placed across the ladder of promotion. A consequence has been an enormous growth in the numbers of such positions relative to the workers they supervise. Twenty years ago, a forty-man road-building crew in a logging division would be managed by one foreman who reported to a superintendent. Since then, the superintendent has been replaced by a road engineer and the same sized road crew has three foremen plus a supervising foreman whose task is to keep track of the other three.

A similar growth has occurred in the ranks of management and among forest workers. The management bureaucracy has expanded vertically and is located chiefly in the head offices and regional offices of the various corporations. The marginal utility of this sector of the corporate world is indicated by the widely held belief in MB during the early 1980s, after almost one thousand head office jobs had been eliminated, that these reductions in bureaucracy led to increases in productivity.

At the labour level, such growth is known as featherbedding, though the IWA calls it job protection. Until recent years, job security was almost nonexistent in the forest industry, for at the best of times logging is seasonal work. Many logging operations are as transient as their workers, moving from one site to another, requiring different systems and equipment. In most cases there is a fine line between eliminating a job out of necessity or out of short-term expediency. The legacy of several decades of unsafe, insecure and uncomfortable working conditions is a general union contract, supplemented in each logging division with a smorgasbord of side agreements that can be, and often are, used as a means of creating unnecessary jobs and spending large sums of money for very small amounts of productive work. There has been constant technological change over the last forty years; the complex and highly mechanized nature of a modern logging operation creates endless opportunities for such "job creation." Most jobs consist of operating machines and are defined in those terms — in a log sorting ground, a worker's job description is not that of log sorter, but rather, stacker operator. The worker is hired to run a machine that was designed and purchased to sort and pile logs. Any operation, such as log sorting, is likely to have a number of small tasks that various machines cannot perform, requiring a few minutes of human work a day — for example, placing the strapping around bundles of very small logs and broken pieces. Common sense might dictate that one of the equipment operators dismount from his machine and perform the task; but the contract between the company and the union will dictate that the operator be paid extra for this work, or even that it be classified as a separate job.

In British Columbia, a major contributor to the growth of corporate bureaucracy is the appraisal-based stumpage system which has almost completely replaced the open market for publicly owned timber. The forest industry, particularly the larger corporations, pays stumpage at a rate determined by subtracting production costs from selling price. Thus, if production costs rise, the agency selling timber and collecting stumpage absorbs the loss, particularly in times of good markets. During the generally favourable markets which have existed since this system came into existence, it has been relatively simple for the costs of an expanded corporate bureaucracy to become absorbed by the stumpage system — a situation partly reflected in the high stumpage rates paid at public timber auctions in Washington and Oregon and the lower rates paid by corporations obtaining timber from public lands in British Columbia.

A measure of the costs involved in the very existence of this extensive corporate bureaucracy can be obtained from a look at another component of the private sector, the so-called independent market and contract loggers. Very few of the first group remain — the number of operators who own the rights to the timber they log and sell has declined drastically during the past thirty to forty years. The legendary independent logger of the type portrayed in Ken Kesey's novel *Sometimes a Great Notion,* or Gordon Gibson's *Bull of the Woods,* is now rare in British Columbia. Most of them either sold their timber rights to the large forest corporations or were squeezed out. By the late 1970s, independent loggers, some owning relatively small sawmills, accounted for no more than 15 per cent of the timber harvested off Crown lands in British Columbia. Their numbers, if not their timber supply, have swelled since 1978, a result of provisions in the new Forests Act to enhance a small business sector in the industry.

By far the largest component of the "independent" sector of the industry are the contract loggers. The contracting sector undertakes close to half the work performed in the portion of the industry controlled by the integrated companies. To some extent, contractors owe their existence to a provision of the new Forests Act which requires that half of the harvesting on Tree Farm Licences be undertaken by smaller, independent logging firms. More recently, the contractors' position has been strengthened by their widely recognized ability to work efficiently — essentially their ability to do any given job much more cheaply than would their counterparts within the bureaucratized corporate structure. It is widely believed, though difficult to document, that contractors work for about half the costs of corporate operators. This is a feeling shared not only by the contractors themselves but also by many in the middle management levels of the large corporations.

Independent and contract logging firms lack the top-heavy management and bureaucratic structures of the larger, integrated companies. Management functions are more likely to be performed by owners and by employees, whose knowledge and authority are based on experience. When these firms need professional expertise, they obtain it from independent consulting firms. Most of the independent companies with more than a few employees are union-organized operators, which undercuts the corporate argument that unions are the main cause of inefficiency.

The large forest corporations have consistently resisted the employment of more efficient contracting firms as required by the Forests Act. Part of the reason is historical. When the major forest corporations were expanding and consolidating their control of the timber available from public lands, it was fairly clear that the major threat to their plans came from the independent sector which could ultilize those same forest resources. During the 1950s and 1960s, many inducements were offered to independent loggers in exchange for their timber rights, including agreements, usually verbal, for future logging contracts on the lands now controlled by the big corporations. It is widely understood throughout the industry that some of these independent logging firms, once they became contractors, were systematically driven out of business. Others were relieved of certain parts of the harvesting operation — road construction, falling, yarding, trucking and so on. A fragmented contracting sector was thought to offer no competition to the integrated licence holders.

This matter of competition has been surrounded by a curious kind of thinking throughout the transition. Ever since World War II, some of the loudest advocates of the competitive, or free enterprise, system have been executives and directors of the corporate bureaucracies of the dozen or so major forest companies that control most of the industry. For most of this period their statements have been echoed by governments formed by the Social Credit party — the self-proclaimed party of free enterprise in British Columbia. But very early in the game the people who ran these corporations, along with the government in power, systematically eliminated the basis of the free enterprise system in the forest industry — competitive bidding for access to the timber supply. The final irony of the situation is that, were it not for the contractor-clause provisions written into the Tree Farm Licences, there might well be no independent sector in the industry today. Free enterprise, in a world of integrated corporate bureaucracies, owes its continued existence to the kind of government regulations it abhors.

The separate and identifiable components of the private sector are organized into, and are in certain ways represented by, a number of associations or interest groups. The largest of these, the Council of Forest Industries, includes most of the large forest corporations and the major independent loggers. Its members account for more than 90 per cent of the product value of the B. C. forest industry. The council serves primarily as an industry lobby and, through its affiliated operation, Forest Industrial Relations, negotiates the bulk of the labour contracts in the industry. On a smaller scale, another form of association has appeared within many Timber Supply Areas, particularly in the Interior, which involves the licencees in that specific area. The basic function of these associations is to resolve conflicts that arise between companies in the same region, particularly those conflicts involving timber allocations. These associations, which naturally have tended to exclude newcomers, also serve to keep the Forest Service at arm's length during the carving up of the resource pie.

Most contract loggers, along with some of the more independent of the independent loggers, belong to or support the B. C. Truck Loggers Association. A similar and smaller organization is the B. C. Independent Logging Association. These groups have formed the most vocal and articulate opposition to the concentration of timber rights in the hands of the few large corporations. For the most part, the members of these two bodies are unequivocal believers in the virtues of free enterprise — and are equally convinced of the vices of big government, big business and big unions.

The labour union component of the forest industry is in many ways a classic model. The first significant forest union in British Columbia was the Industrial Workers of the World (IWW), organized just after the turn of the century. Known as the Wobblies, the IWW had ten thousand members when it was made illegal during World War I. It was succeeded by the Lumber Workers Industrial Union, which organized the industry's first successful strike on Vancouver Island in 1934 and along with other B. C. forest unions joined with forest unions in the northwestern United States to form the Federation of Woodworkers, which in 1937 became the International Woodworkers of America, or IWA, the major forest industry union in existence today.

Initially, the IWA in British Columbia was primarily a coastal union, but the forced labour-management "co-operation" imposed during World War II ignored the demands of unorganized workers and led to the spread of the IWA throughout the province. Immediately after the war, the hysterical anticommunist propaganda that was part and parcel of the campaign to justify Forest Management Licences controlled by large corporations resulted in a painful purging of the more radical factions within the union. By 1979, almost 50,000 of the province's 85,000 forest workers belonged to the IWA, whose international membership stood at 120,000. Although the majority of these members were mill employees, there had been a series of defections from its pulp mill members, eventually leading to the creation of two other industry unions in the province: the relatively decentralized Pulp, Paper and Woodworkers of Canada (PPWC) and the B. C. wing of the 52,000-member Canadian Paperworkers Union (CPU).

Like the companies for which their members work, the forest unions, particularly the IWA, have tended to develop bureaucratic structures, with attitudes to match. In large part, the PPWC and the CPU were formed as a reaction against the sort of union which the IWA had become, following its taming in the late 1940s. There are almost as many opinions on the IWA in the woods as there are people — the most widely held opinion being that it is something one joins in order to get a job.

The IWA is an industrial union rather than a trade union, viewing its jurisdiction as including all trades or occupations within the forest industry, and it is organized into geographical locals. The master agreement or contract is negotiated by the regional or Vancouver office — which effectively runs the IWA as far east as Manitoba. Since 1978, the union has been perceived, both publicly and by many of its members, as a reflection of the personality of its regional president, Jack Munro. The strength of the union during the last decade or two has been its style — its stance in the face of the concentration of corporate power which has occurred in the industry. It projects the image of the straight-talking, no-nonsense, slightly unpredictable Munro. It is widely believed by politicians and corporation executives that successfully doing business with the IWA ultimately involves being able to deal face to face with Jack Munro. What the IWA offers its members is, in essence, a progressive view of its own history; it takes credit, quite justifiably, for the high wages and fringe benefits, including living conditions in the camps, that prevail in the industry, as well as for the safety rules in a traditionally hazardous occupation. And the union is entirely correct in this assertion; there have always been those independent loggers and corporate managers whose treatment of their employees reflects their narrowly exploitative view of the forest resource.

But many workers hold less flattering though equally justified views of the union. In certain respects the IWA is just as much a bureaucratic monstrosity as any of the corporations. Its salaried staff is concentrated in the Vancouver office, and workers in the woods can go for years without ever meeting a paid union representative. The union has always been opposed to the smaller operators in the industry, despite a significant antipathy among workers towards the large corporate organizations. The basic position of the union leadership for the past decade or so has been that the best deal for workers is to be negotiated with the bigger companies and that the best of all possible worlds will be achieved when one corporation holds all the timber rights in the province.

The union's presence is felt largely through the complex, highly detailed master agreement drawn up between its negotiators in Vancouver and the professional negotiators for Forest Industrial Relations. Applying this agreement in most working conditions normally requires a great deal of patience and goodwill on the part of all involved, union members as well as management employees. It is often easy, some would say too easy, for the less enthusiastic members of the work force to use rigid and literal interpretations of the agreement in a way that leads to unreasonably high costs, blatant inefficiencies and bizarre situations. As in any bureaucratic system, the lower levels of the union hierarchy can be taken over by the inept, the incompetent and the lazy — status and authority being derived, not from experience or specialized knowledge, but from a dogged ability to stick around longer than anyone else. That other major bureaucracies in the industry — those of the corporations and the Forest Service — function the same way is beside the point.

It is in the area of broad forest policy that the IWA most resembles the corporate bureaucracies beside which it has evolved. Generally, it opposes reductions in the industrial forest land base. Generally, it resists the idea that the industry is not paying a fair share of its economic rent. Generally, it agrees with the concentration of control over timber rights. And, particularly, it supports the corporate position that the government should allocate vast amounts of money to intensive forest management programs.

This last, the silviculture issue, has in recent years raised a number of questions concerning the essential nature of the IWA itself. Part of the IWA's — or, at least, Jack Munro's — interest in intensive management programs is the prospect that they will provide thousands of jobs. At times, these programs are described as essential to save jobs which already exist, at others as providing vast new opportunities for employment. "In twenty years," Munro has been quoted as saying, "there will be more people working in silviculture than will be working in the harvest."

Naturally, the IWA would prefer that the growing silvicultural work force become part of its membership. That has not yet happened to any great degree. The bulk of silvicultural employment, primarily tree planting, has been done by seasonally employed, migrant crews of contractors, many of them either legal or de facto worker co-operatives. Most tree planting contracts, and all those administered by the Forest Service, are awarded on an open bidding system: the lowest bidder gets the contract. Planters usually work on a piece rate, which can be from 30 to 80 per cent of the contractor's bid price. There is ample evidence to indicate that it is a wide open field for unethical contractors who are as careless in their treatment of employees as they are of the trees they plant. Regardless, there has been a marked reluctance on the part of silvicultural workers — planters and spacers — to unionize.

Most forest companies have tried in the past to do this work with unionized crews, but it is widely acknowledged that they have failed. Apart from questions of efficiency and production, the working conditions and organizational arrangements of an industry set up for harvesting timber are in basic conflict with what is loosely known as the "lifestyle" of silvicultural workers. "Also of importance," the B. C. Forest Service stated in its resource analysis report,

> is the emergence of a trend that appears to signify a change in social values. Many younger people have associated themselves with environmental concerns, not necessarily as an issue to express protest but in the belief that an occupation in this field provides purpose and thus fulfilment in life. In the eyes of many, silvicultural work . . . provides the basis for a satisfying lifestyle. Since one of the functions of our forests is to enhance the well-being of society, this issue must not be overlooked in policy decisions.[4]

Those life style differences are somewhat difficult to define. Some of it is merely a reflection of the moral righteousness of many tree planters — when you're up to your hips in logging slash planting trees in the middle of a 120 ha (300 acre) clear-cut, it is easy to feel morally superior to logging crews. Part of it is that tree planters choose not be be bound by the eight-hour day or the five-day week. Thus, on good ground, a good planter or spacer can earn two to three times as much working on a piece-rate contract as on an hourly rated, forestry union crew.

But perhaps the major issue has to do with the living conditions of silvicultural workers. One of the union's proudest accomplishments has been the abolition of the atrocious living conditions which once prevailed in logging camps. Union agreements include meticulous descriptions of the camp facilities that must be provided for workers: private or semiprivate rooms, showers, toilets, kitchen facilities, recreation facilities and so on. Vast amounts have been spent on these quarters in recent years, all of it eventually deductible from stumpage payments to the public treasury. And while they are in most respects an enormous improvement on former living conditions, they all tend towards a prefabricated, stultifying and sterile existence. For most tree planters, the prospect of spending a few weeks of a planting contract in a 3 m^2 cubicle finished in fake-wood wallboard and taking meals in a catered dining-room along with a few hundred loggers — all men, rarely a woman to be seen — is entirely unappealing.

Typically, successful tree planting, and some spacing, operations use highly portable camps. In certain respects, going to work on a planting contract is like being well paid to go camping. There is variety and change, the food reflects the tastes of the individuals involved, and the atmosphere created by men and women working together is in marked contrast to the overwhelmingly male logging camps. Also involved, according to critics of the often idealized view of silvicultural work, is a widespread intention to work only long enough to qualify for unemployment benefits.

The IWA, whatever its intentions, usually appears devoted to a narrowly defined self-interest that pays scant attention to the basic problems of the industry or to the future of the forest resources, apart from the immediate benefits these resources can provide its members. In large measure, it is a union dominated by its own bureaucracy, a hierarchy that perpetuates itself by courageously leading its members into the battles of a previous era. The best indicator of this is that the newest component of the industry, the silvicultural workers who one day will likely be in the majority, wants practically nothing to do with the union.

The public sector bureaucracy of the forest industry is almost totally contained within the Forest Service. In form, it is a fairly conventional government department. It has a head office in Victoria and six regional offices, which in turn are divided into forty-six districts. During the 1980–81 fiscal year, 2650 permanent employees — plus, at times, a similar number of temporary or auxiliary staff — spent almost $190 million performing their various tasks.[5]

The Ministry of Forests Act defines the purposes and functions of the Forest Service: to maximize productivity of the province's forest and range resources; to manage, protect and conserve those resources, with regard to both short- and long-term economic and social benefits; to plan the use of the resources in a co-ordinated and integrated manner concerning other natural resources; to encourage a viable timber processing industry, and to protect and manage the financial interest of the public in the forests. The Forest Service is responsible to the legislative and administrative centres of government through the minister of forests.

The formal legal structure of the Forest Service, however, provides only one clue to an understanding of its place in the industry. There are other aspects equally relevant. One concerns what could be called the psychology of the organization, a major feature being what is generally perceived as a pervasive inferiority complex. Many in the Forest Service feel this arises from what they consider to be political interference dating from the 1950s and 1960s, the reign of the first Social Credit governments of British Columbia. Perhaps some of the antagonism between the Forest Service and the politicians at that time, described in the earlier chapter on tenure, concerned the Forest Service's 1947 mandate to manage the province's forest on a sustained yield basis. This mandate, which provided the Forest Service with a management rationale quite different from that of maximizing the flow of revenues into the provincial treasury, was bound to put the Forest Service at odds with practically any government that came into power; that it was a Social Credit government merely made matters worse. In addition, the Forest Service took much of the blame for the activities of a corrupt minister. As the instrument of government policy, it presided over the liquidation of the independent operators, though its actual intention had been to transform them into forest farmers.

When the NDP was elected in 1972, there was a widespread belief in most government departments that the democratic socialist party would better serve the "public interest," as opposed to "private interests." It was not that members of the Forest Service particularly favoured a socialist system or the NDP; there was merely a feeling that the new government would probably support forest policies and administrative procedures more in tune with its own beliefs. Thus, at many levels, Forest Service personnel began to assert their authority more than before. The most serious effects of this flexing of bureaucratic muscle were felt, as usual, by the smaller, nonintegrated forest companies. Yet the bigger corporations also began to feel the change. Perhaps the most onerous measures were the logging guidelines established for environmental protection.

Industry people felt that the mounting pressures being put on them were entirely due to the directives coming from the NDP government, and in particular from Minister of Forests Bob Williams. The irony of the situation was that Williams was probably the best hope industry had in the NDP government for working out an equitable arrangement for the private use of public resources. He was in no haste to restructure the industry, assigning that task to a Royal Commission under a known Liberal, Peter Pearse. Meanwhile, the Forest Service was causing Williams considerable frustration by exercising authority in directions which were not government policy. He concluded that the Forest Service was an inadequate administrative mechanism; if he could have got away with it, he might have abolished the ministry altogether.

When asked his opinion, Williams was rarely reluctant to comment upon what he believed to be the department's inadequacies — essentially its lack of talent. The Forest Service's ability to attract competent, capable employees has often been questioned. Most professional foresters come from forestry departments in universities and technical schools, and with the growth of professionally managed forest corporations, graduates are faced with a choice: working for industry or working for government (the Forest Service). For a number of reasons, salary levels being a major one, there has long been a widespread belief among forestry professionals and students that the "best" people work for industry and the "culls" wind up in the Forest Service. Although some professional foresters also believe that working for a private forest company requires the violation of professional principles or ideals, derogatory opinions of the Forest Service have a certain currency within the agency itself, and this fact reinforces its feelings of inferiority.

Like most public bureaucracies in the world, the B. C. Forest Service is highly centralized, not only in terms of policy decisions but in an administrative or operational sense as well. Recent attempts to reorganize and decentralize its structure in order to adapt it to the new Forests Act have merely further concentrated power and authority. The reorganization simply made allowance for technical advances in such areas as communications and data processing. The resulting system made it possible for the centres of power — the regional and head offices — to obtain and process information from the field more easily, while dispatching yet more detailed and restrictive instructions back to the field offices.

The rules of the game as played by the Forest Service are found in a series of written instruction that are applicable to every forest district and to every hectare of Crown forest land throughout the province. The broad outlines are defined in the Forests Act; the fine details are described in the regulations drawn up by the mandarins, while the application of the laws, policies and regulations is defined in greater detail in a series of operations manuals. The intent is to create a system whereby no one working at an operational level in the Forest Service is required to make a decision; it is only necessary to follow detailed instructions for filling out the appropriate forms. The options, in any given situation, are limited to the variety of forms available.

The Forest Service is organized in such a way that those who spend most of their time in the forest are the ones with the least power, authority and experience. The higher a person rises in the hierarchy, the less time they spend in direct contact with the resource itself. The major, certainly — but also and ever increasingly the minor — decisions affecting the forests are made by those farthest removed from them. For example, field staff do not develop management plans for the areas in which they work. Instead, they catalogue the areas according to categories defined in the manuals; they evaluate specific sites in terms of the opportunities they provide for implementing treatment programs — planting, spacing, fertilizing and so on — instituted and budgeted from the regional or head offices, and they administer those programs with procedures, forms and language provided by the central authorities. If on a specific site a problem, an opportunity or a situation arises that is not anticipated in the manuals, its existence is most likely simply ignored.

In 1974 two federal and two provincial cabinet ministers signed the first five-year agreement to implement a $50 million federal-provincial intensive forest management program. Each administrative region was allocated funds, and within the regions each district was given a budget for various types of treatment. As time went on, some districts began to experience difficulty in finding specific sites appropriate to the treatments. For example, a coastal district might find that it did not have any more Douglas-fir sites either productive enough in growth or of the recommended age for juvenile spacing. This information would be passed on to the regional and head offices. Meanwhile, the task being performed at the upper levels of the hierarchy consisted of administering the overall federal-provincial program, the main "problem" being to spend the budget. If the project's money were not spent; its administrative apparatus might be considered redundant — and one thing bureaucracies never do is make themselves redundant. In this instance, instructions would be given to district offices to space older stands of Douglas-fir, even though in some areas this meant cutting trees which were merchantable by the Forest Service's own standards and leaving them to rot. The lost timber volumes on these sites might never be regained by the increased growth the spacing was intended to produce. In such cases, the actual result of the program would be a decrease in the future timber supply.

A different situation arose with research of the root rot problem, which affects coastal Douglas-fir plantations. The federal-provincial program involved no procedures for treating the infected areas, though research people were seeking a remedy. However, many of the juvenile spacing projects were located in diseased areas. It was perfectly obvious to everyone on the sites — the spacers, the Forest Service field staff, the researchers — that spacing these areas was not only a waste of money but would do nothing whatever to check the spread of the disease. But neither the manuals nor the forms revealed any procedure for dealing with the situation. The contract said that the site was to be spaced, and so it was spaced.

Even when this kind of insanity becomes so obvious that it can no longer be ignored, the bureaucratic response is not to relocate the decision-making function closer to the work site, but to create another site category, another form, another standardized procedure. It is entirely conceivable that, in time, a new section will appear at the upper levels of the hierarchy, solely devoted to the problem of root rot. It will have a budget, a staff and office space and eventually will begin to produce its own forms and procedures which will be incorporated into the manuals. And not one of these forms or procedures is likely to have the slightest effect in controlling the disease.

A function overlying the public and private forest bureaucracies is that of the professional forester, whose fundamental role is to maintain the integrity of forest related activities, much in the same way that doctors are expected to safeguard the ethical standards of the medical profession or lawyers the legal system.

By law certain tasks in British Columbia's forests must be performed by Registered Professional Foresters (RPFS) who are certified by their own organization, the Association of B. C. Professional Foresters. The profession is founded on the assumption that forestry requires specialized knowledge to be applied according to certain principles which rank higher than short-term considerations of public policy and private gain.

In order to maintain these high standards, the association has the power to discipline or expel its members. This is a double-edged sword which can and has been used to muzzle RPFS who publicly criticize the forest practices of large forest companies. There are few, if any, instances of the association disciplining RPFS employed by corporations which violate commonly accepted standards of good forest practice. Most of the association's public statements in recent years have argued for increased public spending on forest management or other measures requiring the hiring of additional professional foresters.

In the interaction between public and corporate forestry bureaucracies, there are some significant differences between Canada and the United States. A comparative study of public and private forest bureaucracies in Ontario, Quebec, British Columbia and the United States by Christopher Leman observes that Canadian policy has been to give private corporations much greater responsibility for the management of public timber than their U. S. counterparts enjoy.[6] He also notes that provincial forest services are far more centralized than the U. S. Forest Service. So are Canadian forest companies, compared with those in the United States.

Leman further concluded that, while forest management in a province such as British Columbia is decentralized through the delegation of responsibility to the private sector, this practice of delegation (that is, through tenure provisions) may be incompatible with decentralization of the public bureaucracy. The companies routinely take field level disputes between Forest Service personnel and forest company managers to a higher level. Leman observed that "when the guidance and authorization comes from above, it often seems more sympathetic to the company than the circumstances seem to merit. . . . the receptivity of high-level ministry officials to company complaints leaves a deep mark on the lower levels of the organizations." He might have added that the small, unintegrated forest companies, which have neither the administrative structures, the professional contacts nor the financial resources to take these disputes to a higher level, are much less likely to prevail. In fact, they may well bear the brunt of Forest Service frustrations, thereby increasing the tendency towards corporate concentration.

There are other consequences. A concept often used to justify the creation of large organizations, whether they be forest companies or government agencies, is "economy of scale" — the economic benefits supposedly available from spreading fixed costs over increased production. But there are also diseconomies of scale — inevitable in such administrative arrangements as those used in the B. C. forest industry. The bureaucratic and centralized nature of the organizations concerned, in both the public and private sectors, isolates almost everyone who works for the industry from the consequences of their actions. This is particularly true when those forest management decisions concern silviculture. Tree planters are paid only for putting trees in the ground; the fate of the forest which grows has no bearing on planters' welfare. The corporate field level managers will probably have transferred to another division or been promoted up the ladder before any field assessment can be made of their decisions. Major and minor policy decisions made by Forest Service staff may take a full forest rotation to reveal their strengths and weaknesses.

The result is a system in which no one is quite responsible. All the participants can blame the system for anything that goes wrong, and they regularly do so. In large forest corporations, this isolation from consequences, combined with the system used to calculate stumpage, has created a widely accepted attitude among employees that the corporation for which one works can be endlessly fiddled to provide an unending flow of material benefits. Public service employees, while receiving significantly less pay, have the consolation of knowing that so long as certain minimal levels of public revenues can be extracted from the forests, and so long as they adhere strictly to the established rules, they will have a better chance of holding on to their jobs.

Some in the industry are perfectly happy with this — union members as well as corporate managers, directors as well as shareholders, those at the bottom of the Forest Service hierarchy as well as at the top, small-scale independent operators as well as holders of graduate degrees in forestry. But even in the major forest corporations, there are some employees, including upper-level managers, who believe that the concentration of timber rights in the hands of a few highly centralized and increasingly bureaucratic corporations is good neither for industry nor forest. And there are large numbers in the Forest Service — probably the majority — who know from experience that the centralized bureaucracy of that agency is one of the major threats to the proper management of public forests.

However, the industry as a whole has an enormous capacity to believe its own myths. And there are few, if any, legitimate positions within this complex with the assigned task, or even the freedom, to practise any serviceable self-criticism. Discussing certain issues such as stumpage rates or the value of intensive forest management is near-treason. The serious issues are raised only by those on their way out, such as that endangered species described in Chapter Four by Chief Forester C. D. Orchard, the imperilled independent logger.

The proponents of corporate concentration, bureaucratic centralism, executive-dominated unions and single-crop forests all, of course, deny their obsession with centralism. They argue that these methods of organization and management are efficient, economic and rational, that bigness is not pursued for its own sake, that monoculture is not an end in itself. But somehow three or four decades of so-called progress have failed to convince the skeptical. Increasing evidence suggests that neither the forms of organization nor the established theories and practices of forest management are efficient, economic or ecologically sound.

ELEVEN

What Do We Want from Our Forests?

UNTIL THE MID-1970S, forest management hardly existed in British Columbia. The monolithic corporate structures and the industrial apparatus created in response to the adoption of sustained yield forestry in the province were designed to maximize control of timber rights and facilitate the harvesting of that timber. They were designed for the management of large logging operations rather than the long-term management of forest land. The only silvicultural practice of any significance was tree planting, and even that did not exist on the scale required by the volume of timber being harvested. When the various bureaucracies began to implement what they called "intensive forest management," they shared a fairly uniform approach to the concept.

For a long time, the Rolls-Royce of scientific forest management was JARI, the huge forest complex started in Brazil in 1967. The (reputed) multibillionaire Daniel Ludwig set up the 1 600 000 ha (4 million acre) forest operation to produce wood fibre for a pulp mill which was built in Japan and towed on barges up the Amazon River. The plan was to replace the native forest with melina, a South Asian tree with exceptional growth rates, and with Honduran pine on sandy sites unsuitable for melina. The operation was based on a seven- to eleven-year rotation for melina and eleven years for pine if grown for pulp or sixteen years if grown for saw logs.

JARI was one of the most highly planned and highly integrated forest operations in the world. In addition to its timber operations, extensive agricultural facilities were established to feed the large work force living in elaborate company towns and villages. A huge railway and road system was built, as well as an electrical generating system fuelled by mill wastes and noncommercial native species. One of the more profitable divisions was the mining of kaoline, a fine clay used in making porcelain, paint, a palliative for diarrhoea, and glossy paper. The existence of the enormous kaoline deposits was not known when JARI began.

The strategy at JARI was to cut and burn about 5000 ha (12,350 acres) of tropical rainforest a year, replacing it with melina or pine with a predicted mean annual increment of 200 m^3 per ha (28 cunits per acre). (This compares with 10 to 15 m^3 per ha (1.4 to 2.1 cunits per acre) for coastal Douglas-fir.) The melina harvesting began in 1979 on plantations established in 1970. The plantations were cleared of weed species four times during the rotation, and after harvest melina was regenerated from the stumps. Pine plantations were seeded to grass and used for beef pastures. Of intensive management as it is known in British Columbia, little was practised, though extensive research plots were established to test spacing, thinning, fertilizing and genetically manipulated seedlings.

By the time the first melina harvest was complete, Ludwig had poured almost a billion dollars into JARI, probably the largest enterpreneurial effort ever undertaken by an individual. It was many times over the largest forest operation under a single management plan. JARI implemented the most advanced thinking of industrial forestry; yet within two years of its first harvest, it was bankrupt, Ludwig had pulled out and a consortium of Brazilian corporations, banks and the government was trying frantically to patch together the pieces.

There are several theories concerning the demise of JARI. The first is that it encountered so much bureaucratic and political interference from the Brazilian government that it was unable to proceed as planned. The establishment was so large that it was almost a country within a country; it aroused suspicion and antagonism. Not only was it foreign-owned but it was also an enormous, hierarchical organization set up overnight in an underdeveloped area.

In addition to social and political questions, there was also widespread debate over JARI's forest management practices. Ludwig's forest operation was the most extensive and thoroughgoing application of monocultural forestry ever attempted. It was industrial forestry with a vengeance. By the time JARI's forests came into production, the project was under heavy criticism from most of Brazil's scientific establishment. The main objection was that repeated crops of melina would soon deplete the soil of its nutrients — essentially, that the operation was mining the soil. Other critics claimed that the combined forestry and agricultural operations were so altering the ecology of the entire watershed that the basic economy of the area would be adversely affected. But in the end, the major criticism was that the management plan did not succeed on its own terms: the plantation forests did not produce the anticipated yields; some reports indicated the first crops were 40 to 75 per cent below expectations.

Meanwhile, throughout the 1970s, proponents of large-scale industrial forestry in North America, particularly in Canada, were using the example of JARI to further their own designs. This somewhat mysterious, massive forestry operation somewhere up the Amazon River, implementing the kind of single-crop forestry getting underway here, was held up as a threat. Its mere existence, and hence its "correctness," was put forth as a justification for taking a similar forest management approach to provincial forests in Canada and National Forests in the United States. The logic of the argument was simple: because JARI existed, it worked; because it worked, it was necessary to implement similar management programs here, otherwise the Brazilian forest industry would soon dominate the timber markets of the world.

During the past two or three decades, there has developed a growing body of critical or cautionary knowledge and opinion regarding monoculture forestry — in effect the only approach to silviculture being implemented in the major forest management units at present. The objectives of this type of forest management are, in the short term, economic. In the most immediate sense, the criticisms are primarily ecological; but in the long run, they are economic, too.

The factor common to almost all industrial forestry is the culture of a single crop, usually one but occasionally two or even three species of more or less uniformly aged trees which are grown for a particular purpose, most often for timber. The premise is that by reducing the number of variables, the forest can most easily be managed to a predicted and profitable culmination, or harvest. The object is to concentrate the productive potential of a forest site into the most desirable product. Thus, the coastal regions of British Columbia, Washington and Oregon contain vast plantations of Douglas-fir — commercially the most valuable species — obtained from a relatively narrow genetic base. If the stand is spaced, the tendency towards a single species will be intensified, as will the tendency towards a uniform age. Those sites unsuitable for Douglas-fir will be planted to other species, again in pure stands. One of the central themes of this sort of forestry is that the resource — trees — is being renewed; therefore the practice is responsible and environmentally sound. That is the claim.

There are several objections to monoculture. The simplest reflects a concern for the single crop itself: it may be susceptible to, and even invite, major insect and disease attacks. It is argued that mixed stands are better able to withstand such attacks on one of the species; and even if a single species in a large area is badly damaged, the remaining trees will ensure the survival of the forest itself. An extension of this argument is that single-crop forests will inevitably require the use of herbicides and pesticides to protect them from competition and attack. In reference to agriculture, the noted U. S. biologist Marston Bates has written:

> The single-crop system is always in precarious equilibrium. It is created by man and it has to be maintained by man, ever alert with chemicals and machinery, with no other protection against the hazards of some new development in the wounded natural system. It is man working against nature; an artificial system with the uncertainties of artifacts. Epidemic catastrophe becomes an ever-present threat.[1]

A more serious objection reflects a different perception of what constitutes the resource. The common view has been that trees are the basic resource: hence the stumpage-based practice of charging for the volume of trees cut, not to mention the unqualified belief in the virtues of tree planting or reforestation. An alternative view is that the basic resource is the land itself, with its ability to sustain a whole complex of life forms, including trees. The objection to monoculture in this instance is that, even though it sustains a population of trees, it will weaken the ability of the land to produce the volume and range of products of which it was once capable. This was the chief criticism levelled at the JARI management program: it would deplete the soil, thereby reducing the productive capacity of the land. Although he offered no specific reservations about monoculture in his Royal Commission report, Peter Pearse characterized the essential resource as something more than the current crop of trees: "Present circumstances call for a more flexible approach to yield regulation, with greater emphasis on protecting and enhancing the productivity of forest land and on the economic, social, and environmental implications of harvesting."[2]

Similar concern has been expressed about the attempts at genetic "improvement" that are an integral part of industrial forestry. Some of this concern is fairly straightforward: for example, the fear that geneticists will develop trees which grow exceptionally well for sixty or seventy years and then succumb to a fatal disease. More sophisticated versions of this critique see the forest gene pool as the vital basic resource.

Roy Silen is one of the more important plant geneticists in the Pacific Northwest. He argues that the timber resources of this areas, which are unequalled in the world, cannot be explained by soil or climatic conditions. Superior moisture distribution and soil conditions are found in other parts of the world, yet those areas do not produce trees of the size and quality found between the Rockies and the Pacific coast, from California to Alaska.[3] "When appropriate strains of our world-record species are planted in other temperate forest zones of the world, they usually outgrow native trees by wide margins," Silen argues. "When we try the best species from other forest regions here, as we have for over sixty years, our own species outgrow them by wide margins."[4] Several events contributed to the creation of the northwest forests, he suggests. Perhaps ten million years ago the climate cooled, leading to the replacement of the dominant deciduous species by the conifers growing here today. About a million years ago, the Douglas-fir appeared, and because of its strength and heavy protective bark it was able to dominate the most productive sites between northern California and the top end of Vancouver Island.

A unique geographical feature, the north-south orientation of the mountain ranges, meant that during the various ice ages, forests "migrated" south and returned when the ice retreated. "This was not the case on the Eurasian land mass, where mountains and seas are oriented east to west; there the coming ice must have trapped many fast-growing, cold-sensitive species and strains against the crosswise geographical barriers and eliminated them."[5] Additionally, "There was the rare good fortune that Western man did not arrive here early enough to inflict upon the forest gene pool the drastic disruption that characterized other temperate zones."[6] Natural regeneration practices, condemned by many as neglect of the forests, actually helped insure the survival of the genetic base.

Over the past thirty years, the situation has begun to change dramatically. Natural regeneration of forests has been replaced by tree planting, and the source of seedlings has been narrowed and manipulated by genetic improvement.

> If we look broadly at the path of all genetic improvement, we find really only one philosophy or model. There are strong parallels in it to mining. One prospects the gene pool for the richest sources of the desired genes, refines them into as pure a state as possible, then spreads the product as broadly as the competitive market permits. . . . Prospecting and purifying are in themselves relatively innocuous. It is the replacement of the original gene pool with a more "profitable" one which wreaks the great consequence."[7]

The trends in forest regeneration and genetic improvement described by Silen are merely one facet of the dominant and dominating approach to forestry which influences all phases of industrial forest management. Basically, the tendency is to replace the random, diversified forest with the designed, simplified and profitable forest. In many respects, this is an attempt to create in the forest the conditions of the wheat field. It is the monocultural approach, perhaps the monocultural obsession.

In a way, monoculture is the antithesis of silviculture. Because silviculture is based on life processes, upon the use of living energy to serve human life, one of its primary purposes must be to preserve the integrity of those life processes. It must conform to natural, biological processes rather than to mechanical or economic considerations. The mechanics of silviculture should therefore be derived from the biological conditions, the ecology of the forest. Monocultural forestry has a propensity to use plants, as well as the soil itself, as machines. To illustrate: In Douglas-fir stands, it is common to find an understorey of western red cedar. Cedar is a shade-tolerant species, and grows comfortably under the fir; there is relatively little competition between the two. If the stand is being managed as a fir stand and is spaced at an appropriate age, a decision is required concerning the cedar — should it be left to grow or be removed? There are many pros and cons for either choice, depending on the ecology of the site. A mechanistic view of the cedar, commonly applied, sees it as a "nutrient pump" that is drawing nutrients from the soil and dropping them on the forest floor in the form of litter, where they are more readily available to the fir. A consequence of this perspective might be to cut the top off the cedar 1.5 or 1.8 m (5 or 6 feet) from the ground while spacing, mutilating it to encourage foliage growth. A more sophisticated version of this same point of view is a mechanistic approach to the soil, rather than to the cedar. In this version, the soil is a chemical mass which becomes a growth medium for whatever species is desired. If certain nutrients required by that species are missing or in short supply, they can be added in the form of fertilizer. For instance, the mechanistic perspective can justify the removal of alder from a fir stand, replacing the alder's nitrogen-fixing contribution to the soil with applications of nitrogen fertilizer. And, quite likely, this can be "proven" to be a financially sound decision. But it is monoculture all the same, with all of monoculture's hazards and deficiences.

By the early 1980s, an organizational structure and a management approach that are complementary and mutually sustaining thoroughly dominate the forestry business in North America, particularly in the north and west. Monolithic corporations and government agencies seem able to practise only monocultural forestry. The lack of diversity and variety in organization is reflected in the growing uniformity of the forests being grown.

The rigidity of the industry's organization becomes most apparent in lean times. When the timber harvest cannot be sold, workers cannot be redirected into managing the forests. Instead, they are laid off. In some ways, this may not be a bad thing, considering the apparent deficiencies in present forest management. The evidence presented by silvicultural economists indicates that the intensive management practices are not meeting their primary objectives of increasing the timber supply. This, coupled with the possibility that some of these techniques pose real threats to the basic soil and genetic resources, suggests that from an ecological point of view the inability of the industry to reorganize its energies under adverse economic circumstances is a blessing in disguise. But from an economic perspective it is disastrous.

The separation of ecological and economic considerations, in fact their frequent contradiction, is an obvious feature of contemporary forest management. In attempting to implement the "approved" management programs within the structures that provide and control access to the forests, forest managers often find that the actions indicated by their knowledge, experience and intuition are judged to be inprovident. Conversely, the economics of a particular situation too often require responses that are known to be ecologically destructive.

A current attitude towards public resource administration contributes to the dilemma. This attitude maintains in part that if a "resource" can be identified, it should be managed; every last hectare of forest land should be assigned, classified, evaluated, designated and quantified; one or more ministries should be given jurisdiction over the activities that will occur there. The thrust is towards the elimination of unmanaged land. Wilderness has come to mean those areas that are administered by specialists in wilderness management. Even though the capability to manage everything may not exist, management is seen as a desirable objective.

Combined with this attitude is an assumption that resources can be managed according to certain economic, social and political policies. This is accomplished by enforcing adherence to a plethora of regulations, all of which have the force of law. For example, there is no longer unrestricted access to public land in British Columbia. The day is long gone when it was legal to squat on unoccupied Crown land; now there are areas where the public cannot go without a special permit or licence. Public administration in the field of resource management has come to mean the enforcement of regulations. Except in the case of firefighting, the Forest Service is reluctant to actually perform any work in the forest. It prefers to regulate the activities of others.

A whole area of administration concerns the levying of charges for the use of resources. Some of these charges — stumpage, royalties and rentals, for instance — are designed to generate revenues for the government. Others, such as hunting or fishing licences, are designed to restrict access to the resource. The legitimizing logic of charging these fees is that the resources belong to the Crown, which is interpreted as the citizenry or the public; individual citizens or organizations of people wanting to use these resources in certain ways, primarily for commercial reasons, are considered to be acting in a private capacity. Hence, it is reasonable that they be charged for their use of the resource, in the name of the public and for the public interest. This logic is stretched to the breaking point by government organizations and civil servants who look upon the resource and its administration from a quasi-corporate stance; those in the Forest Service, for instance, who act as though forests "belong" to the ministry of forests.

The strained distinctions between "public" and "private" occasionally lead to some confusing situations. Part of the confusion stems from assigning values to these terms, the "public" interest most commonly ranking higher than "private." Any individual who does not have a professional or proprietary interest in the forest is a member of the public; if he is a logger or a shareholder in MacMillan Bloedel, he belongs to a "private" interest group; if he is a birdwatcher or a member of the Sierra Club, he belongs to a "public" interest group.

It is useful to remember these distinctions when considering the legislation and regulations which influence and determine the nature of forest management in British Columbia. The effect of the 1978 Forests Act is to give the Forest Service almost absolute control over forest management and silviculture on Crown-owned forest land. In theory, certain licences —

notably Tree Farm Licences — give the holders the responsibility or the opportunity to manage the forests therein defined, subject to the approval of the Forest Service. In addition — and this is where the real control lies — Section 88 of the act stipulates that the costs of reforestation and other silvicultural treatments undertaken on Crown land shall be credited against stumpage payable by the licencee on the harvested timber. As well, the Forest Service directly oversees the silvicultural work performed on areas outside the Tree Farm Licences.

It is in the nature of a public bureaucracy such as the B. C. Forest Service that, ideally, its practices and procedures are standardized throughout its jurisdiction; the same rules apply in Atlin as in Abbottsford. Organizationally, silviculture in the province is supervised by silviculture crews working out of district offices within the six regions of the province. But management practices and procedures are defined in the silviculture manual prepared in Victoria. In precise detail, the manual stipulates how silviculture will be planned, administered and evaluated. To a major extent, it determines the precise nature of the silviculture that is practised throughout the province. The effect of applying these regulations, along with others defining such aspects as tenure, harvest schedules and so on, is to restrict the practice of silviculture in British Columbia to very narrow confines.

The result is an "official," or "approved," silviculture that inclines inexorably towards monocultural forestry. To understand how this happens, one need only compare certain silvicultural treatments conducted under Forest Service control with those performed on private forest land or on Tree Farm Licences prior to 1978. When, for instance, the Forest Service undertakes a juvenile spacing project, a very small portion is sampled, usually one-half of 1 per cent of the stand. Using tables, charts and detailed directives supplied from the Silviculture Branch's head office in Victoria, the field staff computes the specifications to which the stand will be spaced. Forestry contractors submit bids based on these specifications, with the contract almost always being awarded to the lowest bidder; only in extreme cases does the contractor's competence become a factor, it being far more important for a public bureaucracy to appear fair than for it to be capable.

When the work has been performed, the contractor is assessed according to criteria provided by the central office. The field staff put the appropriate numbers on the proper forms and make certain calculations, and the final figure represents the payment the contractor receives. The result is that the contractor "spaces to the contract." The trees are left a specified distance apart, the species mixture has been decisively ranked and the age-class distribution has been narrowed, all as defined in the contract. Diversity is replaced by uniformity. When everyone involved works strictly according to the book, as is quite often the case, the system is relentlessly mechanistic in terms of the ecology of the stand. That is the basic problem with the bureaucratic system: it is capable of functioning even under the most ridiculous circumstances, so long as everyone does what they are told.

By contrast, some of the spacing on Tree Farm Licences — at least until recently, when the Forest Service became involved in monitoring — proceeded in a somewhat different manner, particularly if the work were being done by a crew employed directly by the forest corporation managing the TFL. The specifications for the treatment would not be so clearly defined. The spacers — people actually cutting out the unwanted trees — would be paid by the hour; they could be given a different and much wider set of variables within which to work. Because there was no predetermined set of specifications which had to be met, they could "space to the stand" — the distance between the trees could vary according to an infinite variety of site-specific conditions; the species priorities could be adjusted to suit the most appropriate tree to the specific spot; largely for the sake of economy, there was less obsession with obtaining a narrow age stratification. The result, while not all that noticeable in comparison to a Forest Service–spaced stand, was a somewhat less uniform forest, one where diversity had not been narrowed quite so much. When a spacer is required or encouraged to cut or leave trees according to the dictates of a specific site as well as the broadly defined directives of the corporation's head office and its wood supply division, he has to think about what he is doing as he does it. The forest he leaves behind will reflect those thoughts: his knowledge, his skill, his personality and the way the sun shone through the trees that day. These diverse factors, anathema to the bureaucratic system, are the basis of culture, of silviculture.

Unfortunately, because of the nature of corporate structure and organization, silvicultural practices do not evolve significantly in the big forest companies. The forest worker — spacer, planter or other member of the team — has no long-term connection to the forests on which he works, except occasionally on privately owned forest lands. He is an employee; he will soon move on to a less physically demanding job, or a higher paying one with a contractor; the union, with its bureaucractic priorities, becomes involved. There is no residency on a Tree Farm Licence. It exists only to grow timber and provide jobs, not to provide a birthplace and a home for a culture, even silviculture.

The failure of the monolithic, monocultural approach to forest mangement is not merely in its tendency to eliminate diversity for the sake of uniformity. The problem is that actions taken for bureaucratic reasons too often violate both the ecology of the forest and the economy of the enterprise at hand. Although economic and ecological considerations are often seen as contradictory, they are inextricably related. Economics, as Marston Bates considered it, is the ecology of man; ecology is the study of the economy of nature.

The attitude towards red alder in the northwestern rainforests reveals a great deal about the nature of orthodox industrial forestry. The industry in this region was built on coniferous or softwood species; alder is a deciduous hardwood, short-lived and in short supply in an untouched forest. It has taken over large areas of logged-off lands and, in spite of its qualities, has until recently been looked upon as a weed tree of no commercial value. In fact, alder is as useful and valuable a hardwood as many of the eastern North American and European species such as birch and maple.

One of the rare features of alder is that it can take nitrogen from the air and deposit it in the soil; no other tree in the region has this capability. Coniferous species growing on sites previously covered with alder or in stands containing some alder trees grow at rates that can be matched in pure coniferous stands only with the repeated application of expensive nitrogen fertilizer. In addition, red alder may prove to be part of the solution to the Gilbertson root rot problem.

At certain stages — in British Columbia until the late 1970s — the bureaucratic strategy regarding alder has been to eliminate it and convert the tens of thousand of hectares to species that are considered commercially more valuable. To this end, the Forest Service began planning and establishing a number of reclamation projects designed to replace alder stands with fir. Some of these projects consisted of simply destroying the alder, with herbicides, machines or by falling them, and leaving them to rot, providing nutrients for the fir crop that, usually, was planted on the site. At that time, there was only a very small market for alder, and its value was perhaps a third or a fourth that of fir.

But the market changed. Rising petroleum prices led to a proliferation of wood-burning stoves and furnaces throughout the country, assisted by government conversion grants; alder is a superior fuelwood. At about the same time, fashions changed and light-coloured woods were in demand for furniture and interior finishing; alder is a light-hued wood, with qualities that make it highly suitable for furniture-making. As the general market decline of the early 1980s was cutting the price of fir logs by a half or two-thirds, the price of alder was rising. At the point when alder logs were selling for as much as or more than fir, the Forest Service had managed to clear the bureaucratic hurdles with its reclamation program. While loggers were clamouring for alder logs and the public for firewood, the Silviculture Branch of the Forest Service was launching a program to exterminate the species, in some cases without the wood being utilized in any manner. And during the same period, large amounts of money were being spent on the aerial application of nitrogen fertilizer. This type of "intensive forest management" program is what some major forest corporation executives, some union leaders, some Forest Service mandarins and some professional foresters are talking about in their campaign to have hundreds of millions of public dollars spent on forest management.

There is an aspect of the alder situation that reveals a central feature of the organization of the forest industry and forest management. In the areas where it grows, alder is the favoured domestic fuelwood, partly owing to its nature and partly to its never having been of great industrial value. In particular areas, it is an extremely valuable commodity; it is an easily and cheaply available source of energy for a large part of the rural population. At the risk of exaggeration, one could say that in this regard it has a certain strategic value. It is an energy supply not dependent on transmission lines, supply routes, transportation facilities and the vagaries of national and international energy politics. For the rural coastal population, alder provides one of the basic necessities of life, and it is literally at everyone's doorstep. A realistic forest policy, as part of a wider, reasonable economic policy, would at least be capable of acknowledging such a fact. The connection between alder and energy certainly does not constitute a major issue, but the failure to recognize this connection is symptomatic of the inability of rigid administrative structures to deal with basic social, ecological and economic issues.

The declining availability of fuelwood is one result of the decades-long trend towards urbanization. The energy needs, both real and frivolous, of urban areas explain, and in some cases justify, the vulnerable and precarious distribution systems which have been established. There is a considerable amount of sense involved in energizing a large city with transmission- and pipelines. The logistics of heating a city with fuelwood, not to mention the air pollution which would result, are enormous and impractical. In a city such as Vancouver, the predominant use of petroleum oils and electricity for energy makes sense, despite the protestations of urban environmentalists. But it is a different matter to impose the same energy-use patterns on hinterland areas. There is something fundamentally absurd in an organization which, at great cost and inconvenience, transports petroleum fuels hundreds of kilometres to forest industry installations where it used to generate electricity which, in turn, is used to heat living quarters for forestry workers. It is especially ridiculous in areas where projects are underway to apply herbicides to one of the highest energy-content species in the area. A conventional economic analysis that can justify such a state of affairs is as cockeyed as our ecological perspective.[8] Further, there is something sad and even frightening about a culture which expends energy striving to eliminate the plentiful, cheap and historic fuel of its pioneering ancestors in favour of an expensive and ever-diminishing alternative.

Of the many criticisms levelled at the corporate and bureaucratic superstructure, the most common is that institutional arrangements such as those that have evolved in the forest industry are repressive and inhuman; that big business, government and unions are concerned only with money and profits and are unresponsive to human needs. The same, essentially the economic, motivation is blamed for the environmental damage that forest companies are reputed to be inflicting on the forests. Much of this criticism contains an unstated assumption that the forest corporations are models of economic efficiency, with the ability to milk every last cent from the timber they harvest. It follows from this assumption that if these efficient corporations, along with the Forest Service, were made to practise intensive forest management — planting, stand tending and the like — on a major scale, then all would be well in ecological terms.

To consider the first point: it is difficult to find the repressed and exploited workers portrayed by some of the critics. It would be both perilous and futile to attempt to take advantage of a MacMillan Bloedel logger or millworker. Similarly, and despite the claims of some people in organizations like the Sierra Club, individuals within these corporations and bureaucracies can occasionally exhibit an environmental awareness and sensitivity beyond the comprehension of the most ardent urban eco-freak.

So to the second point, the most common complaint from within the industry is that, far from being models of efficiency, the structures in fact do not work, that they are not reasonable or efficient operations in economic terms. The evidence, particularly in British Columbia, is that the monolithic integrated forest corporations squander the resource. Control of timber rights and forest land is not so much a function of MacMillan Bloedel's or Crown Forest's supposed efficiency in managing the forests or the mills as of their political ability to manipulate the mechanisms that allocate the resource — the tenure provisions. The forms of tenure so fundamental to the industry and to the particular pattern of its administrative apparatus are equally fundamental to the problems which plague all forms of forestry.

There appears to be a need for some different approaches. If the forests of an area such as British Columbia are to be anything more than second-growth wilderness, then we must learn to grow trees properly. This is particularly important for timber production, but for other uses as well. If we learn how to grow trees, we will be able to grow forests and shape them to our needs. We need to develop a silvicultural capability which will be a reasonable alternative to the present monolithic, bureaucratized management methodology that is neither economical nor good for the environment. This capability will have to be learned, not in trade schools or universities — though these have a useful function — but in the forests, by people working for years, decades and generations. It will be of prime importance that these individuals live and work in particular individual forests, planting trees, watching them grow and harvesting them — if not in one lifetime, then in succeeding generations, between which there is a continuity.

There needs to be decentralization, a dispersal of the role of defining what is and what is not silviculturally acceptable. We are at a point where many approaches must be tried, and tried in a context where those who undertake to manage the forests will remain, as farmers do, to bear the consequences of their actions and reap the fruits of their labours. We need a means of doing this whereby the decisions concerning forests are made *in* the forests, by the people who work in the forests. We must find ways to build a tradition of silviculture. Forest management needs to function at the field level. This is not to be confused with what William Duerr called the "doctrine of absolute standards," a sort of tyranny of the site, where all off-site considerations — economic, social or political — are ignored. It means that those considerations, along with the relevant body of silvicultural knowledge, must be brought right to the actual site instead of being hoarded away in some central location where decisions will be made by "experts" assigned to their special, isolated tasks.

The bureaucratic hierarchy presently assigned the task of defining and administering intensive forest management, the Forest Service, is drastically in need of functional revision before silviculture can be practised on the lands under its jurisdiction. Historically, the Forest Service's role has been to protect the forests and administer the activities of a harvest-oriented industry. It has been the police force of the woods. A tradition of silviculture will not evolve out of a strict enforcement of rules and regulations; like any form of culture, it requires creative people to exercise their creative abilities, communicating their discoveries to like-minded souls not only of their own generation but to subsequent generations as well.

The ultimate arrogance of the bureaucratic system is its assumption that individuals working within it do not possess the creative faculties that could and should be applied directly to the site. The bureaucratic mind believes that "creativity" is an essentially irrational activity performed by creative experts known as artists. Loggers, foresters, tree planters and the like are not artists; they are employees performing tasks assigned to them by the hierarchy, and therefore they must perform their tasks according to proper rules. But the occasional maverick within the bureaucracies, taking advantage of the occasional fortuitous opportunity, has shown the facts to be otherwise. It is not that employees are uncreative; it is that the hierarchies deny them opportunities to be so.

What is required for the development of silviculture in British Columbia is a Forest Service which will provide more support for and less control of the people working in the woods. After all, the Forest Service is the logical body to act as a clearing-house and dispensary, bringing possibilities, knowledge and the experience of others to those actually practising silviculture. Police are necessary in any society, but they are not generally looked upon as the agents of enlightenment. What is needed between those who work in the woods and those whose task is to look after the public interest is a relationship that admits and encourages an element of co-operation. We are facing the awesome task of learning how to grow the forests that will determine the future wealth and well-being of the people of British Columbia, a task in which the co-operation and communication of all parties is crucial. Yet one of the most regrettable aspects of the Forest Service's present mandate is that its members, most of whom are capable, competent and indeed creative individuals, are provided with job definitions that make them appear as the enemy to most others working in the woods.

In the long run, the forests of the province would probably benefit more if the money now spent on intensive forest management were diverted to broadening the base of silvicultural knowledge. This does not particularly mean the training of more professional foresters, though it would help if those already being trained knew a little more about silviculture; until recently, for example, there was only one professor of silviculture at the University of British Columbia's school of forestry. The primary need is for the dissemination of the existing arcane knowledge of silviculture and forest ecology among the main body of forest workers. What is known is not known widely. There is even a tendency on the part of some forestry professionals to hoard their meagre store of knowledge, perhaps for competitive advantage, but also like priests of a religious cult whose power lies in their control over the secret myths and rituals of their calling.

Up to a point, it is useful to compare forestry to farming, silviculture to agriculture. But it is difficult to make such comparisons from a structural point of view; the evolution of North American forest farming is quite different from that of good farming. Yet with some major qualifications it is possible to compare certain developments in Soviet agriculture with the forest industry in parts of North America. Under Stalin's collectivization program, control over agricultural production was taken from several million small, independent, land-owning farmers — the kulaks — and reorganized into large communal farms whose operations were co-ordinated with overall state planning. In certain ways, there are parallels between this reallocation of resources and the concentration of timber rights and control of forest land that has occurred over the past twenty or thirty years in British Columbia. The major difference, of course, is that under Stalin the kulaks were starved or shot; in British Columbia, such stern measures were not required, and many independent operators were well compensated for relinquishing their rights. But in the end, the results were not that dissimilar: the Soviets were left with an agricultural system that cannot feed them and which is only fractionally as efficient as an independent small farmer on the Canadian Prairies or the

American Midwest; British Columbia has inherited a forest industry which, though utilizing one of the world's most productive forests, is only fractionally as efficient as the small independent operators who compete for their timber in Washington and Oregon. The Soviet system stays in place due to the coercive powers of a totalitarian state; the B. C. system continues to function, in no small part, because the surplus value — the conversion return, or the economic rent — is sufficient to cover the monumental inefficiencies of a monolithic corporate structure that is all too secure in its rights.

One of the fundamental characteristics of any orthodoxy is its assumption that it knows what is "right," that it has or can find the proper response to any situation. The management practices of industrial forestry, as approved and defined by the "official" agency, the Forest Service, constitute orthodox forestry in British Columbia. It is an approach to forestry that seeks no alternatives; it is not open to different ways of looking at, of relating to or of approaching a forest. Opinions or viewpoints which contradict the orthodox are considered heretical, however widely held they may be. If heresies cannot be purged, they can at least be prevented from having any practical effect.

For instance: one of the basic assumptions of orthodox forestry is that forest management can be practised only by large organizations, governments or corporations. Therefore, attempts to legislate small-scale forestry into existence, in the case of Woodlot Licences in the 1978 Forests Act, are dealt with simply by neglecting to implement the legislation. Thus Woodlot Licences, currently our best hope for a new approach, fare no better than other heresies, including those pertaining to silviculture, which are dealt with in a similar manner.[9]

Contemporary forest management in many areas of North America has evolved out of exploitation. The corporate structure, the regulatory apparatus, the operational practices and the very mentality of the industry are rooted in exploitation — harvesting the bounty of nature. To make such a statement is not to pass judgement, merely to note a historical reality. The fly fisherman is also an exploiter: he makes use of what is there, doing nothing to nurture the resource. The orthodox approach to silviculture is in many respects an extension of the exploitative mentality. It is "intensive forest management," a mechanistic application of various techniques which makes use of the soil and the genetic pool to produce wood fibre. This is the dominant, almost the exclusive approach to forest management on much of the private and all of the publicly owned industrial forest land.

The problem is not that this narrowly defined, monolithic and monoculturally oriented forestry exists; forests managed from radically different assumptions might be much the same as those presently being engineered. The difficulty lies with the lack of diversity in approach, with the implication that there is a "right way" to manage forests and that the right way is known and practised. This attitude excludes possibilities which would, if pursued over time, form the basis of silviculture.

Silviculture is not just a set of techniques, nor is it an occupation, a specialization or a profession. It involves more than the kind of knowledge which can be transmitted in institutions or by training. Neither is it something so subtle and refined as to be possessed only by a select and sensitive few. Silviculture is something a society acquires over time; it is the product of generations of experience. Silviculture advances as much from what is "wrong" as from what is "right." It embraces diversity and variety. It is science as well as technology, and it is also an art which has as much to do with the psychology of the human beings who practise it as with the biological imperatives of a living, growing forest. It is not a luxury, an unaffordable dream, but a necessity.

Today, silviculture is being denied by the very bureaucratic apparatus established to bring it into being. And as silviculture is denied, so too is our hope of a vital tradition of forestry. Advocates of such a tradition are no mere mawkish sentimentalists. The vital principle of tradition is its practicality: however dim, it nevertheless represents our brightest light to illuminate a murky and uncertain future.

The lengthy time spans involved with forestry place most of the major issues — biological, ecological, economic and social — in the realm of speculation. The final judgements of who is right and wrong will be written only in the nature of the forests that will exist many centuries from now. Ultimately, the future is an unknowable abyss. Thus, the practice of forestry is a profound act of faith: if nothing else, faith that there *is* a future. This, in itself, is an increasingly rare phenomenon in our society.

The evolution of forestry, or more precisely, of silviculture, has been contingent upon an acceptance of uncertainty. An essential feature of the enterprise is that the fruits of a century's effort can be destroyed, quite literally, by a bolt from the blue. The essential strength of forestry is that its very existence denotes a willingness to respond to such a cataclysmic event. If the forest burns, replace it. And endure another century of lightning strikes before reaping the benefits.

A faint indication that the industry may just possibly be in healthy transition is that although it is rapidly becoming an interlocking series of corporate and public bureaucracies, its employees, from top to bottom, are developing some profound reservations about the nature of their work. The people who like, trust and are willing to commit their creative energies to these institutions are becoming fewer. The most complacent members of the Forest Service and the large forest corporations are those whose job definitions involve the growth and expansion of the bureaucracies themselves. But among the more thoughtful employees of the Forest Service, there is hardly one who is not daily confronted with the frustrations of trying to function in a bureaucratic quagmire. There is hardly one reflective employee of a forest corporation who is not painfully aware of the inefficiencies that seem to be the inescapable consequences of the corporate structure itself. What is remarkable in this situation is not the individual cynicism, indifference or despair that is engendered, but the willingness to carry on in the belief that there is more to the industry than a monthly paycheque, that at some level it is intrinsically worthwhile, despite the Forest Service or despite the particular corporation for which one works.

The forest industry now coming into existence after a century or so of timber exploitation is attempting to establish a silvicultural capability that is equally based on exploitation. The resources being exploited by intensive forest management practised on an industrial scale are more basic and, finally, more important than the trees which until now have been considered the primary, renewable resource. At issue now are the land itself — the soil that determines the quantity and quality of the trees grown — and the legacy of centuries past that is stored in the genetic pool. Although what is being offered as silviculture today is most often only a more profound form of exploitation, the activity is wrapped in a sanctimonious mantle which is largely a response to the moral outrage of the industry's critics. The representation of intensive forest management practices as a moral issue obscures the possibility that some of these practices may be more destructive to the forest ecosystems than progressive clearcut logging.

The final irony of the current situation is that the widely heralded need to reorient the forestry business towards the growing of trees, a task that will require a small army of forestry workers to be employed in the forests, comes at a time when most parts of North America have reached the highest levels of urbanization in history. The labour force required to nurture the forests and the traditions of tomorrow largely lives in the cities. The whole trend of public policy and bureaucratic expediency has for decades been to force people out of the rural and into the urban areas. City dwellers require money to sustain themselves, and much of that money is siphoned from the rural resource areas. The lack of a stable, indigenous rural work force, and the lack of access to the land that would sustain such a work force, means that the bulk of forestry work is performed, at great expense, by nonresident workers, transients both geographically and occupationally. What is urgently needed if we are to succeed as forest farmers is a secure economic base for those engaged in the task. To provide that economic base will not be easy. It will require no less than a restructuring of the industry, a rewriting of our rules and regulations and a reformulation of many of our thoughts and ideas about forests.

TWELVE

Do We Have the Answers?

OUR FORESTS ALREADY PROVIDE us with countless benefits. More gifts await, almost within our grasp; but certain conditions are preventing us from reaping the potential bounty. To receive all that our forests can give, we must restructure our forest industry, our tenure arrangements, our forest management and even, to some extent, ourselves.

Whether the industry is capable of such a reformation is, at best, a moot question. The general depression or recession of the early 1980s has shown that, with its present structure, the forest industry lacks the flexibility to adapt to a poor market. In 1979 the industry had one of the best years in history — British Columbia recorded its highest annual cut ever, and world forest product prices were high. Large amounts were being reinvested in plant expansion and modernization, and intensive forest management expenditures were increasing rapidly. The experts were confidently predicting a constant rise in demand, to be accompanied by a slow but steady increase in forest product prices. Yet just three years later, more than half the employees in the British Columbia forest industry were unemployed, many of them permanently.

The effect of market decline seemed to be least severe on the small independent operators. Loggers cutting their own timber and selling on the open market were getting by, as were small sawmills buying on the same market. The large integrated operations seemed to be hit hardest. They were stuck with high operating costs that were uncomfortably close to the selling price of the various products. How tight the margin on which the big companies were operating could be measured by comparing the low stumpage rates which the major British Columbia corporations were paying with those paid by their less-integrated counterparts who were buying timber at competitive auction on U. S. National Forest lands in Washington and Oregon. In British Columbia, prices did not have to drop very far before the stumpage rates hit their prescribed minimums, after which industry began to absorb the losses.

If they could, B. C. corporations bailed out altogether — Rayonier and Crown Zellerbach, for example. The rest held out as long as they could, shutting down their least efficient operations first. By the end of 1982, a higher proportion of the integrated industry was shut down than at any time since its emergence after World War II.

Perhaps the most serious long-term effect of this situation concerns the implied promise — indeed, the age-old justification — of the integrated corporate system: that it could provide the financial stability and continuity to weather adverse times. This supposition, shared by Fernow, MacMillan, Sloan, Clyne, Orchard and a legion of other shapers of the industry, had never been seriously tested until the recent debacle. Even employees of the big forest corporations had come to regard the idea as an Eternal Verity, assuming that, apart from the usual seasonal layoffs, their jobs were reasonably secure. The 1980s have severely strained their faith, particularly when they observed that the smaller independent operations have continued to function.

More surprising is the possibility that in certain respects the forest industry of the Pacific Northwest, and perhaps of British Columbia in particular, may have lost its "economic advantage," its ability to produce specified goods or services more efficiently than other products can be produced in the same region. Without this economic advantage, the existence of a timber resource does not necessarily guarantee the existence of a forest industry. At various times in British Columbia's history, the economic advantage has lain with the fur industry, the mining industry and the fishing industry. Throughout most of this century, the forest industry has had the advantage. Now that situation may be changing: in this region, the forest industry was one of the first, not one of the last, to be seriously affected by the general economic slowdown of the early 1980s.

From time to time, the problems and contradictions within the forest industry have been noticed, and various solutions have been proposed. The most time-honoured of these remedies is a return to a competitive bidding system for public timber. There are at least two schools of thought among those advocating this change. One, which calls for a return to old-style free enterprise, is supported by most independent operators and contract loggers. This solution would at least remove large integrated corporations from Public Sustained Yield Units. Other critics, such as Gordon Gibson, advocate the removal of all noncompetitive timber tenures, including Tree Farm Licences. Gibson maintains that everyone, including the big companies, would be better off if the timber were harvested by small independent loggers and sold to the large processing mills, which would then be forced into efficiency by having to buy their timber on an open market.

Gibson's proposal has much to recommend it: the big companies have very little invested in the Crown-owned portion of the Tree Farm Licences; most of their expenditures have been covered by stumpage offsets. The corporations' long-standing argument — that they require control of their future timber supplies — is contradicted by experience in a number of other areas and countries. In the southeastern United States, for example, where timber processing is largely controlled by multinational corporations, including MacMillan Bloedel and Crown Zellerbach, most mills obtain their timber on the open market, much of it supplied by small forest land owners. This region's industrial efficiency is acknowledged by Canada's corporate forest establishment: the campaign for increased government spending on forest management portrays the small southeastern forest farmers as a formidable threat to Canadian industry.

Competitive timber sales would also have the virtue (to some, the vice) of increasing public revenues from the forests. It is for this reason that some factions of the political left support the idea of drastically revising the procedures for allocating timber, though a counterargument maintains that any such gains would be more than offset by inefficiencies consequent from the public sector assuming management functions now performed by private corporations.

The argument for competitive timber sales has a more fundamental weakness: it assumes that the resource being allocated is timber. Yet it is becoming ever clearer that the important resource is the forest land itself, control of which is of crucial economic importance. It is far more difficult to allocate rights to this resource competitively because the revenues on which the market values and economic rent will depend are presently unknown. Woodlot Licences, if they ever come into existence, will be allocated on a competitive basis, but competitors for those licences will still be bidding on stumpage. Further, much of the competitive element will be missing from the system because bidders will not be bidding the full stumpage; they will instead be bidding the bonus over the appraised stumpage rate, or upset price, which they are willing to pay for some period into the future. This is the same system the Forest Service now uses to determine charges on noncompetitive timber allocations. The alternative — fully competitive bidding for timber free of long-term management tenures — is generally looked upon as contributing to economic instability; speculative bids in times of rising prices would lead to bankruptcies when prices drop,[1] whereas licences obtained in periods of low prices would lead to windfall gains and a failure of the government to collect full economic rent when prices rise. The obvious solution to this problem, indexing the stumpage and expressing it as a fraction of current end-product selling prices, would work only in an open, nonrigged selling market.

The final problem with the approach of Gibson and the political left is that it would entrust the Forest Service with the task of growing timber which it would then sell on an open, competitive market. This solution assumes that the Forest Service is capable of the task. There are very few people in either the private or public sectors who would agree.

Woodlot forestry, the small-scale approach, has found support for decades from many directions. Essentially, this solution proposes allocating relatively small parcels of public forest land to what are basically individual or family forest operations. From time to time, this has been a popular idea. In his 1956 Royal Commission report, Sloan recommended that tracts of less than 400 ha (1000 acres) of Crown forest land be sold for small-scale management. Sloan's recommendation had the enthusiastic support of even some executives from British Columbia's major forest corporations, such as H. S. Foley of the Powell River Company. Many of these supporters argued that legislation should be enacted to prevent large companies from acquiring these tenures. In contrast to the positions taken by the managers of the major companies today, these earlier managers insisted that the participation of independent forest operators was essential for the future of the free enterprise system, and even for the well-being of the large forest companies themselves.

The woodlot concept has always had considerable support from professional foresters, especially those in the best positions to judge the forest management practices of the Forest Service and the large corporations. Although this viewpoint flies in the face of orthodox forest management theory, nevertheless a considerable number of knowledgeable and experienced foresters are convinced that if they had control and operation of a relatively small tract of forest land, they could not only practise better forestry but they could do so more efficiently. At the same time, they could free themselves from the largely bureaucratic roles they now fill in both the public and private sectors.

Perhaps the most articulate expression of woodlot forestry was contained in a brief to the Pearse Commission by Jim Collins, a Vancouver forestry consultant. He suggested a tenure much like a Tree Farm Licence but, like Sloan's proposal a quarter of a century before, limited to 400 ha (1000 acres). Collins's suggestion was incorporated, almost unchanged, in Pearse's report and later in the 1978 Forests Act. But there it lies in suspended animation; the Forest Service has not chosen to breathe life into it.

A modified version of the woodlot tenure is widely discussed in regard to the National Forest lands in the northwestern United States. There it is talked about as "landed" or "holistic" forestry. The idea has evolved out of the experience of relatively numerous small-scale forest land owners who successfully operate in that area, and it has a wide appeal among the large and growing numbers of contract silviculture workers. The great virtue of this conception is its acknowledgement of forest ecology, in contrast to the intensive management practices of corporate industrial forestry. There is less talk of free enterprise and a greater emphasis on both preserving environmental integrity and the life styles this would make possible. In this respect, the development of a silvicultural tradition is almost implicit, but one of the weaknesses of the holistic version of forest management is that it often tends to see timber harvesting as, at best, a necessary evil.

The Woodlot Licence has a major deficiency: conceived as a very narrowly defined alternative to a Tree Farm Licence, it springs from a somewhat idealized vision of the individual entrepreneurial forest manager. Nor was the licence an integral part of the new Forests Act. Similarly, Pearse's chapter on small-scale forestry was a "throwaway" chapter; it could have been omitted entirely without affecting any of his other recommendations. As elsewhere in his report, Pearse appears here to have been a good Liberal party member, including the woodlot suggestion in an attempt to please everyone.

The failure to propose fundamental changes in the structure of the forest industry is the major criticism of Pearse's Royal Commission report, otherwise the most comprehensive collection of suggestions, solutions and recommendations ever prepared in British Columbia for resolving the major differences in forest policy and practice. Pearse recognized most of the weaknesses of the present system, including its conflicts and contradictions. He noted the shift underway from a harvesting towards a growing industry and realized that the ultimate resources were the forest land and the forest soil. He detailed and deplored the concentration of timber rights in the hands of a few corporations. Yet overall, Pearse upholds the status quo. Although he tinkers with the system, he concludes that the present mechanisms are fundamentally sound. People have wondered what he would have proposed if the New Democratic government, which established his commission, had remained in power until his report was completed. Perhaps the most significant criticism of the report is the consensus, which Pearse has never refuted, that it *would* have been different. If so, then his report was true to the traditions of such investigations: he told the established powers, if not exactly what he thought they wanted to hear, then what he thought they would accept — specifically, what the new Social Credit government might act upon.

The value of Pearse's report lies in his exhaustive investigation of the industry. It is a remarkable document that contains vast amounts of information otherwise unavailable, some provocative analyses and a unique overview of provincial forest resources and the uses to which they are being put. However, his recommendations need to be read with due regard for the political context in which they were offered.

There are some curious conventions concerning politics and forestry, the chief one being that the two do not mix. With the notable exception of Gordon Gibson, few if any B. C. politicians have had experience in the forest industry. This is particularly true of forest ministers: Robert Sommers's chief qualification appears to have been a summer job with the Forest Service; Ray Williston was a school teacher; Bob Williams, an academic urban planner; Tom Waterland, a mining engineer. Politicians, in power or out, traditionally view forests as a source of public revenue, a readily available supply of funds; something to be exploited. Their primary concerns, and therefore the major political questions, have to do with policies and procedures for extracting money from forest users and with the control of access to the forests. The political resolution of most forestry issues is dominated by two considerations: the financial return to the government and the control of timber rights. More fundamental questions — the balancing of urban and rural interests, the ecological implications of forest management, the growth of public and corporate bureaucracies — are far less important.

Politicians increasingly consider themselves professionals, specialists in public policy and administration. They tend to think that other "experts," such as foresters, have everything within their fields well in hand and that the essential poltical task is to define policy, which will promptly be executed. Thus, the nature of intensive management practices is considered a technical question; of such practices, only the costs and returns are relevant. Techniques are left to the experts.

Consequently, a political issue, such as the allocation of timber rights, is handled in a vacuum. While in power in British Columbia in the 1970s, the NDP took the approach that the public interest would be best served by giving control of timber rights to Crown-owned corporations. This policy ignored the most common public complaint: that the large, private forest corporations were large, not that they were private. A great many people around the industry could imagine only one thing worse than multinational corporate control over forests: control by equally large Crown corporations. The monolith to end monoliths in the province is B. C. Hydro; throughout the hinterlands, the idea of such a monster roaming loose in the forest industry was appalling. By the time the NDP was thrown out of office, some of its more intelligent members had begun to share Minister of Forests Bob Williams's view that there were virtues in the smaller independent operations in the industry. Indeed, Williams's actions had begun to reflect this attitude more strongly. But generally the party looked upon increased competition for timber rights mainly as a way of increasing government revenues.

The newly elected Social Credit government talked a lot about allocating timber rights and boosting the fortunes of "free enterprises," and about protecting hinterland interests from the growing power of urban bureaucracies and corporations. At the same time, however, the government strengthened the timber rights of the large tenure holders and launched a reorganization of the Forest Service that increased its bureaucratic nature, making it even more capable of designing and implementing a monolithic monocultural approach to forest management. Social Credit's solutions, like those of the NDP, were founded on the belief that the basic resource is timber rather than land and on the questionable assumption that the Forest Service, through its legislated ability to define what is and what is not "orthodox" silviculture, is capable of renewing that resource.

The political approach has created a system of forest management in which only a few people are assigned to seek alternatives — and those in very narrow, specialized ways. One of the consequences of limiting forest politics to the generation of revenues and the allocation of timber rights is that politicians and the political process are ill prepared to deal with the combined chorus of corporate managers, government bureaucrats and union leaders which insists that intensive forest management is the solution to every ill of the industry and every ailment of the forests.

In Canada, the demand for intensive forest management is part of a long political tradition. Large corporations, flying the false colours of free enterprise and extolling the virtues of the entrepreneurial spirit, have always been able to convince governments to spend money on their behalf. As usual, there is the promise of great public benefit, in this case an increase in the timber supply, the protection or creation of jobs and the exercising of environmental responsibility. The possibility is rarely considered that vast public spending in these areas might be at best a waste of money and at worst a means of destroying the forest ecology. There is no evidence that pouring money into the inefficient forest management system that dominates British Columbia's forests will help to retain or regain the economic advantage which, in the early 1980s, appears to have been lost. We are still woefully inexperienced at growing trees in this province, and in this country. The proposition that by spending hundreds of millions of dollars annually on a very narrowly defined type of forest management, controlled by inefficient corporations and government agencies, we can somehow buy an economically viable industry and healthy forests, is simply not credible.

Any examination of the industry clearly shows the great need for flexibility in our forest policies, with any or all participants free to express their conclusions without fear of bureaucratic black marks. Modern agriculture was not devised solely in research institutions, agricultural colleges and government departments; most of it was learned by farmers working on the land. There is no question that the academy, the research institution and the various public and private bureaucracies have much to contribute, but in the end silviculture will be created in the woods, by the people who work in the woods. It seems only sensible that their knowledge and experience should be cultivated and incorporated into the search for solutions. All too often, however, this kind of experience is ignored.

There is an assumption built into the way we do many things that the only valid means of expanding a field of knowledge is through research, and this almost always means formal, scientific, test-tube research. When it is applied to silviculture, this research most often involves testing certain propositions in isolated, controlled research plots. A major problem of such research is that much of it relates to phenomena occurring over decades or centuries — the rotation of a forest, for instance, or the life span of a Douglas-fir tree. Another problem is that there is little evidence of research results finding their way into operational forestry. On the one hand, we cannot wait a century or two for the results to come in; on the other, we have a system in which research and operational forestry are so isolated from each other that they are mutually irrelevant. This, and the ignoring of practical, on-site experience by forest managers, is a waste of potentially creative cross-fertilization of knowledge.

The managed forests now replacing virgin stands in most of Canada and the western United States require the development of a new and appropriate technology. This is particularly true in the Pacific Northwest, where logging the enormous trees of the coastal rainforest has led to the development of big machinery capable of hauling 2 m (6 foot) diameter logs out of some of the roughest country in the world. By the 1980s, logging conditions and technical advances have resulted in a highly capital-intensive industry, with most large-scale logging operations requiring about $300,000 worth of equipment for every worker. The equipment needed to harvest the managed stands now being grown in these same forests will be quite different. In the first place, a significant portion of the future timber supply will be obtained from commercial thinnings or other types of selective cuts. A $500,000 yarder designed to haul out first-growth Douglas-fir and cedar is not the appropriate piece of equipment for thinning a forty-year-old plantation, or for clearcutting the relatively small sites that replace progressive clearcutting in many areas. For both silvicultural and environmental reasons, the economics of second-growth harvesting is shifting towards a more labour-intensive approach. During the 1970s in Washington and Oregon, a number of smaller forest companies implemented drastic retooling programs, increasing their number of employees and dropping their capital investment to $30,000 or $40,000 per man. This will eventually occur in British Columbia.

There are several aspects to the technology involved in the evolution of the forest industry. The first is that practically none of the equipment that will eventually be needed is being produced in North America. The yarders used in commercial thinning operations are either imported from Europe or pieced together from obsolete machinery once used here for other purposes. Second, from the perspective of local economic and social stability, there can be a tremendous advantage in a change in the labour-capital ratio. Replacing a $1-million machine employing three men with a $200,000 machine capable of yarding the same number of logs a day but employing twice as many people, really means twice as many jobs for one-fifth the capital investment.

There is another facet of the labour-capital ratio which is critically important, and involves the policies and outlook of the major forest industry union, the IWA. At present, a major obstacle to innovative silviculture is the union's rigid approach to defining job descriptions. For instance, as far as the IWA is concerned, a faller is a faller, whether he is falling old-growth Douglas-fir in steep country or the small trees taken in a commercial thinning operation. The union insists that the same rates be paid and the faller not be engaged in other tasks, such as working on the rigging, which would improve the falling and increase the overall productivity of the operation. Even more important is the IWA's antipathy to the kind of small operations which are necessary if silviculture is ever to become an established fact.

The capital requirements of a silviculturally oriented forest industry create certain problems for corporate economists and accountants. From their point of view, the greatest advantage is in a high ratio of capital to labour. A million-dollar piece of logging equipment is an asset; it can be depreciated, sold or traded. Furthermore, if it happens to be the "approved" piece of equipment for logging certain forests, it has the virtue of restricting competition for that timber to those loggers who can afford it. Additionally, most of this equipment is produced by large equipment-manufacturing corporations that are part of the multinational corporate network, and it has been the nature of these corporations to prefer producing a single million-dollar machine to ten hundred-thousand dollar ones.

There is an important silvicultural aspect to the issue of appropriate technology. Oversimplified, the general rule is that the more costly the piece of equipment, the more reduced the silvicultural options. For instance, small patches of diseased or insect-infested forest cannot be treated and salvaged with a

27 m (90 foot) steel spar worth $1 million; but they can be with a $50,000 yarder powered by a farm tractor. The degree to which the appropriate technology is unavailable or hard to obtain is the degree by which we are unable to develop a silvicultural capability — and ultimately unable to compete on the world market.

Above all, the growth of silviculture in British Columbia requires the diversification of forest land tenures. At present, the only really effective means of obtaining the right to grow trees on Crown land is the Tree Farm Licence. There are thirty-four such licences ranging in size from the 7600 ha (18,800 acre) licence operated by the city of Mission to an area of almost 2 700 000 ha (6.7 million acres) in B. C. Timber's TFL no. 1 near Prince Rupert. Most TFLs are several hundred thousand hectares in size, and several companies hold a number of licences. Woodlot Licences, which at present exist mostly in theory, are limited to a maximum size of 400 ha (1000 acres).

A far wider variety of tenure arrangements must become available — a wider variety in the size of tenures as well as in their form. Such a change would also involve a much-needed re-examination of Crown ownership of forest land. The main objection to privatizing land — that the land might be removed from the forest base — could be countered by privatizing only that land which is best suited to forestry and which is located in relatively undeveloped areas. Forest land should also be protected by zoning regulations and tax measures. The major advantage to be gained from selling a specified portion of the provincial forests, say 10 to 20 per cent, would be the evolution of private forest management practices, free from the domination of the Forest Service. This is needed not because the Forest Service is so bad, but because in British Columbia its influence is so pervasive. A degree of privatization would create opportunities for alternative approaches.

New management tenures are chiefly required in the Public Sustained Yield Units now managed by the Forest Service. In addition, a range in tenure size is needed, from 200 and 300 ha (500 and 750 acre) blocks to parcels of several thousand hectares. They should be of a size and forest-cover composition that would attract individuals as well as small- to medium-sized independent logging and silvicultural contracting operations.

One of the main objections to this type of tenure on the land is, of course, bureaucratic. It originates in the mechanisms used to calculate harvest levels and allocate timber rights. Basically, the argument goes, it is impossible to create these forms of tenure because sooner or later they will entail harvesting timber, and the allowable cuts of most areas are already fully committed. If, for example, a long-term land tenure is granted containing a forty-year-old stand calculated to "mature" at age ninety, in fifty years, when it does mature, the timber on that land will not be available for distribution via the various forms of harvesting licences now available. In essence, this argument seeks to perpetuate the present system whereby harvesting in Timber Supply Areas is performed by logging companies while the forest is actually managed by another agency — the Forest Service. The basic proposition is that the Forest Service should retain the business of growing the trees, which will be sold to the private sector for harvesting.

The alternative proposal here is to give both the existing harvesting industry and the silvicultural contracting industry the chance to transform themselves into a forest farming industry. This would simply recognize the changing nature of the resources being utilized. A good deal of diversity in tenure arrangements would be required, partly because there is a great amount of diversity in the province's forests, but largely because the business of growing trees is a new undertaking, best approached from a number of directions.

The future of the Tree Farm Licences is more complicated. They are supposed to be forest management tenures, but there is little evidence that any of the corporations, at the executive policy-making level, view TFLS as serious silvicultural operations. At best, they do what is required under the terms of their licences. In reality, TFLS have been valued by their corporate holders as the source of a secure, inexpensive timber supply. More important, they have produced enormous capital gains and made it possible for the forest corporations to raise money for their processing mills.

What the poor markets of the 1980s have indicated is that some TFLS, particularly on the coast, are becoming liabilities to the integrated companies. In many cases, the companies could get their timber more cheaply on the open market, to the limited extent that such a market exists. Further, they could obtain the grade and species they want without having to log large volumes of timber not suited to their mills.

Thus far, the issue of TFL tenure has been politically sensitive, with one extreme demanding the cancellation of these rights and the other advocating that the terms be lengthened and made more secure. In the future, it may be more productive to look at the question differently. The integrated companies do not make the bulk of their profits from timber harvesting; they will make even less growing trees. They make their money in the sawmills, pulp mills and other processing facilities. Increasingly, as the first-growth forests on the TFLs are harvested, it is reasonable to expect that some of the companies will want, or be willing, to relinquish their tenures. If that occurs, it would make sense to reallocate these lands in some form of tenure to those whose interest lies in silviculture. In many instances, the people involved would be those now employed by the major corporations.

The indispensable requirement of forest management tenures ought to be to encourage people, individually and in groups, to form long-term associations with specific tracts of forest. Forest workers, professional and otherwise, should be permitted to live as well as work in the forests, much as farmers live on the land. These people must be able to form a cultural attachment to the forests, in contrast to the transient, exploitive relationship presently characteristic of harvesting. This is not possible now, mainly for reasons of bureaucratic expedience: the Forest Service does not want to bother with the massive amount of paperwork its own bureaucratic procedures would generate if people were to live as well as work in the woods. There are no inherent reasons why foresters should not live where they work; it is simply forbidden because it is administratively inconvenient.

New forms of tenure should also be designed to allow licencees to develop equity. This would help offset a tendency towards short-term exploitation as well as encourage silvicultural treatments which take a long time to provide a return. There would also have to be a mechanism to prevent or limit capital gains to be realized from the mere acquisition of a tree farming tenure. These gains are actually another expression of the economic rent, and that rent properly belongs to the public. When a logging company works its forest farming tenure, it does more than chop trees. It affects everything on that land — trees, birds, deer, fish, mosquitoes. Further, it restricts the access of other people to the land. The economic rent should reflect this broad usage; it should be calculated on the resource really being exploited — the land itself.

By contrast, rent based on stumpage is based only on trees, a mere by-product of that land. It distorts both the ecological and economic activities by placing undue emphasis on the timber-producing functions of the forest at the expense of its other values. As a form of tax based on production, stumpage encourages cutting yet discourages the growing of new timber. It also distorts silvicultural judgements. A stumpage system applied to a forest farming tenure is based ultimately on an appraisal method. The Forest Service has shown how difficult it is to find an appraisal system that accurately reflects the worth of timber; it could not possibly manage such a system if it also had to include the costs of growing that timber.

If British Columbia is to sustain a silvicultural capability, a policy of rural or hinterland development must be pursued. At present, most of the province's resources are siphoned through the urban centres, where the corporate and bureaucratic headquarters are located, with a diminished portion returning to the area whence it came. A 1974 study of the Slocan PSYU found that direct government revenues from the area in the previous year had totalled $1.1 million, with only $235,000 being spent by the government on the management of all the natural resources in the PSYU.

Rural British Columbia needs repopulating for more than nostalgic reasons. Undoubtedly, part of the North American psyche yearns for a rural life style. This yearning, if tapped, could develop into the powerful creative force needed to develop a viable silviculture. Further, rural repopulation as a consistent and clearly articulated policy also has strategic value. The ultimate strength of a resource-based economy, such as exists in British Columbia, rests with the people who perform the basic and actual conversion functions. For several decades, there has been a trend described by Premier Bill Bennett in November 1978 as "the growing erosion of the rural life style which is the strength of this province." He was speaking to resource bureaucrats and warned that if necessary he would "bring forward legislation that will provide an incentive to improving the quality of life for rural British Columbians."

The premier's sentiment is a fine one. Regrettably, fine sentiments alone will not reverse the process of urban concentration that has taken place in British Columbia for the last half-century. Specific, and in some cases even drastic, measures are required. For instance, many political resource questions — until recent years regarded as purely technical in nature and decided by bureaucrats — should instead be decided by local political institutions such as the regional district boards. The present system concentrates an inordinate amount of detailed power in the hands of the provincial cabinet and its committees — principally the Environment and Land Use Committee. The stability of rural economies would be better served if many of these decisions were made at the local level. It is not more participation in the lower levels of a centralized decision-making process that is required, but a decentralization of the process itself.

The availability of industrial or commercial financing also needs revision. It is far more difficult to obtain a business loan in a rural area than in an urban centre. Hinterland financial institutions mainly provide consumer and mortgage loans. This rural handicap was a major factor in concentrating timber rights in the hands of urban holders, and it has contributed in other ways to the urbanization of the provincial economy. The re-creation of a vigorous hinterland economy depends on readily available capital, with the same terms and conditions as in urban centres.

The publicly owned forest lands of the North and West can be considered from two broad perspectives. Our forests and forest industry can be seen as an immense, complicated set of problems, a shrinking resource, the object of growing conflict. Invariably, the solutions to these perceived "problems" require spending more and more money; thus our forest resources, in their various stages of growth and development, appear as liabilities rather than assets. We have a forest products industry that is organized and financed on the assumption that government will grow the trees and forests needed in the future. Our present knowledge is such that this task is more intimidating than inspiring.

Alternatively, the forest can be viewed as a place of opportunities and possibilities. One of these opportunities, already mentioned, is to make the business of growing trees a means of tapping creative energies now being wasted and of integrating this creative enterprise into the overall economic and social fabric.

The business of growing trees also holds out the possibility of developing a significant new component of the economic resource base. Many observers have noted that there will soon be more people employed in the growing of trees than in their harvesting. Silviculture is an entirely new sort of resource industry that will complement rather than replace the present users of the forests. It is difficult to appreciate this opportunity because of a long and widely held idea in Canada that there is something wrong with being "hewers of wood," that a modern and sophisticated society should not be engaged in such primitive tasks as cutting down trees in order to make a living. Manufacturing or other technologically sophisticated occupations enjoy a higher status than agricultural or resource occupations. Hewing wood, however, is highly profitable for the hewers. Most people who actually work in the woods consider themselves fortunate that they are not stuck in some industrial ghetto created by the architects of modern, industrialized America. There is nothing wrong with hewing trees, and probably even less with growing them. Certainly the world will always need forests, even if the demand for timber declines — and that is unlikely. Growing those forests and providing that timber can be as pleasant and — if we are good at it — as profitable a way of life as any.

Silviculture also gives us a chance to redefine our human relationship with the natural environment. If we are to become silviculturally adept, we must establish ourselves in a symbiotic rather than a parasitic relationship with the forest ecosystem. In fact, symbiosis will have to be integral to whatever silvicultural traditions we develop. This is, surprisingly, also an economic imperative. The response of any ecosystem to a parasitic organism is to deprive it of sustenance. In a diseased forest, the species under attack disappears and is replaced by another which is useless to the parasite; the organisms that cause root rot in a Douglas-fir forest disappear with the fir. On the other hand, the mycorrhizic relationship between mushrooms and some trees, in which each provides the other with certain nutrients they are unable to obtain on their own, is a symbiotic relationship that benefits both. In terms of human values, the symbiotic relationship is both the preferred and the profitable option.

The solutions proposed here are based on the assumption that a varied forest, variously managed for a variety of social and economic uses, is preferable to a monocultural forest, monolithically managed for the primary purpose of producing maximum income for the government, the corporations and the unionized workers in the forest industry. For too long the management of our forests has been entrusted to a few professionals and corporations whose goals are restricted to harvesting an ever-increasing supply of merchantable timber. This has led not only to a depletion of the forest resource and damage to the forest ecology but also to conflicts between the managers and others — fishermen, recreationists, conservationists, farmers, ranchers and rural residents — whose interests are not being served by current forest policies. Intensive management, as advocated by corporations, professional foresters, unions and the Forest Service, will not alleviate these conflicts because "scientific" management is narrowly focussed on economic values. It is also financially wasteful, ecologically suspect and impractical, given the present state of silvicultural knowledge.

The argument for alternative forms of forest management, and thus of forest tenures, should not be confused with a romantic yearning for a more primitive, less complicated phase in our history. The possibilities of a silvicultural evolution offer no escape from the modern world. On the contrary, the ability to create and sustain healthy, productive forest ecosystems is a challenge to our most visionary perceptions of ourselves as a society and as a species. As human beings, we are so dependent on the forests that, in a global sense, our survival depends to a large extent on whether or not we are able to meet that challenge with the political and silvicultural skills worthy of a modern technological age.

If we succeed, our forests will be as generous to us in the future as they have been in the past. If we fail — even though we should succeed in journeying to the stars — our voyage into the universe will be no more than a desperate leap for survival. We will go not as emissaries of a healthy, vibrant biological community, but as refugees from a devastated, hostile ecosystem.

The Pacific rainforests of North America once contained the most valuable trees the world has ever seen: firs, cedar and spruce that were five and six or more centuries old when they were cut and put to human use. Dare we imagine a time when we will be able to profitably replace those forests as they once were — a time when we will again be able to stand beneath gigantic trees on a still summer night, gazing up through the branches at the stars?

The final great gift of the forests is this: when we plant a seedling in the ground, we can see a future measured in centuries.

Appendices

Appendix 1 Amounts Charged Against Logging Operations, 1980, rounded to nearest dollar

Forest Region	Royalty	Misc.	Interest	Scaling Fees and Expenses	Stumpage	Rentals, Cruising, Advertising, Transfer Fees	Totals
Cariboo	112	735 998	628 412	3 797	16 847 094	735 696	18 950 884
Kamloops	281 228	943 232	429 014	4 962	25 595 329	1 086 999	28 340 763
Nelson	130 015	904 901	417 085	4 959	11 261 385	1 330 975	14 049 319
Prince George	120 634	1 575 761	2 125 527	6 303	42 796 150	2 778 704	49 403 079
Prince Rupert	2 732 918	998 314	449 166	622 042	61 270 682	2 722 877	68 795 999
Vancouver	10 422 691	866 465	443 775	2 713 891	175 688 133	6 088 587	196 223 541
Totals 1980	13 687 373	6 024 671	4 492 978	3 355 954	333 458 773	14 743 837	375 763 585
1979	12 910 812	5 961 595	—	3 092 980	489 801 320	15 582 570	527 349 277
1978	8 306 627	5 107 149	—	2 984 822	214 617 487	1 283 656	232 209 741
1977	8 610 617	5 064 910	—	2 728 374	67 074 287	2 066 413	85 544 602
1976	6 897 259	5 074 294	—	3 123 280	48 592 302	2 877 315	66 564 449
1975	6 074 175	4 438 210	—	2 834 921	28 389 508	1 989 319	43 726 134
1974	8 221 172	3 841 146	—	3 066 601	169 698 770	1 213 665	186 041 352
1973	6 804 684	3 876 214	—	2 892 161	251 777 437	1 917 706	267 268 202
1972	5 231 474	2 510 947	—	2 399 416	96 595 978	1 921 977	108 659 792
1971	5 519 237	1 930 657	—	2 531 007	55 347 358	2 341 637	67 669 896

Source: B. C. Ministry of Forests *Annual Report* 1980 (Victoria: B. C. Ministry of Forests, 1980), p. 58.

Appendix 2 Average Stumpage Prices Received on Timber Scaled from Tree Farm Licence Cutting Permits, by Species and Forest Region, 1980[2]

FOREST REGION	BALSAM Volume (m^3)	BALSAM Price (per m^3)	BALSAM Price Range (per m^3)	CEDAR Volume (m^3)	CEDAR Price (per m^3)	CEDAR Price Range (per m^3)	CYPRESS Volume (m^3)	CYPRESS Price (per m^3)	CYPRESS Price Range (per m^3)
Cariboo	15 525	2.64	0.92– 6.40	—	—	—	—	—	—
Kamloops	92 983	2.26	0.39–13.05	22 513	3.27	0.39–25.54	—	—	—
Nelson	132 349	2.28	0.80– 9.95	283 324	5.31	0.80–34.05	—	—	—
Prince George	101 211	3.92	0.94– 9.30	[1]	2.27	2.27	—	—	—
Prince Rupert	366 592	2.83	0.89– [1]	411 100	6.36	0.74– [1]	58 565	63.89	54.89– [1]
Vancouver	1 546 135	13.24	3.51–14.20	1 569 768	10.92	3.06–15.99	193 952	70.50	[1] –83.02
Totals	2 254 795	9.96	0.39–14.20	2 286 706	9.33	0.39–34.05	252 517	54.15	54.89–83.02

FOREST REGION	DOUGLAS-FIR Volume (m^3)	DOUGLAS-FIR Price (per m^3)	DOUGLAS-FIR Price Range (per m^3)	HEMLOCK Volume (m^3)	HEMLOCK Price (per m^3)	HEMLOCK Price Range (per m^3)	LARCH Volume (m^3)	LARCH Price (per m^3)	LARCH Price Range (per m^3)
Cariboo	42 471	13.41	3.15–31.24	38	1.05	0.96– 9.43	—	—	—
Kamloops	85 686	6.17	0.39–42.33	14 744	1.22	0.39– 9.99	12 408	17.79	0.91–25.87
Nelson	96 546	5.74	1.01–26.65	337 280	0.29	0.23– 2.86	26 712	3.37	0.31–20.38
Prince George	6 819	16.27	0.98–32.64	1 093	2.54	0.90– 9.30	—	—	—
Prince Rupert	—	—	—	1 556 699	5.26	[1]	—	—	—
Vancouver	585 482	19.05	3.38–25.79	3 036 118	12.70	[1]	—	—	—
Totals	817 004	15.81	0.39–42.33	4 945 972	9.46	0.23– 9.99	39 120	7.94	0.31–25.87

FOREST REGION	LODGEPOLE PINE			SPRUCE			WHITE PINE		
	Volume (m^3)	Price (per m^3)	Price Range (per m^3)	Volume (m^3)	Price (per m^3)	Price Range (per m^3)	Volume (m^3)	Price (per m^3)	Price Range (per m^3)
Cariboo	10 023	3.90	1.05–10.93	34 013	8.03	1.10–15.89	—	—	—
Kamloops	268 444	2.31	0.39–15.74	279 279	5.90	0.39–17.93	1 709	14.99	0.39–48.71
Nelson	163 558	1.57	0.89– 8.73	264 139	4.78	0.96–19.33	90 537	12.39	1.88–45.22
Prince George	20 812	4.72	1.00–10.33	342 173	11.36	1.09–19.20	—	—	—
Prince Rupert	54 865	1.42	[1]	397 976	31.30	[1]	5	7.15	[1]
Vancouver	46	12.85	[1]	67 806	44.10	[1]	16 915	9.35	[1]
Totals	517 748	1.61	0.39–15.74	1 385 386	16.25	0.39–19.33	109 166	11.96	0.39–48.71

FOREST REGION	OTHER SPECIES			ALL SPECIES		
	Volume (m^3)	Price (per m^3)	Price Range (per m^3)	Volume (m^3)	Price (per m^3)	Price Range (per m^3)
Cariboo	206	0.99	0.50– 1.23	102 276	9.04	0.50–31.24
Kamloops	836	2.96	0.39–27.90	778 602	4.30	0.39–48.71
Nelson	531	2.93	0.44–23.55	1 394 976	3.72	0.23–45.22
Prince George	13	3.89	0.50	472 122	9.52	0.50–32.64
Prince Rupert	11 112	2.04	[1]	2 856 914	9.85	[1]
Vancouver	3 360	6.27	[1]	7 019 582	14.84	[1]
Totals	16 058	2.89	0.39–27.90	12 624 472	11.59	0.39–48.71

[1] Information not available. [2] Excludes firmwood rejects and waste.

Source: B. C. Ministry of Forests *Annual Report* 1980 (Victoria: B. C. Ministry of Forests, 1980), p. 55.

Appendix 3 Average Bid Stumpage Prices on Cutting Permits of Timber Sale Harvesting Licences and Timber Sales, by Species and Forest Region, 1980

FOREST REGION	BALSAM			CEDAR			CYPRESS		
	Volume (m^3)	Price (per m^3)	Price Range (per m^3)	Volume (m^3)	Price (per m^3)	Price Range (per m^3)	Volume (m^3)	Price (per m^3)	Price Range (per m^3)
Cariboo (C)[1]	23 287	1.16	1.16	—	—	—	—	—	—
Cariboo (I)[2]	317 302	1.69	0.92– 61.03	270 164	1.87	0.95– 6.21	—	—	—
Kamloops	867 860	1.90	0.92– 13.98	771 304	3.31	0.40– 19.15	—	—	—
Nelson	545 866	1.27	0.28– 12.99	880 343	4.49	0.37– 16.86	—	—	—
Prince George	2 396 475	2.56	0.81– 12.24	121 628	1.62	1.03– 12.47	—	—	—
Prince Rupert (C)	354 480	3.05	1.99– 6.09	795 090	8.30	0.74– 32.43	55 103	59.61	4.35–105.65
Prince Rupert (I)	1 059 390	2.42	0.40– 16.95	68 040	2.66	1.18– 14.00	—	—	—
Vancouver (C)	944 962	11.76	0.75– 22.47	853 205	11.02	0.71– 40.00	250 266	77.13	1.09–111.14
Vancouver (I)	85 672	6.64	1.06– 14.32	20 587	6.12	1.60– 15.30	—	—	—
Totals	6 595 294	3.69	0.28– 61.03	3 780 361	6.22	0.37– 40.00	305 369	73.69	1.09–111.14

FOREST REGION	DOUGLAS-FIR			HEMLOCK			LARCH		
	Volume (m^3)	Price (per m^3)	Price Range (per m^3)	Volume (m^3)	Price (per m^3)	Price Range (per m^3)	Volume (m^3)	Price (per m^3)	Price Range (per m^3)
Cariboo (C)	—	—	—	—	—	—	—	—	—
Cariboo (I)	1 036 379	6.29	0.92– 26.94	50 709	1.11	0.82– 1.32	—	—	—
Kamloops	1 063 537	6.09	1.02– 25.34	492 754	1.28	0.26– 16.20	64 501	3.77	0.95– 17.37
Nelson	373 471	4.10	0.30– 19.76	671 792	0.36	0.21– 7.93	99 522	2.70	0.43– 18.95
Prince George	210 317	11.39	1.23– 31.68	75 364	1.02	0.39– 1.35	—	—	—
Prince Rupert (C)	142 080	15.74	2.67– 21.76	1 231 690	9.17	0.62– 29.04	—	—	—
Prince Rupert (I)	—	—	—	899 024	1.12	0.65– 5.72	—	—	—
Vancouver (C)	628 242	17.91	0.71– 48.31	2 667 990	9.17	0.71– 27.49	—	—	—
Vancouver (I)	36 523	9.14	1.15– 16.63	87 204	5.31	1.80– 10.06	—	—	—
Totals	3 490 549	8.80	0.30– 48.31	6 176 527	6.19	0.21– 29.04	264 023	2.96	0.43– 18.95

FOREST REGION	LODGEPOLE PINE			SPRUCE			WHITE PINE		
	Volume (m³)	Price (per m³)	Price Range (per m³)	Volume (m³)	Price (per m³)	Price Range (per m³)	Volume (m³)	Price (per m³)	Price Range (per m³)
Cariboo (C)	1 394	0.26	0.26– 0.27	912	1.11	1.06– 1.16	—	—	—
Cariboo (I)	3 337 737	1.97	0.25– 21.47	1 413 507	5.57	0.88– 77.50	—	—	—
Kamloops	2 166 074	1.60	0.30– 15.72	1 948 918	4.78	0.95– 19.39	67 128	13.14	0.50– 32.73
Nelson	2 215 332	1.27	0.23– 18.75	1 180 872	3.66	0.30– 14.31	189 354	18.40	0.44–101.96
Prince George	3 640 238	2.46	0.83– 14.03	8 990 331	6.51	0.93– 25.95	—	—	—
Prince Rupert (C)	—	—	—	392 580	36.80	2.20–118.82	1 940	1.35	0.32– 1.93
Prince Rupert (I)	2 117 030	2.35	0.23– 12.19	1 211 620	4.25	0.40– 17.65	—	—	—
Vancouver (C)	1 077	2.21	1.82– 3.86	90 330	49.91	3.71–154.06	1 317	2.39	1.56– 3.71
Vancouver (I)	12 760	1.01	1.00– 1.22	20 380	6.15	1.15– 12.68	—	—	—
Totals	13 491 642	1.98	0.23– 21.47	15 249 450	6.83	0.30–154.06	259 739	16.83	0.32–101.96

FOREST REGION	OTHER SPECIES			ALL SPECIES		
	Volume (m³)	Price (per m³)	Price Range (per m³)	Volume (m³)	Price (per m³)	Price Range (per m³)
Cariboo (C)	—	—	—	25 593	1.10	0.26– 1.16
Cariboo (I)	12 510	2.27	0.50– 19.15	6 438 308	3.43	0.25– 77.60
Kamloops	63 369	14.97	1.05– 30.15	7 505 445	3.48	0.26– 32.73
Nelson	25 138	4.29	0.39– 11.30	6 281 690	2.81	0.21–101.96
Prince George	24 469	0.50	0.50	15 458 822	4.93	0.39– 31.68
Prince Rupert (C)	—	—	—	2 972 963	13.09	0.32–118.82
Prince Rupert (I)	81 500	0.50	0.50	5 436 604	2.55	0.23– 17.65
Vancouver (C)	50 505	2.53	1.00– 12.25	5 487 894	14.60	0.71–154.06
Vancouver (I)	—	—	—	263 126	6.19	1.00– 16.63
Totals	257 491	4.92	0.39– 30.15	49 870 445	5.54	0.21–154.06

[1] Coast forest region.

[2] Interior forest region.

Source: B. C. Ministry of Forests *Annual Report* 1980 (Victoria: B. C. Ministry of Forests, 1980), p. 56.

Notes

Chapter One

1. *The Outlook for Timber in the United States* (Washington: U. S. Department of Agriculture, 1973).
2. F. L. C. Reed and Associates, *Selected Forest Industry Statistics for Canada* (Toronto: Canadian Forest Congress, 1980), pp. 113–28.
3. The allowable annual cut is the annual harvest permitted in an area using sustained yield criteria.
4. In the western United States the harvest from the National Forests increased rapidly following World War II. The average annual cut reached 53 000 000 m^3 (1.9 billion cubic feet) during the 1960s, then dropped about 11 per cent during the 1970s. In 1977 the U. S. Forest Service recommended a program that would increase harvest levels to 93 000 000 m^3 (3.3 billion cubic feet) by the year 2000. But independent observers argue that this forecast does not take into account reductions in harvesting to come from implementing the 1976 National Forest Management Act, the creation of new wilderness areas and a variety of other federal acts designed to protect or enhance other forest and environmental resources. Some of these critics suggest that the annual cut will drop even further, perhaps to 42 000 000 or 43 000 000 m^3 (1.4 to 1.5 billion cubic feet). Such a drop, combined with the reduced cutting levels expected from the depleted industrial forest lands, lead these critics to predict that between 1985 and 2000, the West's annual cut will decline by 20 000 000 m^3 (706 million cubic feet).

   See 1982 and 1983 issues of *Forest Planning* (Eugene, Oregon).
5. *Forest and Range Resource Analysis Technical Report* (Victoria: B. C. Ministry of Forests, 1980).
6. Ibid., Appendix D5.

7. *Progress Report, March 1981* (Ottawa: B. C. Ministry of Forests and Government of Canada, Department of Regional Economic Expansion, 1981).

Chapter Two

1. Andrew D. Rodgers, *Bernhard Eduard Fernow: A Story of North American Forestry* (Princeton: Princeton University Press, 1951), p. 90.
2. Bernhard E. Fernow, *Economics of Forestry* (1902; reprint: Ayer, 1972), p. 90.
3. Ibid., p. 273.
4. Ibid., p. 345.
5. Rodgers, *Fernow,* p. 388.
6. Fernow, *Economics of Forestry,* p. 141.
7. Rodgers, *Fernow,* p. 464.
8. Ibid., p. 506.
9. Ibid., p. 518.
10. *Report of the Royal Commission on Forest Resources* (Victoria: Queen's Printer, 1976), p. 20.
11. Mensuration on a global scale produces an interesting picture of worldwide forest distribution. Canada's land mass covers about 10 000 000 km^2 (4 million square miles), the U. S.'s 9 000 000 km^2 (3.6 million square miles). British Columbia occupies about 5 per cent of the continent's total. A third of the North American continent, just over 6 000 000 km^2 (2.4 million square miles) is classified as forest land. British Columbia contains about 8.5 per cent of this.

    About two-thirds of North America's forests, or about 4 000 000 km^2 (1.6 million square miles), are defined as productive or commercial forests. The remaining one-third consists of land incapable of growing enough timber for profitable harvesting, as well as parks, wilderness areas and other areas where harvesting is prohibited. The term "productive or commercial forest" means two things: first, that the forest can produce industrial crops of wood, and second, that harvesting these crops is not prohibited by law. British Columbia, with 482 000 km^2 (192,800 square miles) of productive forest land, accounts for 12 per cent of the North American total and 24 per cent of Canada's productive forests.

Harvest figures show a much different pattern. In 1978 North America's timber harvest amounted to 494 750 000 m^3 (17.5 billion cubic feet). Sixty-eight per cent of this came from U. S. forests. In the same year British Columbia cut 75 200 000 m^3 (2.7 billion cubic feet) — 15 per cent of the North American cut and 48 per cent of the Canadian. Thus, British Columbia, with 24 per cent of Canada's productive forest, supplied double that proportion of the Canadian timber harvest.

North America cut 19 per cent of the 1978 world timber harvest of 2.6 billion m^3 (92 billion cubic feet). South America cut 9 per cent, Asia 29 per cent and the Soviet Union 14 per cent, while Africa accounted for 29 per cent and Europe (including Scandinavia) 12 per cent. Mexico, Central America and the South Pacific, which have negligible timber production at best, are omitted from this discussion.

A different pattern of distribution characterizes the world export of forest products, which in 1978 was calculated to be worth U. S.$37.2 billion. Canada shipped 22 per cent of the total and the United States 10 per cent. South America exported only 1.5 per cent and the Soviet Union just 6 per cent; Africa burned almost its entire harvest for fuel. Scandinavia exported a surprising 21 per cent of the world total. It is worth noting that 70 per cent of Canada's exports of forest products went to the United States, which was itself shipping out forest products worth nearly $4 billion.

The volumes of timber available for harvest show yet another picture. North American forests contain about 16 per cent of the world's outstanding timber, South America's enormous 27 per cent, Asia's 15 per cent and the U. S. S. R.'s a full one-third — 33 per cent — of the world's timber volume. Africa's share is 2 per cent and Europe's 5 per cent.

Those volumes may be compared with global forest land distribution to provide a good index of the present productivity of those lands. Of the estimated 20 000 000 km^2 (8 million square miles) of productive forest land in the world, about 19 per cent lies in North America. South America and Asia each account for 17 per cent and the Soviet Union for about 34 per cent. Africa's forest land amounted to 2 per cent and Europe's to 6 per cent.

F. L. C. Reed and Associates, *Selected Forest Industry Statistics for Canada* (Toronto: Canadian Forest Congress, 1980), pp.113–28.

12. G. M. Bonnor, *Canada's Forest Industry* (Ottawa: Environment Canada, 1981).

Chapter Three

1. Martin Allerdale Grainger, *Woodsmen of the West* (Toronto: McClelland and Stewart, 1964), p. 55.
2. *Final Report of the Royal Commission of Inquiry on Timber and Forestry* (Victoria: King's Printer, 1910), p. 58.
3. Bernhard E. Fernow, *Economics of Forestry* (1902; reprint: Ayer, 1972).
4. Ibid.
5. Orchard Papers, File 8-15, Special Collections, University of British Columbia Library, Vancouver, B. C.
6. Gordon M. Sloan, *Report of the Commissioner Relating to the Forest Resources of British Columbia, 1945* (King's Printer: Victoria, 1945), p. 127.
7. Gordon M. Sloan, *Report of the Commissioner Relating to the Forest Industries of British Columbia, 1956* (Victoria: Queen's Printer, 1957), p. 222.
8. *Forest and Range Resource Analysis Technical Report* (Victoria: B. C. Ministry of Forests, 1980), Appendix B2.
9. A built-in fallacy of this procedure is the assumption that a tree will grow differently and have a different point of maximum growth if it is logged at an earlier age.
10. *Report of the Royal Commission on Forest Resources* (Victoria: Queen's Printer, 1976), p. D4.
11. J. P. Kimmins, "Sustained Yield, Timber Mining, and the Concept of Ecological Rotation; a British Columbian View," *Forestry Chronicle* (Feb. 1974): pp. 27–31.
12. Fernow, *Economics of Forestry*, p. 119.
13. Ray Raphael, *Tree Talk* (Covelo, Calif.: Island Press, 1981), pp. 71–79.
14. For debates on this topic, see the *Forestry Chronicle*, June 1969, Oct. 1969 and Aug. 1970.
15. Peter Pearse, "Conflicting Objectives in Forest Policy: The Case of British Columbia," *Forestry Chronicle* (Aug. 1970): pp. 281–87.
16. *Royal Commission Report*, p. 225.
17. W. Young, speech, *Truck Logger* (June 1980).

Chapter Four

1. E. K. DeBeck and Aird Flavelle, interviews, Sound and Moving Image Division, B. C. Provincial Archives, Victoria, B. C.

2. These are the first known predictions of timber famine in British Columbia. See chapter six for more on this topic.
3. Fulton Report Estimate of Land Alienations — 1910

	acres	ha
Vancouver Island Crown grant timber	318,000	129 000
Mainland Crown grant timber	552,000	223 000
E & N Railway Co.	375,000	152 000
CPR, unpublished timber leaseholds	619,000	250 000
Special timber licences	9,000,000	3 650 000
Pulp leaseholds	387,000	156 000
Totals	11,251,000	4 560 000

Source: *Final Report of the Royal Commission of Inquiry on Timber and Forestry* (Victoria: King's Printer, 1910), p. D-17.
4. Orchard Papers, interview no. 42, transcript, Special Collections, University of British Columbia Library, Vancouver, B. C.
5. Ibid., p. 120.
6. Ibid., pp. 122–23.
7. The companies implicated were Tahsis Co., Empire Mills, Church Sawmills, East Asiatic Co. and B. C. Forest Products.
8. *Report of the Royal Commission on Forest Resources* (Victoria: Queen's Printer, 1976), pp. 26–27.
9. Orchard Papers, interview no. 42, pp. 111–12.
10. *Royal Commission Report,* pp. 39–40.
11. F. L. C. Reed and Associates, *Selected Forest Industry Statistics for Canada* (Toronto: Canadian Forest Congress, 1980), p. 120.
12. *Royal Commission Report,* pp. 60–62.
13. Ibid., pp. 86–87.
14. B. C. Ministry of Forests, *Policy Manual — Timber,* Section 006 (Victoria: B. C. Ministry of Forests, 1981), p. 15.
15. Ibid.
16. Gordon M. Sloan, *Report of the Commissioner Relating to the Forest Industries of British Columbia, 1956* (Victoria: Queen's Printer, 1957), pp. 146–47.

Chapter Five

1. Mason Gaffney, interview by Derek Reimer, transcript, Sound and Moving Image Division, B. C. Provincial Archives, Victoria, B. C. p. 7.
2. Ibid., pp. 1–2.
3. Ibid., pp. 3–4.

4. Robert D. Cail, *Land, Man, and the Law: Disposal of Crown Lands in British Columbia 1871–1913* (Vancouver: University of British Columbia Press, 1974), pp. 270–71.
5. For a more detailed description, see Ken Bernsohn, *Cutting Up the North: History of the Forest Industry in the Northern Interior 1909–1978* (Vancouver: Hancock House, 1981), pp. 86–91.
6. *Forest Insight* (16 Feb. 1981): p. 5.
7. *Annual Report, 1980* (Victoria: B. C. Ministry of Forests, 1980).
8. *Alternatives for Crown Timber Pricing* (Victoria: B. C. Ministry of Forests, 1980), p. 7.
9. Ibid., p. 23.
10. The expectation of determining this cost and otherwise engaging in the market was one of the most compelling reasons for Minister of Forests Bob Williams's purchase of the Crown Zellerbach and Columbia Cellulose operations.
11. J. J. Juhasz, "Methods of Crown Timber Disposal," in *Timber Policy Issues in B. C.*, ed. W. McKillop and W. J. Mead (Vancouver: University of British Columbia Press, 1976), p. 64.
12. *Second Report of the Task Force on Crown Timber Disposal* (Victoria: Queen's Printer, 1974), pp. 75–92.
13. *Annual Report, 1979* (Victoria: B. C. Ministry of Forests, 1979), p. 51.
14. *Canadian Forestry Statistics* (Ottawa: Statistics Canada, 1979), p. 37.
15. *Annual Report, 1979,* pp. 61–62.
16. Ibid., p. 63.
17. David Haley, "A Regional Comparison of Stumpage Values in B. C. and the U. S. Pacific Northwest," *Forestry Chronicle* (Oct. 1980).
18. Council of Forest Industries (COFI), "A Brief Examination of Comparative Factors Affecting the Forest Industries of the Pacific Northwest and B. C.," Oct. 1981.
19. There are many, Gaffney and Williams among them, who argue that the forest unions have been "bought off" through wages higher than the market would normally allow. Essentially, they have a cut of the economic rent that should go to the public.
20. COFI, "Brief Examination," p. 15.
21. *Forest Insight* (16 Feb. 1981): p. 7.

CHAPTER SIX

1. *The Forest Imperative,* proceedings of the Canadian Forest Congress (Toronto, 1980), p. 32.

2. *Victoria Times-Colonist,* 5 Dec. 1981.
3. Ibid.
4. R. B. Forster, "Myths in Forestry," 1979.
5. Ibid.
6. *The Forest Imperative,* pp. 32–35.
7. Ibid.
8. *Forest and Range Resource Analysis Technical Report* (Victoria: B. C. Ministry of Forests, 1980), pp. 753–74.
9. *Forest and Range Resource Analysis and Five Year Program Summary* (Victoria: B. C. Ministry of Forests, 1980), p. 5.
10. T. A. Snellgrove and David Darr, "Lumber Potential for Cull Logs in the Pacific Northwest," *Forest Products Journal* (July 1976): p. 51.
11. Project Whole Tree Utilization, *Final Report* (Stockholm: Royal College of Forestry, 1977).
12. W. S. Duval and F. F. Slaney, "A Review of the Impacts of Log Handling on Coastal Marine Environment and Resources" (Vancouver, 1980).
13. Canadian Forestry Service, "The Other Way," 1978.
14. Paul Diggle and Ray Addison, *Management Options in the Sayward Forest* (Victoria: B. C. Ministry of Forests, 1977), p. 93.
15. J. R. Collins, "Forest Farms: A Complementary Tenure Concept," brief to the Royal Commission on Forest Resources, 1975.
16. *Technical Report,* pp. 775–77.
17. *Beale's Letter* 217 (May 1980).

Chapter Seven

1. Alan Chambers, "Toward a Synthesis of Mountains, People and Institutions," in *Integrated Management of Resources,* ed. Graham Drew (Vancouver: University of British Columbia Press, 1978), pp. 137–38.
2. Ibid., p. 143.
3. Ibid., p. 138.
4. M. Apsey, "Resource Management in British Columbia," in *Integrated Management of Resources,* ed. Graham Drew (Vancouver: University of British Columbia Press, 1978), p. 15.
5. Ibid., p. 17.
6. Tsitika Planning Committee, *Tsitika Watershed Integrated Resources Plan,* vol. 2 (1978), p. 4.
7. John Chittick, memo, 1982.
8. *Report of the Royal Commission on Forest Resources* (Victoria: Queen's Printer, 1976), p. xiv.

Chapter Eight

1. C. D. F. Reventlow, *A Treatise on Forestry* (Denmark: Society of Forest History, 1960).
2. Stanley D. Richardson, *Forestry in Communist China* (Baltimore: Johns Hopkins Press, 1966), p. 122.
3. "Management Opportunities in the Sayward Forest" (Victoria: B. C. Ministry of Forests, Special Studies Division, 1977).
4. G. W. Wallis, *Technical Report No. 12* (Canadian Forest Service, 1976).
5. John Small, "Intensive Management Boosts Yield 300 Percent," *Hiballer* (March 1979): p. 81.
6. Robert Curtis *et al.*, "Intensive Forest Management of Coastal Douglas Fir," in *Loggers Handbook,* vol. 33 (Washington: U. S. Department of Agriculture, 1973).

Chapter Nine

1. F. L. C. Reed and Associates, *Selected Forest Industry Statistics for Canada* (Toronto: Canadian Forest Congress, 1980), p. 138.
2. Ibid.
3. Ibid., p. 134.
4. W. G. Burch, "The Need to Intensify Forest Management Costs and Benefits," in *The Forest Imperative* (Toronto: Canadian Forest Congress, 1980), p. 63.
5. Ibid.
6. Ibid.
7. Reed, *Industry Statistics,* p. 114.
8. Bernhard E. Fernow, *Economics of Forestry* (1902; reprint: Ayer, 1972), p. 134.
9. *An Analysis of Forest Management Options for the Okanagan Timber Supply Area, Kamloops Forest District* (Vancouver: Crown Zellerbach Canada, 1980).
10. L. C. Promnitz and R. F. Strand, Crown Zellerbach Research Manuscript no. 25, 1979.
11. *Annual Report, 1980–81* (Victoria: B. C. Ministry of Forests, 1981).
12. Fernow, *Economics of Forestry,* p. 132.
13. Marion Clawson, *Forests For Whom and For What?* (Baltimore: Johns Hopkins Press, 1975), p. 86.

Chapter Ten

1. Donald MacKay, *Empire of Wood: The MacMillan Bloedel Story* (Vancouver: Douglas and McIntyre, 1982).
2. MacKay, *Empire of Wood,* p. 272.
3. MacKay, *Empire of Wood,* p. 277.
4. *Forest and Range Resource Analysis Technical Report* (Victoria: B. C. Ministry of Forests, 1980), p. 205.
5. *Annual Report, 1980–81* (Victoria: B. C. Ministry of Forests, 1981), p. 25.
6. Christopher Leman, "The Canadian Forest Ranger: Bureaucratic Centralism and Private Power in Three Provincial Natural Resource Agencies," paper delivered to Canadian Political Science Association, Halifax, 1981.

Chapter Eleven

1. Marston Bates, *The Forest and the Sea* (New York: Random House, 1965), p. 261.
2. *Report of the Royal Commission on Forest Resources* (Victoria: Queen's Printer, 1976), p. 235.
3. Roy Silen, "The Care and Handling of the Forest Gene Pool," *Pacific Search* 10 (8).
4. Ibid.
5. Ibid.
6. Ibid.
7. Ibid.
8. On a larger scale, the B. C. government subsidizes the forest industry through B. C. Hydro by selling massive amounts of electricity to pulp mills at extremely low rates, often below the costs of production. A major justification for construction of the controversial Chekeye-Dunsmuir transmission line to Vancouver Island was to provide electricity for the expanded facilities at the Elk Falls mill in Campbell River — at rates less than half of those charged to domestic consumers. As a report prepared for the Canadian Forestry Service concluded, "Recent investigations into energy sources for Vancouver Island's short term requirements, at least half of which are to meet the needs of the forest industry, appear to have overlooked the opportunities of using forest biomass, a renewable source of energy." (*Energy From Forest Biomass on Vancouver Island,* Canadian Forest Service, 1979, p. 135.)

9. This particular example of death by neglect is somewhat unusual. In most cases, such "window-dressing" legislation is undone to death by prior inaction of the government. Measures passed by the legislature are not referred to the lieutenant-governor for proclamation; thus they are in limbo, and if not proclaimed by the end of a legislative session, they die entirely. By contrast, the woodlot legislation has been proclaimed and is enforceable law. It is merely being neglected at the bureaucratic level.

Chapter Twelve

1. During the March 1982 debate in the United States about charging tariffs on imports of Canadian forest products, the producers in Washington and Oregon were shown to be in just such a predicament.
2. Slocan Valley Community Forest Management Project, *Final Report,* 1974, pp. 3–7.